Practicing
Counseling AND
Psychotherapy

D0145305

Practicing Counseling and Psychotherapy

INSIGHTS FROM TRAINEES, SUPERVISORS, AND CLIENTS

NICHOLAS LADANY

JESSICA A. WALKER

LIA M. PATE-CAROLAN

LAURIE GRAY EVANS

Routledge
Taylor & Francis Group
New York   London

Routledge
Taylor & Francis Group
270 Madison Avenue
New York, NY 10016

Routledge
Taylor & Francis Group
2 Park Square
Milton Park, Abingdon
Oxon OX14 4RN

© 2008 by Taylor & Francis Group, LLC
Routledge is an imprint of Taylor & Francis Group, an Informa business

Printed in the United States of America on acid-free paper
10 9 8 7 6 5 4 3 2 1

International Standard Book Number-13: 978-0-415-95739-7 (Softcover) 978-0-415-95738-0 (Hardcover)

Library of Congress Cataloging-in-Publication Data

Practicing counseling and psychotherapy : insights from trainees, supervisors, and
     clients / Nicholas Ladany ... [et al.].
          p. ; cm.
     Includes bibliographical references and index.
      ISBN 978-0-415-95738-0 (hardcover : alk. paper) -- ISBN
     978-0-415-95739-7 (softcover : alk. paper)
          1. Psychotherapy--Vocational guidance. 2. Counseling--Vocational guidance. I.
Ladany, Nicholas.
          [DNLM: 1. Psychotherapy--methods. 2. Counseling--methods. 3. Professional Role.
     4. Professional-Patient Relations. WM 420 P8953 2008]

     RC440.8.P73 2008
     616.89'140023--dc22   2007022107

Visit the Taylor & Francis Web site at
http://www.taylorandfrancis.com

and the Routledge Web site at
http://www.routledge.com

To all those who aspire to help others

Contents

Preface

Practicing Counseling and Psychotherapy is a book for graduate students learning how to become mental health practitioners from multiple disciplines that include counseling, counseling psychology, clinical psychology, school psychology, social work, psychiatry, and psychiatric nursing. *Practicing Counseling and Psychotherapy* is a guide to help new practitioners in the field understand and handle issues and dilemmas most frequently encountered as they begin their training experience with clients. Our book covers a myriad of issues from what do to with a client in the first therapy session to termination of the therapy relationship. We also look at how to conceptualize a client, as well as how to get the most out of supervision. The topic areas are practical and include real-life cases for illustration.

Before we began writing this book, we asked our students what type of book they wished they had had for their practicum or fieldwork course. They wanted a practical, "how-to book" that included real-life examples (the good, the bad, and the ugly) and spoke to them in a voice that reflected that they were colleagues-in-training. They also wanted to know about things that happen in therapy that are not often discussed in graduate training programs such as how to manage a difficult supervisor or what it means to be bored with a client. To answer these questions, we wrote this book.

Although we believe that this book is useful in a practical sense, it is also theoretically and empirically informed. The issues and strategies for working with clients are intended to be pantheoretical in nature, as well as applicable across mental health disciplines. Our approach is purposefully multidisciplinary and inclusive. We also use an accessible and, at times, humorous writing style that is intended to make the reading more real for students.

We envision our book as a companion text to a practicum, fieldwork, or intern course where trainees are beginning to see clients, typically in their first or second year of training. We also believe that training sites may want to offer our book to their practicum trainees or interns as a means to ensure that critical elements of seeing clients are available. Although our book is focused primarily on first- or second-year students, we believe it can also serve as a supplement to a supervision course as the cases of therapy and supervision can be directly applicable. In some instances, the book may be used in a prepracticum course as a preparation text that will continue in its use in a practicum course. Finally, we hope that our book is a book that students will turn to throughout their training experience as the issues discussed are likely to be revisited and worth reexploring with experience as a partner.

Overview of the Book

Practicing Counseling and Psychotherapy consists of eight chapters, each of which addresses particular aspects of therapy work. In "The Journey to Becoming a Therapist," we provide an overview of a bird's-eye view of therapy and supervision intended to help trainees see the bigger picture. "The Work in Therapy" attends to the nitty-gritty of what is involved in seeing clients, from what to consider with a first client to how to develop a therapeutic alliance, to the types of therapy skills one uses. We then move to "Understanding Your Self as a Therapist" and "Conceptualizing and Understanding the Client." In these chapters, we address critical factors that need to be considered when completing a case conceptualization of a client, as well as how to conceptualize oneself as a therapist. "Getting the Most Out of Supervision" addresses the essential components of supervision and how trainees can use supervision to help them become more effective therapists. In "Lydia's Story," we take a novel approach to an actual case of a trainee, Lydia. We follow her through her trials, tribulations, and successes as a new therapist and supervisee across 89 therapy and supervision sessions. Finally, in "The Next Steps in the Journey," we consider goals in which to aspire and look at the elements of master therapists and explore the issues of therapist self-care. Throughout, we attempt to offer a realistic and honest look at what happens in therapy and supervision, warts and all!

At the end of each chapter, we include a set of exercises intended to be thought-provoking, stimulate self-reflection, and perhaps initiate lively debate for the classroom and among peers. The questions are intended to reflect the notion that there is still a great deal unknown about how therapy works, and that continuous examination of assumptions is a healthy enterprise.

Throughout, our book is informed by a large-scale study that provides an inside look at therapy and supervision. The study followed four trainees, their clients, and their supervisors over a 2-year period. Quantitative (e.g., outcome measures) and qualitative (e.g., postsession interviews with trainees, clients, and supervisors) data are integrated throughout the text to illustrate the topical discussions.

In addition, we have included an Appendix that offers a closer and more expansive look at the results of this study. At times in the chapters, we point to the Appendix as a place for additional information about the topic at hand. We thought this format would best serve you such that you could choose when you want to go more in-depth with a particular topic area or wait until another time. For example, you could refer to the Appendix when you want to see more examples of what trainees are thinking but do not tell their clients, look at ways that therapy outcome changes over time, or the many different types of learning that can occur in supervision.

Ultimately, our hope is that trainees will find our book meaningful, educative, and enjoyable!

Acknowledgments

The authors wish to thank a number of people who have helped in the development of this book.

First, we would like to express our sincere appreciation to our partners, Kris Bronson, Eric Frey, Sylvester Carolan, and Cliff Evans, who offered their support and encouragement throughout the writing of this book.

The authors would like to thank a number of people who served as mentors, advisors, and colleagues, and who offered advice and feedback throughout the development of our book, including Janine Bernard, DiAnne Borders, Robert Elliott Mike Ellis, Micki Friedlander, Charlie Gelso, Rod Goodyear, Jeff Hayes, Clara Hill, Claus Jacobsen, Mike Lambert, Lester Luborsky, Lee Nelson, David Orlinsky, Larry Shulman, Bill Stiles, Barbara Thompson, David Tune, Barbara Vivino, William West, and Dori Yusef.

Many assisted with aspects of the large-scale therapy process and outcome study and their combined contributions were instrumental and noteworthy. Special appreciation goes to Andrea Bak, Sandy Banks, Melissa Brown, Barb Burkhardt, Amanda Busby, J. P. Caloiero, Amy Centofante, Tracy Clayton, Cindy Cole, Jen Crall, Ada Cruz, Chris Cunningham, Mike Facine, Megan Flack, Emily Fleck, Shana Flicker, Adrian Foley, Whitney Gaumer, Brenden Gegwich, Brandi Gilmore, Lisa Gobarty, Jackie Gower, Britney Hanson, Gretchen Hill, David Hurwitz, Marcia Kaufman, Nick Kehrwald, Amy Klesse, Lauren Kulp, Mandi Levine, Cara Levitt, Kristin Linde, Katie Loomis, April Martin, Rebekah Masters, Valerie McDonald, Janet Muse-Burke, Katie Powers,

Manju Pradhan, Susan Rarick, Jenny Ribeiro, Christy Rothermel, Peg Schutt, Maura Seidel, Ed Shapiro, Tim Silvestri, Prang Snitbhan, Katja Spradlin, Courtney Stein, Caroline Streicher, Emi Takeshita, Amanda Tyson, Eda Ulus, Julie Wolf and Mary Yotter.

We also want to offer special thanks to Frank Datillio for his generous contribution that went toward some of the laboratory facilities.

List of Tables and Figures

LIST OF TABLES AND FIGURES (Appendix)

CHAPTER 1

The Journey to Becoming a Therapist

Two roads diverged in a wood and I—
I took the one less traveled by,
And that has made all the difference.

—Robert Frost, *The Road Not Taken*

Without a doubt, one of the most important jobs in the world is that of a therapist. Equally, without a doubt, one of the most difficult jobs in the world is that of a therapist. As a therapist, you are asked to emotionally invest yourself in others, spend years of study learning about interpersonal approaches to working with clients, engage in lifelong self-examination, and eventually settle with the knowledge that much of your work will not provide immediate results. All of this is done for, at best, a modest salary. So then why do it? Perhaps the best answer to this question is because of the love of the work and the knowledge that simply being with a person who is suffering can be healing and offer comfort. How many greater goods are there?

Our book is intended for those who are interested in learning the ins and outs of what it takes to become an effective therapist. We rely on our experiences that began when we were students up to the present time as educators and practitioners. We approach this work with an honest and frank assessment of the ups and downs we have experienced. We also depend on information from a large-scale study we conducted as a guide for offering real-life data from the mouths of trainees, their clients, and their supervisors. In essence, our goal is to offer a realistic, behind-the-scenes, and in-front-of-the-scenes look at the training and practice process.

Some notes about terminology. Throughout the book we primarily use the term "therapy" as a synonym for words such as counseling and psychotherapy. The basic premise that underlies these terms is that psychological models, theory, and research inform practice. In some circles, these terms connote unfortunate turf battles between disciplines that have little grounding in real life situations. We have all known excellent master's and doctoral-level counselors, clinical psychologists, counseling psychologists, social workers, and psychiatrists, just as we have all known their incompetent counterparts. Throughout our book we will talk about that which makes therapy effective and leave the turf battles for the professional organizations. To that end, we don't limit ourselves to literature from only one discipline but, rather, incorporate the literature from all of the aforementioned disciplines, thereby hopefully offering a rich understanding of the work of therapy. Our hope is that trainees in each of the disciplines will find our book useful and bring therapists together for the common good of helping clients.

In a similar fashion, we are not convinced that operating from a singular theoretical approach is prudent (nor is it adequately supported by research). Although we do not eschew theory, we believe that working with clients involves a comfort with being informed by multiple theoretical perspectives. The Dodo Bird Verdict still seems to be true: "Everybody has won and all must have prizes" (Luborsky et al., 2002; Rosenzweig, 1936). We also agree with Bruce Wampold, who states in his meta-analytic review of treatment approaches in *The Great Psychotherapy Debate*, "The essence of therapy is embodied in the therapist" (Wampold, 2001, p. 202).

In addition, we prefer the term "client" to "patient." Carl Rogers first used the term "client" to minimize or decrease the hierarchical implications around the term "patient." The use of "client" also highlighted a more optimistic view of people's ability to change and was therefore more empowering to the help-seeker. We, too, believe that "client" is a more humanistic (i.e., less dehumanizing) term to refer to those with whom we work. We also believe that using the term *client* keeps therapists in the mind-set of the collaborative nature of the therapeutic work, an element of successful therapy.

We mentioned previously that a study we conducted informs the chapters throughout our book. In order to understand the therapy training process we decided to undertake a large-scale research project examining the ins and outs of therapy and the training experience from the perspectives of everyone involved. We learned pretty quickly why no one had conducted such a naturalistic investigation (i.e., the undertaking just about sent us to the undertaker!). The official name of the study was the Psychotherapy and

Supervision Research Project, but from this point forward we will simply refer to it as the Study.

Basically, the Study involved tracking four beginning therapists, their clients, and their supervisors for a little over a 2-year period. The basic structure of the Study was that we observed four therapists, each of whom worked with four to six clients, and each of whom worked with one or two supervisors. We videotaped and audiotaped all of the therapy and supervision sessions. We used quantitative measures at multiple points in time including pretreatment, presession, postsession, and posttreatment. We conducted qualitative interviews after every therapy session with both the trainees and their clients, and after every supervision session with both the trainees and their supervisors. In all, 4 trainees, 16 clients, and 6 supervisors were studied across more than 250 therapy and supervision sessions. A summary of the methodological protocol, as well as the quantitative and qualitative variables, can be found in Table 1 in the Appendix.

When applicable, we use data from the Study to illustrate concepts and ideas about therapy. In that way, the concepts are grounded in real-life examples. In our examples from the Study, we altered the demographic information about the volunteer participants to protect their anonymity. Although we do use actual data from the questionnaires the participants completed and the interview information they provided, we did not believe changes in the demographics compromised the integrity of the concepts we attempt to convey.

As can be anticipated, the data set was enormous but also quite rich. We were very pleased with the findings and use them to illustrate the practices we discuss. Although we provide examples of what worked well, we also provide examples for when things did not go well because learning takes place from our failures as well as our successes.

We thought the qualitative and quantitative results of the Study would be useful to illustrate concepts we discuss throughout the book. However, because there was so much data we thought it prudent to attend to the *nuggets* of data that were most illustrative to the topic at hand so that the text would not be too cumbersome with tables and figures and lose focus on the points we were attempting to illustrate. That said, we also realized that the data from the Study could prove useful to explore the topics more in depth that in turn could stimulate more reflection and further discussion (e.g., many types of secrets that therapists do not share with their clients). To that end, we have included the bulk of the results of the study in an Appendix, and encourage you to refer to it as desired.

The overarching structure of the book is represented in Figure 1.1. In essence, we examine therapy process and outcome in relation to supervision process and outcome, all in the context of client, therapist, and supervisor characteristics and external-therapy events. To be sure, therapy process and therapy outcome are not clearly distinguishable. Like many constructs in the therapy field, they seem to be solid in the middle and a little a fuzzy on the outside. That said, generally speaking, therapy process can be seen as what happens in therapy sessions (e.g., therapist and client behaviors) whereas therapy outcome pertains to short and long-term changes in the client (e.g., decrease in depression) that result from therapy processes (Lambert & Hill, 1994). To be sure, there is overlap in what can be labeled a process variable from what can be labeled an outcome variable. However, the labeling system can prove useful as a heuristic manner of looking at psychotherapy. Supervision process and outcome can be similarly defined. For a more extensive appreciation for the primary therapy and supervision variables attended to in the book, please see Table 2 in the Appendix.

Each chapter takes a close look at a subset of these variables. To be sure, there are many other variables to be considered; however, we have found that these are the primary ones that you will run across as a therapy trainee. We begin by looking at therapy process variables and consider the essential skills used by therapists. In the next chapters, you will learn ways to conceptualize clients and conceptualize yourself as a therapist. You will then be provided with ways to conceptualize therapy outcome to the point of termination. Next, we attend to supervision variables related specifically to how you can get the most out of supervision. We bring it all together with *Lydia's Story,* which is a narrative that captures the entire first training experience of "Lydia," a beginning trainee. We conclude with a look at how to engage in therapist self-care and what we know leads one to become a master therapist.

At the end of each chapter, we include a set of exercises intended to be thought-provoking, stimulate self-reflection, and encourage debate among your peers. There is still a great deal unknown about how therapy works, and we contend that continuous examination of assumptions is a healthy enterprise. Indeed, self-awareness is a skill that is consistently practiced by the most accomplished therapists.

We use "we" throughout the book in reference to our group consensus about ideas that we all tend to believe. At times, we may get more personal, such as when we refer to a specific example from our training or our current professional work. In these cases, you will see one of our initials in parentheses following these statements (i.e., NL, JW, LPC, LG).

We have also set up a Web site for the book to answer your questions and hear your reactions to the things we say (http://www.routledgementalhealth.com/ladany.com). We recognize that becoming a master therapist is a lifelong endeavor, and we want to hear about how you are doing along the way. It is also a place for others to share their experiences so we can all learn from one another. We look forward to hearing from you!

What Makes an Effective or Ineffective Therapist?

This question is perhaps the overriding query of the entire book. We boil down the answer into three key features that make for an effective therapist: empathy, managing countertransference, and the ability to tolerate ambiguity. Although on the surface, having only three things to learn seems rather simple. However, it is our belief that to adequately learn each of these skills takes years of practice and self-examination. It is also likely the case that most therapists never reach an adequate level of each of these skills, which may explain the variations found in therapeutic outcome. Although we will be discussing each of these skills more throughout the book, they are worth mentioning here to set the framework for our basic assumptions. First, in relation to empathy, or in essence, the ability to understand another person "as if" you are that other person, we believe it is vital for therapists to understand a client's framework to be able to help them. It is not sufficient to sympathize, or feel sorry for the client. The essence of empathy is the notion that you yourself could be in that client's shoes given the same life circumstances. The closer you can get to that belief, the more empathy you will have. The further from that understanding, the more blocked you likely are, and, by default, the more countertransference is operating.

In a nutshell, countertransference is how your biases as a therapist are interfering with your ability to empathize with a client. We all have countertransference, and as can be seen by the definition, we see countertransference as a pantheoretical construct. The key to managing countertransference is to first identify it (no longer allow it to be a blind spot) and second to work through the feelings associated with the biased belief (whether they originate from your past and/or the client's behavior).

Finally, we believe that it is therapeutically beneficial to be sitting with a client and every now and then say to yourself, "I don't know what the hell is going on right now." Of course, as a beginning therapist, this thought may be entering your head more than every now and again. However, expert therapists have indicated that getting comfortable with, and tolerating, the inherent ambiguity of therapy allows for an openness of new ideas to enter the treatment, as well as ultimately assist in therapeutic outcome. Therapists who are the most dogmatic about an approach also tend to be the least open to alternative ways of thinking. As a result, this may stifle their ability to learn and help their clients. So the lesson here is to learn how to be comfortable with not knowing.

We began this chapter by noting that becoming a therapist is a noble thing to do. As with many noble adventures, the road is less traveled for a reason. In the end, though, we believe the adventure is worthwhile and we wish you the best in your journey!

Discussion Questions and Exercises

Discussion Questions

- What made you want to be a therapist?
- What setting do you eventually want to work in (e.g., Hospital? College counseling center? Community mental health center? Veteran Affairs? Prison system? Children and Youth advocacy?)? Why do you want to work in that setting?
- What are some of the chance events in your life that led you to the therapy profession?
- If you were not going to be a therapist, what occupation would you like to have? How can you keep aspects of these other occupational interests as part of your avocational life?
- What do you think will be your greatest challenge in this field?
- What do you think will be your greatest strength in this field?

Exercise: Professional Informational Interviewing

Career counselors will tell you the best way to learn about a profession is to interview people already in the field. To that end, your task is to interview a professional in a specific mental health occupation in which you are interested. Consider places in which you would like to work once you have graduated. Also, think about the types of clients, potential mentors, and so on. Use what resources you have to identify a person you would contact for an interview. Don't be afraid of rejection. Most people love to have their ego stroked! If needed, you can do this interview on the phone. As a general structure for the interview, look at it as something that would last about 45 minutes. Some guidelines for what to focus on include the professional's (a) experience entering the field (i.e., training, obstacles, chance happenings); (b) current tasks; (c) likes and dislikes of present job; and (d) match with expectations from when he or she was a graduate student. Rinse and repeat as desired!

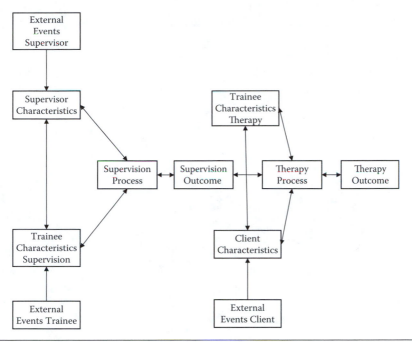

Figure 1.1 Categories of Therapy and Supervision Variables.

CHAPTER **2**

The Work in Therapy

All adventures, especially into new territory, are scary.

—**Sally Ride**

Do you feel ready to be doing therapy? Typically, when I (NL) ask my students this question, I receive a resounding "No!"

I counter, "But you have had multiple courses on theory and research. You have taken helping skills classes with great professors (most of the time!), and have received extensive training in what it means to be an ethical professional."

Silence ensues along with a number of head drops. Then I am reminded how scary it can be to venture into new territory. I typically have to explain to my students that you never really feel ready to begin seeing clients. I've taught master's and doctoral students in counselor education, counseling psychology, clinical psychology, social work, and psychiatric nursing at three universities and have rarely met students who say they are completely ready to see their first client. They can provide, though, numerous reasons for why they aren't ready, and how much more training they need. In the end, it is important to embrace your *nonreadiness*. In fact, you are probably as ready as you'll ever be. In reality, you were probably ready enough before you began your training. After all, you were the one who your friends and family members came to when they needed someone to listen to them and empathize with their experience. Sure, your training thus far has helped refine some of these skills, but the real refinement will come after you are able to see an actual person.

To that end, this chapter is about what it's like to see a client for the first time and then keep seeing them. We begin by addressing the importance of the therapeutic relationship, the key to how effective or ineffective therapy is likely to be. We then talk about the most important skill to have in your arsenal: empathy, followed by a way to conceptualize and use your skills in therapy.

The Therapeutic Relationship: It's All That It's Cracked Up to Be and More

The foundation on which effective therapy is based can largely be determined by the therapeutic relationship. Over and over again, we learn from the literature that a primary predictor of therapeutic outcome is the therapy relationship (Horvath, 2006; Horvath & Greenberg, 1994; Orlinsky, Grawe, & Parks, 1994; Wampold, 2001) even over and above specific techniques from therapeutic approaches.

We find that the most heuristically appealing way to conceptualize the therapy relationship is through Bordin's (1979, 1994) model of the therapeutic working alliance. In addition, a scale directly corresponding to Bordin's model has proven to be psychometrically solid and has been used extensively as a research tool to examine the influence of the therapeutic alliance in relation to therapy outcome (Horvath, 2006). The working alliance emerges consistently and is positively related to improved client outcome (Fitzpatrick, Stalikas, & Iwakabe, 2001; Hill & Kellems, 2002; Horvath & Symonds, 1991; Weerasekera, Linder, Greenberg, & Watson, 2001). From this work, we offer Bordin's conceptualization along with an enhanced understanding of specific issues related to the therapeutic working alliance.

Relying largely on Sterba (1934), Menninger (1958), Zetzel (1956), and Greenson (1967), Bordin conceptualized a pantheoretical model of the therapeutic alliance that consists of three components: (a) a mutual agreement between the therapist and client on the goals of therapy, (b) a mutual agreement between the therapist and client on the tasks of therapy, and (c) an emotional bond between the therapist and the client.

First, in terms of a mutual agreement on the *goals* of therapy (Bordin sometimes referred to these goals as *change goals*), the client and the therapist should collaborate on the types of outcomes they will be working toward. Typically, these goals are stated in the first session, but new goals may emerge throughout the therapeutic work, as old goals are achieved. Common goals include decreasing depression, anxiety, and distress;

working through traumatic experiences; providing assistance with deci-sion making (e.g., career, relationship, etc.); and increasing self-esteem, happiness, and so on. For each therapeutic goal, there has to be a meeting of the minds between the client and the therapist for a reasonable under-standing of what they will be working on together. Bordin holds a high premium on the negotiation aspect of this collaboration. In addition, the goals will likely be along an explicit to implicit dimension, typically falling somewhere in the middle.

As goals are negotiated and decided, so to are the *tasks* assigned to the client and therapist. Tasks vary and should be linked to the goals. Also, tasks are often a function of the therapeutic approach used by the therapist for a given client. This is not to say that a therapist should only work from one theoretical approach. Rather, therapists should be flexible and be able to draw on multiple theoretical approaches depending on the client's needs and presenting concerns. Just because you are first trained to use a ham-mer doesn't mean that you should forever treat everything like a nail!

Some common therapeutic tasks include exploring the client's feel-ings, challenging the client's thought patterns, having the client engage in homework assignments, processing the therapeutic work in the here-and-now. As can be seen, tasks can vary across theoretical approaches such as behavioral treatment (e.g., self-monitoring, relaxation), client-centered (e.g., reflections), gestalt (e.g., two-chair), and psychodynamic (e.g., free association). Bordin recognized that the *type* of task is less relevant than the *agreement* on the tasks. It is through this negotiation that the alliance is built, and may become stronger or weaker. Hence, the client becomes an active participant in the negotiation, thereby diffusing to some extent the hierarchy in the therapeutic relationship.

The final component of the therapeutic working alliance is the *emo-tional bond* between the client and the therapist. The emotional bond con-sists of a mutual caring, liking, trusting, and respecting between the client and the therapist. Without a reasonably strong bond, the tasks of therapy may become strained. One thing we noticed about our clinical work is that whenever we are unable to feel a sense of caring or liking with our clients, it often points to countertransference reactions we are having. We don't believe with the simplicity of the adage that "we will never like all of our clients." The reason this adage rubs us the wrong way is that the implica-tion is that when we feel dislike toward a client, we can just accept that and move on, as should the client. An alternative perspective that we prefer is that when we find ourselves not liking a client, we should look deeper at our countertransference reactions and work toward working through these nonfacilitative reactions to get to a place where we can understand the client's pain. We talk more about this in Chapter 4, but for now, suffice it to say, err on the side of not giving up on a client, or yourself!

Research suggests that the therapeutic working alliance generally takes between three to five sessions to develop adequately (Horvath & Greenberg 1994). Therefore, therapists must recognize the importance of attending to the alliance in the early phase of therapy and not overestimate the strength early in the therapeutic work. It is true that for some clients, an alliance may attain adequate strength in the first session, or first five minutes! However, for many clients, it takes longer and for some clients can take much longer than the three- to five-session average (e.g., clients with a history of trauma).

In addition, the client's perception of the working alliance is not always in sync with the therapist's beliefs. As examples, Figures 2.1–2.4 show different patterns of alliance for clients and therapists in the Study. Trainee III consistently rated the working alliance lower than that of the Client (AH). Alternatively, Trainee I consistently rated the working alliance as stronger than the Client (OD). The data remind us that the working alliance can form in many different ways and over different periods of time. Or, in other words, it's a relationship, and it's going to be different for each of us. And different it was for Trainee II and Client (OC). Look at Figure 2.3. Trainee II and Client (OC) perceived the working alliance differently for almost every session, and especially early in their work. Finally, just when you thought all the patterns had been illustrated, in Figure 2.4 you can see the working alliance taking four to five sessions to develop between Trainee I and Client (AJ). But then, a rupture in the working alliance seems to occur and they never seem to get back on track. As these figures illustrate, the alliance is a dynamic construct, can change on a dime, and is something that therapists should be attuned to.

A good way to keep a conceptualization of the relative moment-to-moment strength of working alliance in your mind is to consider the alliance existing within a figure-ground state. In the early session of therapy, or when things get rough in therapy, the alliance becomes the figure. When the alliance is strong, it becomes the ground, allowing other aspects of the therapeutic work (e.g., therapeutic techniques) to take center stage. As we mentioned previously, whenever we are stuck as therapists, invariably it is because our goals and tasks do not match our clients' goals and tasks. At this point it becomes important to make the alliance the figure rather than the ground.

So, a good question at this point is, how do therapists create a strong working alliance? The answer leads us back to our basic therapy skills: those that we learn when we first become therapists. They include skills such as listening, reflection of feelings and thoughts, and empathy. When attending to the goals and tasks components, we believe that reflections allow the client to hear herself or himself, and the therapist to gain and offer perspectives on the clients presenting concerns. Through these reflections, and to some extent clarifications and validation, the client and therapist can negotiate the goals and tasks of therapy. Reflections also attend to the bond component; however, nothing beats strengthening the bond like empathy. We believe so much in the power of empathy that we give it its own section.

If You Do Nothing Else, Empathize!

On the surface, empathy appears to be a relatively easy skill to exhibit. However, it is our experience that empathy comes easy to some but not so easy to most, and never substantively develops for many. Without a doubt, empathy can take years to develop. Our general view is that all therapists, all people for that matter, have the capacity to empathize; however, most do not put forth the effort it takes over time to delve into the myriad of experiences that each new client brings to us. That said, if you want to be a productive therapist, we encourage you to make empathy a lifelong skill to practice. In particular, especially when just starting out, or whenever you are not sure what to say with a client, a good general rule to follow is that if you do nothing else, empathize. Even if you engage in an *empathic miss* (e.g., you try to understand but do not truly relate to what another person is feeling), the client will likely recognize your attempt to understand her or him and will let you know how close you were to empathy. And, when you have an *empathic hit* (e.g., you can accurately feel what another person is feeling and communicate that understanding), it works toward strengthening the working alliance (typically the emotional bond component), which in and of itself is never a bad thing.

Banks (2007) in recent review of the literature examined empathy and how it has been defined and investigated empirically. She put forth the following definition that does an excellent job of summarizing and capturing what empathy is:

> The construct of empathy is defined as an ability to (a) genuinely feel care for the client, (b) accurately perceive the client's experience both cognitively and emotionally, (c) comfortably and unconditionally accept the client's situation while withholding judgment, (d) predict the client's reactions, and (e) sensitively and accurately communicate this experience to the client. (p. 6)

As can be seen by the multiple components of this definition, empathy involves the therapist accurately experiencing the client, accepting the client, and communicating this understanding to the client. Although it can be reasonably argued that a therapist can never completely empathize with a client's experience, the point is to approximate the experience closely, and the closer the approximation, the more the empathy conveyed. Moreover, attempting to empathize with a client rarely creates problems in the therapeutic work, which is why we think that it is the one intervention that is worth trying at any time. So, it bears repeating, if as a therapist you can do nothing else, empathize!

Helping the Client Understand What Therapy Is All About: Role Induction and the First Session

You have been through multiple courses and have likely learned about many theoretical approaches to therapy, ethics, research, and perhaps even engaged in a prepracticum therapy skills course. You are ready to see your first client. Or, you are about as ready as you are going to be regardless of what you actually think! But that's okay. As mentioned earlier, most beginning therapists never believe they are quite ready to start and may, in fact, still question whether the graduate admissions committee was in error. However, it should always be kept in mind that although credentials such as undergraduate GPA, GRE scores, and so on may predict academic achievement in graduate school (although only somewhat mildly and primarily GPA), there appears to be no evidence to suggest that these criteria predict clinical performance. So, if you are in graduate school, accept it for what it is, try to become the most effective therapist you can, and don't worry about whether or not the admissions committee made an error because it doesn't matter anyway!

So, what are the key components of a first session? First and foremost is a review of the taping procedures and to receive consent for taping. It is our belief that the best training sites require that therapists-in-training record (e.g., audio or video) all of their sessions. Without direct observations, it is nearly impossible to make accurate, reliable, and valid evaluations (Ellis & Ladany, 1997). In any recording consent, mention should be made of the limits of confidentiality or who listens to the recordings (e.g., supervisors, peers, etc.) and how long the recordings will remain before being erased, and the purpose of the recording (i.e., to assist the trainee with understanding the client better and to receive alternative perspectives on how the trainee approaches therapy). Most clients will consent to having sessions recorded without much question. In most cases they are aware that they are working with a therapist in training and appreciate the multiple eyes and ears that will be helping them. Occasionally, a client will have questions about taping and trainees should respond in a forthright and honest manner. For example, the client may want to check the limits of confidentiality or how long the recordings will exist before they are erased. Or, they may want to clarify or process their discomfort with the recording. Reassurance on the part of the trainee usually does the trick. The times when we have witnessed the most difficulty is when the therapist is reluctant to record the sessions, or has not practiced recording and presenting the recording to clients, and this reluctance gets communicated directly or indirectly to the client. If there are large numbers of clients who don't want to be taped, the problem usually resides in the therapist's presentation rather than a unique set of clients, all of whom have recording anxiety. All that said, in cases in which the client is too uncomfortable to continue, then we recommend that the client receive a referral before the work begins, thereby respecting the rights of the client, as well as the ethical and training obligations of the therapist and training site.

Once the recording consent has been secured, the therapist should begin by clarifying the limits of confidentiality. These limits include times when the client indicates he or she is likely to hurt oneself or others, if a child or elder is being abused in some fashion, or by court order. As with recording, most clients understand the limits of confidentiality and roll with what is said. However, at times, clients may need to process what confidentiality means and how it may influence them. It is imperative that therapists talk about confidentiality right away. If not, the therapist may be caught in a situation where the client is expressing suicidal thoughts while the therapist is describing how confidentiality will be breached. Not the best situation!

Once the recording and confidentiality issues are covered, something that typically takes only a few minutes, the next thing to do is open it up to the presenting concerns or problems. This is the bulk of the session. An open-ended statement such as "Tell me what brings you here," or "How may I help you?" are effective ways of getting the ball rolling. The key at this point is to explore and reflect each of the client's presenting concerns. In addition, it is important not to lose sight of offering empathic comments as the client discloses. These empathic moments will affect the bond component of the alliance and will likely help the client explore the concerns with breadth and depth. Of course, because this is a first session to gather information, there may be a limited amount of depth that is acquired. As each of the concerns is expressed and explored, we encourage therapists to see if the client has any preliminary goals in relation to the presenting concerns. For example, if the client is anxious and worried about many things in their life, they may offer that they want to be less anxious and worried. Obvious, yes, but linking the concerns with preliminary goals can be useful way to ensure that the goals component of the alliance is adequately addressed.

Another key component of a first session is to assess client suicidality or suicidal risk. If you do therapy, you will likely have multiple clients over the course of your work who have mild to moderate levels of suicidal risk. In addition, across a therapist's professional life, there is a reasonable chance that a client will attempt or commit suicide while in therapy (Chemtob, Hamada, Bauer, Torigoe, & Kinney, 1988; Jobes & Berman, 1993). Hence, it is crucial that the risk of suicide is assessed. Of course, risk is a matter of degrees and there is never certainty. That said, there are factors associated with risk that are worth assessing any time a client exhibits a depressed mood or feelings of hopelessness or helplessness. Actually, as a matter of every first session, we think it's a good idea to assess suicidal risk even if it seems the client is not suicidal based on the presenting concerns. We have just had too many experiences in which clients seem to have no risk (e.g., career clients) but end up exhibiting significant suicidal risk.

In terms of assessing suicidal risk, we think that the best way to start things out is simply ask the question, "Have you had any thoughts of hurting yourself?" Of course, at first, this question can feel awkward to ask, but over time and with practice, it becomes second nature. Next, we encourage therapists to consider five primary factors (plan, means, time, place, and willingness to contract in verbal or written form that the client will not hurt herself or himself) and six additional factors (things that would prevent suicidal behaviors, previous attempts, family attempts, social support, substance abuse, and impulsivity) with the affirmation of each factor adding to the suicidal risk. It should be noted that the risk factors for suicidality are similar for homicidal risk and can be used to assess homicidal ideation and risk. In addition, therapists-in-training should never feel alone. Any time there is concern about suicidal risk, we encourage you to consult with a supervisor to get a second opinion about procedures. As a matter of good practice, we believe that consultation and supervision, regardless of training level or professional experience, is the sign of a mature professional. And, of course, we always encourage clear and thorough documentation of the client work and consultation in relation to the suicidal assessment. For more information about suicidal risk, we refer you to additional publications (American Association of Suicidology, 2001; Jones, 2001; Mattas-Curry, 2000; Murray & Wright, 2006).

Along with assessing the primary presenting concerns, therapists may choose to gather background information about the client (e.g., family, occupational, etc.; see Chapter 4), as well as gather diagnostic information. Some training sites utilize very structured intake forms such that there is little room for exploration. As already mentioned, although we are not sure we can mention it enough, it is important that even in the most structured of intake sessions, therapists do not forget about the therapeutic alliance, specifically the bond component that is attended to by reflections, restatements, and empathy, all done in a culturally sensitive manner.

At the end of the session, we usually like to check in with the client to see how they experienced therapy. This checking in also allows for an assessment of how the client experienced the tasks of therapy (i.e., the task component of the alliance). So, we might ask something like, "How was it to meet today and talk about your concerns?" or "Were you able to express many of the things you needed to today?" "How did this first therapy session compare to the expectations you had about what therapy would be like?"

Therapist Skills

A good theory teaches us *how* to conceptualize the client's difficulties and should guide us about how we should treat the client. And although most theories do this fairly well, they rarely indicate how we should *be* with our clients in moment-to-moment interactions. For example, exploring a client's past certainly seems reasonable as an approach to understanding the client's presenting concerns. However, what does one actually say to explore a client's past? What are the nitty-gritty verbal statements for doing this? And, what happens if the client doesn't want her or his past explored? What types of thoughts may the client have? To understand the answers to these questions, we first must define a context from which therapy skills can be judged.

Hill (1982, 1986) and Stiles (1979, 1986) offered frameworks for categorizing different levels of therapy skills. We believe a modification of these frameworks can be quite useful for beginning practitioners to conceptualize what they are doing in the therapy session. Essentially, we conceptualize therapy process skills along four levels, ranging from those that are directly observable to those that are highly abstract. These levels include (1) nonverbal behaviors (e.g., head nods, eye contact, etc.), (2) response modes (i.e., how and what is said), (3) covert processes (i.e., internal thoughts and feelings of the members of the dyad), and (4) therapeutic strategies and techniques (i.e., theoretically based techniques for change such as the two-chair technique, cognitive restructuring, free association, etc.).

Level 1: Nonverbal Behaviors

Nonverbal behaviors are critical to convey that the therapist is listening and attending to what the client is sharing (Fretz, 2001). The basic nonverbals include nodding your head, keeping an open body posture (arms and legs uncrossed), and leaning forward toward the client. In addition, you need to be sensitive to how you are perceived in cross-cultural situations such that you are aware of how your nonverbals might be conveyed to clients from other cultures. Of course, in the end, your nonverbal stance should reflect a relaxed state of "you." Who you are needs to be conveyed, even in nonverbal ways, so that you don't end up looking like Magritte's statue of *The Therapist*.

Although these general guidelines seem self-evident and easy to pull off, it isn't always the case. Perhaps for unconscious reasons, we are not always aware of how we may be coming across to our clients. During our review of the therapy sessions from the Study, one of the things we learned anecdotally is that we could tell the general tone of a discussion without the audio. By simply looking at the client's nonverbal behaviors, we could tell when the client was listening (e.g., direct eye contact) or tuning the therapist out (e.g., crossed arms). In addition, it was striking how some of the therapists presented themselves. There was one therapist who at times would cross his arms and look away from the client. We later learned that the therapist was bored with the client, although we probably didn't need him to tell us that. We could see for ourselves! In another case, the therapist would excessively nod her head, and while it likely didn't affect the therapeutic work (in fact, it definitely conveyed she was listening!), the head nodding behavior could have been altered by simply having seen herself on the video. At some point in your training, we strongly encourage you to review a video recording of your therapy work. Apart from the morbid discomfort most trainees feel about seeing themselves on video, the experience can prove incredibly enriching.

Level 2: Response Modes

We believe that the response modes level is where we find most of the action. Response modes are the most easily identifiable and manageable to keep in your head when first seeing clients. To be sure, theoretically based strategies can guide these pantheoretical response modes, but it is the response modes that are happening moment to moment. There are two types of verbal response mode systems that we will mention. The first involves the *type* of verbal exchange (e.g., *how* they communicate) and the second involves the *content* of the verbal exchange (e.g., *what* they communicate).

In type-based systems (e.g., the Hill Counselor and Client Verbal Response Modes Category Systems: Hill, 1986, 2004; Hill & O'Brien, 1999; Microcounseling: Ivey, 1971; Verbal Response Mode system: Stiles, 1979/1986) the *type* of verbal exchange is labeled and defined. For example, a therapist may *challenge* the client and the client may respond by feeling *scared*. These methods have proven useful in describing the therapeutic encounter, as well as a method for teaching therapy skills (Hill, 2001).

A second version of client and therapist interactions was developed out of the Study and is a *content-based* system of verbal responses. Instead of focusing on *how* something is said, a content-based system assesses *what* is being said. So, for example, a therapist question such as "How are you feeling today?" would be labeled an *open question* in a type-based system. Alternatively, this same question would be labeled the *therapist attempts to gather information about client affect* in a content-based system. Both systems offer different yet useful perspectives of the same thing. The one advantage of the content-based system is that preliminary research has indicated that it may do better at predicting therapeutic session process and outcome. Because we believe both offer valuable insights for therapists-in-training, we review both methods.

Type-Based Method of Verbal Response Modes   Hill (2004) offers a useful model for understanding the therapeutic work and the skills associated with that work. Although there are multiple response mode systems, we believe the Hill model has a number of advantages: it is empirically derived, couched in the context of a theoretical model, widely used as a training model, and very user friendly. Moreover, the system attends to three levels of therapy process skills: response modes, covert behaviors, and therapeutic strategies and techniques.

At the response mode level, the Hill Counselor Verbal Response Category System—Revised (HCVRCS-R) identifies a variety of verbal response modes initiated by the therapist that include attending and listening, open questions, restatement, reflection of feelings, challenge, interpretation, self-disclosure, immediacy, information giving, and direct guidance. A similar system for clients (the Client Behavior System) describes client behaviors including resistance, agreement, request, recounting, cognitive-behavioral exploration, affective exploration, insight, and therapeutic changes. Using these systems, therapists can learn these skills through practice via role-plays as part of a therapy skills prepracticum course. However, they also can be used to examine how therapists are with real clients.

One advantage of understanding verbal modes response to therapists-in-training is the ability to hear one's own style and preferences when talking with a client. For example, there may come a time when you are feeling stuck with a client because the client seems to answer minimally (e.g., with only one-word responses). When listening to a recording of yourself, you may come to learn that the client is simply responding to the many closed-ended questions you ask. Another advantage of understanding verbal response modes is that you can ensure that you are using skills that are conducive to the type of work you are trying to accomplish. If, for example, your client and you agree that it's important to explore the client's feelings in session, you should expect that are using the skill *reflection of feelings* fairly regularly and not predominantly using restatement of client thoughts.

Content-Based Method of Interpersonal Response Modes   Moving the therapy lens for a different view, one can go from *how* things are said (type-based) to *what* is said (content-based). Pate-Carolan (2004), using the data from the Study, as well as tapes from expert therapists, developed the Interpersonal Response System that identified what was said by both the client and the therapist. She identified 18 content-based responses for the client and 19 content-based responses for the therapist. In both cases, the bulk of the responses boiled down to information giving and information gathering responses (see Tables 3 and 4 in the Appendix). *Information Giving Responses* are statements used to convey information and *Information Gathering Responses* are inquiries with the goal of obtaining information. This system is intuitively appealing for beginning therapists and their supervisors because it offers clear and observable verbal responses that can be identified and discussed in relation to what actually occurs in therapy.

Like the type-based systems, the content-based system offers certain advantages such as discovering stylistic preferences for each therapist and ensuring that the responses are consistent with the theoretical approach used. In addition, the content-based system has been found to be related to therapeutic process and outcome. Specifically, Pate-Carolan (2004) used the system to measure the concept of congruence, or how well the therapist and client are matching in terms of their exchanges. At the simplest level, if the therapist asks the client, "How are you feeling today?" and the client responds, "Sad," there is congruence between the therapist's statement and the client's response. However, if the therapist asks, "How are you feeling today?" and the client responds, "I think I'm not going to look forward to tomorrow," there is not congruence. Essentially, the therapist asks about feelings and the client responds with a thought. Presumably, the greater the congruence the better the flow and session outcome. In fact, this is what she found in her research. Specifically, she found that for both therapist and clients, across therapy sessions, the greater the extent of congruence, the stronger the working alliance and the greater the session impact (as assessed by session depth and smoothness). Conversely, the lesser the extent of congruence, the weaker the working alliance and lesser the session impact (more work is to be done to continue to validate this type-based response system).

Both the type-based and content-based verbal response systems have intuitive appeal. For some beginning therapists, the type-based response works better and for others the content-based is more appealing. Both systems can fit under the Three Stage Model of Helping (Hill, 2004) that will be discussed shortly. We encourage you to consider which one works best for you.

There are two response modes in particular that warrant further attention, particularly because they seem uniquely notable for beginning therapists: silence and self-disclosure. Silence, which can be defined as a recognizable pause where neither the therapist not the client is speaking (Hill, 2004), is a skill that therapists can use for multiple purposes (Hill, Thompson, & Ladany, 2003; Ladany, Thompson, Hill, & O'Brien, 2004) including to convey empathy, facilitate reflection and expression of feelings, challenge the client to take responsibility, or give themselves time to think about something to say. It's quite amazing that such a simple thing as not talking can have such a wide range of effects!

Our experience with training therapists tells us that using silence is a skill that takes a while to master. Initially, many therapists are reluctant to let the pause in the dialogue go long enough. This makes sense, though. We've spent years knowing when it's our turn to talk in a conversation. The challenge in the beginning is to know when not to talk. Typically, if therapists gave clients just a little more time, more will come out (Hill, 2004). We also find that using silence is difficult for potentially two alternative reasons: The therapist may have been raised in a family in which (1) silence was used as a form of punishment or (2) there was rarely any silence in the home. It's worthwhile to look back on how silence is used in your own family of origin in addition to how silence played a role in your client's upbringing. That way, when it occurs in session you can know more about what the client may be experiencing. A simple statement such as "what was that like to have silence between us?" can prove quite useful and illuminating after a silence has occurred.

A second response mode that tends to be of interest to new therapists is the use of self-disclosure. As a skill, self-disclosure is something we recommend that therapists use sparingly, although it can prove quite meaningful to clients. Some therapists believe that self-disclosure is never okay; however, we generally believe *ne dis jamais jamais,* that is, "never say never." In fact, self-disclosure can prove therapeutic, particularly as it can help build the alliance, normalize the experience of the client, or support the client (Hill, 2004). However, a few things should be kept in mind about self-disclosure. First, the self-disclosure should be relevant to what the client is discussing. Second, the self-disclosure should be in the service of the client. Although it may benefit the therapist, there has to be the client's best interests in mind when making a self-disclosure. Finally, the self-disclosure may range from intimate to nonintimate, the level at which will depend on the second point, that is, the usefulness to the client. Good questions to ask yourself are (1) How comfortable are you with self-disclosure in general? and (2) How might this comfort level influence how you would be able to use self-disclosure in therapy?

Level 3: Covert Processes

In addition to the therapist and client response modes, Hill (2001) developed a system for classifying covert processes for the therapist and the client. For the therapist, she identified helper intentions that include set limits, get information, give information, support, focus, clarify, instill hope, encourage catharsis, identify maladaptive cognitions, identify maladaptive behaviors, encourage self-control, identify and intensify feelings, promote insight, promote change, reinforce change, deal with resistance, challenge, dealt with the relationship, and relieve helper's needs. Alternatively, a client reactions system was developed that labeled client covert reactions that include positive reactions: understood, supported, hopeful, relieved, negative thoughts or behaviors, better self-understanding, clear, feelings, responsibility, unstuck, new perspective, educated, new ways to behave, challenged; as well as negative reactions: scared, worse, stuck, lacking direction, confused, misunderstood, and no reaction. As can be seen, there is quite a bit going on in the session that is not directly observable but certainly can affect the therapeutic work!

One form of covert processes that is clinically meaningful and has been studied some is client secrets (Hill, Thompson, & Cogar, 1993; Hill, Thompson, Cogar, & Denman, 1993). As it turns out, there are a number of important things left unsaid in therapy by the client and the therapist, many of which can be negative. To a large extent, this makes sense. One of the things clients come to therapy for is to resolve past conflicts, and typically, people are not readily willing to work on conflicts. We find this is also true of many therapists! For clients, it takes quite a strong alliance to feel comfortable bringing things forward to their therapist. In addition to conflicts in their past, there are conflicts with the therapist. If we believe that clients will reenact their past relationships with a therapist, then it makes sense for some of these conflicts to occur. For example, imagine Janice, a client whose parents were chronically critical of everything she does. Even to this day, whenever she calls her father, he finds a way to criticize something about Janice's life. Janice sees Tom as a therapist. They decide together that Janice will work on self-affirmations to counteract her critical internalized voice of her father. However, Janice ends up not engaging in this self-affirmation homework. She ends up canceling her next scheduled therapy appointment and comes 30 minutes late for the following one. In the end, Janice may be reenacting how she deals with conflict or believing she is disappointing others, that is, through avoidance. Tom's task is an extremely difficult one. Janice is playing her role in a pattern that may prompt Tom to express criticism and disappointment, thus inadvertently acting out the role of her father.

In addition to conflicts, clients may feel reluctant to bring up things that are difficult or embarrassing, such as experiences of sexual assault or embarrassing habits (e.g., counting habits as may be the case with someone who has an obsessive-compulsive disorder or excessive masturbation that may have some bearing on a presenting concern). In the Study, there was a client who was having an affair outside her marriage. Although she was not willing to share this with her therapist, she gladly shared it with the research interviewer during the postsession qualitative interview. She indicated that the reason she didn't share this information with her therapist, something she very much wanted to talk about, is that she believed he would be judgmental of her based on his religious leanings (something he had alluded to in a previous session). What was even more interesting is that the therapist informed the researchers that he believed she was not disclosing she was having an affair because she thought he would judge her, which he agreed was accurate. As a result, this important discussion never occurred.

A few things are highlighted here. Both the client and the therapist had things that were left unsaid in the therapy session. In addition, they both have reasons for why these things were left unsaid. One of the aims of the postsession interviews of the Study was to explore a little more the things that clients and therapists do not tell one another, and may never tell one another, as well as what therapists think the client may not be telling them. In most instances, the clients and the therapists could not identify things of importance that were not disclosed. As a result of the low frequency of nondisclosures by clients, clear categories did not emerge for classification. However, occasionally there were things not disclosed that may have been clinically meaningful. During the times clients could identify nondisclosures, they pertained to internal states or processes, personal issues, and being confused by the therapist's question. One client told an interviewer, "He asked me some things about my childhood, and I kind of sidestepped some of that." Another client reported, "There's that whole sense of well if I really told him every little detail, he would be disappointed in me." It seems clear that clients were adept at disclosing and not disclosing things as they saw fit.

Therapists, too, left things unsaid in the therapy sessions. In some cases, the therapist did not inform the client about an interpretation, such as noticing the client was replicating a dynamic in the therapy relationship that occurs for them in other significant relationships. This is a type of nondisclosure that often can benefit the client from hearing, although it can be difficult to mention and should happen only when the alliance is strong enough for the client to hear it. Alternatively, there are a number of categories of nondisclosures that are probably best left unsaid by the therapists (e.g., personal issues), particularly because they were not therapeutically indicated. For example, perhaps they had no clinical justification for sharing the disclosure, or they thought the disclosure might be countertherapeutic or even harmful to the client. Moreover, therapists did not disclose information that might turn the focus of the session away from the client and onto the therapist. In over one-fifth of the sessions, trainees withheld disclosures with the intent to "Empower the Client" to come to realizations, insights, or decisions on their own. Again, such decisions suggest that the therapists were patiently trusting in the clinical process, understanding that, to help clients improve, therapists are more effective when they empower the client rather than foster dependency on the therapist for answers and guidance. In the end, these data highlight an important task for therapists, that is, to not only reflect on what happened in the session, but also reflect on things that happened behind the scenes (see Tables 5–8 in the Appendix for a complete set of nondisclosure content and reasons).

Level 4: Therapeutic Strategies and Techniques

To understand how and when the response modes are used, Hill (2004) developed a Three-Stage Model of Helping, which falls under the highest level of therapy process work: therapeutic techniques and strategies. The three stages include exploration, insight, and action, and generally, each of these stages correspond to the use of a particular helping skill. In the exploration stage, when the therapist establishes rapport, builds the relationship, and explores the client's issues, the skills most often used include attending and listening, open questions, restatements, and reflection of feelings. During the insight stage, therapists are likely to use challenges, interpretations, self-disclosure, and immediacy. And, in the action stage, therapists can be found using information giving and direct guidance. Moreover, these three stages generally correspond to three different theoretical approaches: Exploration—Humanistic, Insight—Psychodynamic, and Action—Cognitive-Behavioral. Thus, therapists can go from moment-to-moment behaviors and understand the general theory that is guiding the work. In addition, they can go from the general theory that is guiding the work and understand the moment-to-moment behaviors. And this, along with their internal thoughts and feelings (i.e., covert processes), is by and large what therapists do in therapy.

This, of course, probably sounds a lot more complicated than it is. In reality, therapists have a general belief about what they are going to do with a client (e.g., explore an issue), and then engage in behaviors that fulfill that approach (e.g., reflections of feelings, restatements, open questions). If you have had a therapy skills course, this may seem like old hat to you. Even if you haven't, this process of going from theory to skills will come naturally in a very short period of time. Typically, the exploration skills are easiest to begin with and use throughout the session. Fortunately, most of the work with clients involves exploration. Around particular issues, though, the work with clients moves along a typical pattern: begin with exploration, move into insight, and eventually move into action. One of the key tasks of a beginning therapist is not to move into the action phase too quickly. Generally, we recommend not worrying about action until you have connected empathically and focused on building the alliance. After all, how can you suggest something to the client until you really know the client and have developed a strong alliance (which likely takes about three to five sessions to develop)?

The Three-Stage Model of Helping is one theoretical approach toward working with clients and integrates three of the most common theoretical approaches. Of course, there are numerous theoretical approaches that we all learn about in graduate school, all of which have many things in common. In fact, most of the theoretical approaches to therapy have constructs that largely overlap one another. The interested reader is directed to Dollard and Miller (1950), who long ago converted psychoanalytic theory into behavioral terms. Over the past couple of decades, a number of integrative models also have emerged (e.g., Norcross & Goldfried, 2005; Prochaska & Norcross, 2005). As we mentioned previously, given that the effectiveness of therapy is more due to common factors than specific therapeutic techniques, we encourage you to learn about multiple theoretical models and apply the techniques and approaches to fit the specific client needs in a forthright manner. In addition, it behooves all therapists to become familiar with the latest emerging and cutting-edge models of multicultural theoretical approaches (Ponterotto, Casas, Suzuki, & Alexander, 2001). For all of these models, there are skill sets that have subcomponents linked to verbal response modes. We talk more about these skill sets in Chapter 6 in relation to trainee evaluation.

It's Normal to Feel Out of Sorts

With everything going on for a new therapist, it's a wonder that we can keep it all straight. The fact is, when we first start conducting therapy, we are naturally a little anxious and have a lot on our mind. But that's okay. As long as we can rely on reflecting and trying to understand the client, we rarely will go wrong. One thing that is common for beginning therapists is a slightly heightened level of anxiety and awareness about what's going to take place in sessions. A little anxiety can actually be a good thing, so we recommend you embrace it and use it to your advantage. How the anxiety can help you is by ensuring that you are prepared for the session. That means having all the taping equipment prepared in advance, having the forms ready to review, and knowing in advance many of the things you may want to cover, particularly in a first session. One thing we have found to be helpful is to take notes during the session. Although it may be just as easy to review the recording (and probably something you should do anyway in the beginning), writing on a pad of paper may be a way to release some of the built up tension. In addition, the pad can have on it particular things you may want to have at the ready should you feel like you may get stuck. These things include statements such as, "Remember to empathize," "Explore the issue," "Tell me more," and "How does that feel?" Furthermore, it's good to have a list of the things you should be asking in the event the client is suicidal (e.g., method, means, time, place, contract). If you don't have a pad of paper, we recommend that you at least have an index card with the things to note when assessing suicide. It never hurts to have a backup.

As just mentioned, one of the feelings you are likely to experience is anxiety. This is a normal reaction. Figures 2.5–2.8 show data from the Study of Therapist II's experience with anxiety over time with a few clients. First, let's point out that the client (OC) was her first client of the entire study. Her anxiety with that client was really high before that first session. But then look what happens to her anxiety. It seems to decrease, level off, and remain lower across sessions with that client. There are some peaks in anxiety along the way, but her anxiety level seems very different from Session 1 to Session 2. Now look at her anxiety levels with three of her other clients. Again, there seem to be some peaks across treatment. Can you think of something that might have made her more anxious during the course of treatment? I (LPC) think this view of Trainee II's experience with anxiety across treatment with a few different clients is a good illustration of what can really happen across a therapist's caseload. First, there might be clients with whom you feel less anxious. Maybe their presenting issues seem more manageable, or perhaps you establish a therapeutic relationship with them easily. Second, just because your anxiety level drops a little one session doesn't mean there isn't going to be something in the next one that doesn't make you feel a bit apprehensive or worried. As with any new skill, the more you do it, the more comfortable you become.

Along with some working anxiety, some working self-awareness of what is happening in the therapy session and how you as the therapist are doing can also prove useful. In fact, there is research to suggest that some low to moderate levels of self-awareness may be a good thing for beginning therapists (Fauth & Williams, 2005; Williams & Fauth, 2005). This self-awareness skill is similar to what psychoanalysts refer to as the observing ego and the analyzing ego. Essentially, experienced therapists are able to observe what is going on in session while analyzing what may be happening for the client and the therapist. The self-awareness piece (e.g., internal thoughts, feelings, and reactions) can prove quite useful and, similar to a bit of working anxiety, should be embraced. Similar to anxiety, too much of a good thing can take away from the therapeutic work, so it's important to monitor and make sure that the anxiety and self-awareness are helping the therapeutic endeavor rather than hindering it.

Conclusion

You have spent a great deal of time learning what is involved in being a therapist, including theoretical models and interventions. It is our hope that this chapter served as a chance to step back and appreciate the multitude of relevant factors outside of theoretical orientation that play a significant role in therapy. You now have a framework for the therapeutic work, including a template for the important pieces of the first session, and some classic skills that, when in doubt, you can pull out of your hat. Finally, you have some more to think about in terms of your personal issues with silence and disclosure.

Ultimately, you may never truly feel "ready" to begin as a therapist, and we acknowledge that adventures into new territories are indeed scary. However, trust that what you have left to learn, you will learn during therapy sessions, not beforehand. It is truly during the course of our work (rather than our courseload of classes) when we learn how to best conceptualize and understand our clients.

Discussion Questions and Exercises

Discussion Questions

- Think of a time when you needed help or support and the person you were talking to showed empathy. What did that feel like? How was it helpful? Think of a time when you reached out for support and experienced something other than empathy. How did that feel?
- How was silence used in your family-of-origin? How is it used in your current relationships? How might these dynamics reveal themselves in your therapeutic work?
- Can a therapist ever really choose not to disclose anything about herself or himself? For example, is wearing a wedding band

disclosure? What about how the office is decorated? Or what books are on the shelf? Pictures on the desk? Clothes the therapist wears?

- What kind of personal information do you feel comfortable disclosing to your clients?
- What are you most nervous about when going into your first therapy session? What are you most confident about?
- What are the implications of eating or drinking in a session with a client? Is eating or drinking a form of self-disclosure?
- What are the advantages and disadvantages of knowing only one theoretical approach to therapy?
- How would you handle a client wanting to give you a hug at the end of your first therapy session?
- If a friend were to describe you, what would he or she say are your greatest attributes?
- If a person who dislikes you were to describe you, what would he or she say are your greatest weaknesses?

Exercises

Exercise 2.1: First Session Role-Play

Find a partner and act out how you would begin a first session, including consent to be recorded, limits of confidentiality, and an open-ended beginning question. Then switch partner roles and provide one another feedback. Also, role-play the conclusion to a first session including scheduling follow up appointment and processing your client's reactions to their first session.

Exercise 2.2: Working Alliance Role-Play

Pair up with a partner and act out the beginning of therapy session. As the therapist, practice negotiating and agreeing on the therapy goals and tasks. Switch partner roles and provide one another feedback. Pay attention to developing the emotional bond component of the working alliance even while you are establishing the goals and tasks of therapy.

Exercise 2.3: Challenging Your Empathy

Choose a client issue that you believe would challenge your ability to be empathic with a client and that would ultimately have a bearing on your performance as a therapist. Your task is to explore the issue by (a) reading up on the topic, (b) describing where you think the difficulties with this issue originated, and (c) engaging in encounter-like experiences (e.g., actual or role-play) in which you interact or interview people who have this particular issue and consider the extent to which you have been able to enhance your empathic abilities through this work.

Exercise 2.4: Nondisclosures in Therapy

Reflect back on a recent session with a client or use an example from your instructor. Consider what things the client may not have told you and why that information was not disclosed. How well do they fit with the categories listed in Tables 5–8 in the Appendix?

Exercise 2.5: Nondisclosure in Your Personal Therapy

Reflect back on an experience of your own therapy. What things can you remember not disclosing to your therapist? Why not? What things do you wish your therapist might have disclosed to you and why?

Exercise 2.6: Practice Using Silence

Find a partner and practice sitting in silence for 5, 10, and 30 minutes. Following each exercise, reflect on your thoughts, feelings, and reactions to the silence and where these reactions originated. Practice asking your partner what the silence was like for her or him. Explore those feelings with your partner.

Exercise 2.7: Looking for Patterns

Review one of your therapy recordings and look for patterns of response modes. Is there a response mode that you tend to lean on? Are there ones that you could have used more frequently?

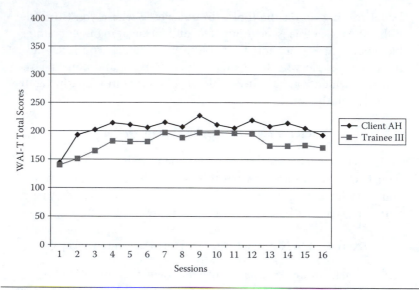

Figure 2.1 Example #1: Client and Trainee Working Alliance Scores Across Sessions. (Note: Greater scores indicate a stronger working alliance.)

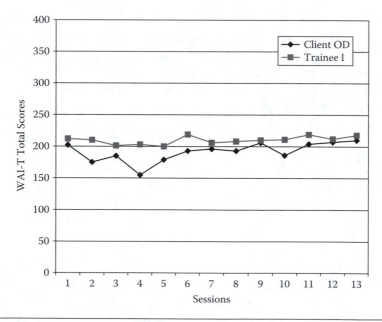

Figure 2.2 Example #2: Client and Trainee Working Alliance Scores Across Sessions. (Note: Greater scores indicate a stronger working alliance.)

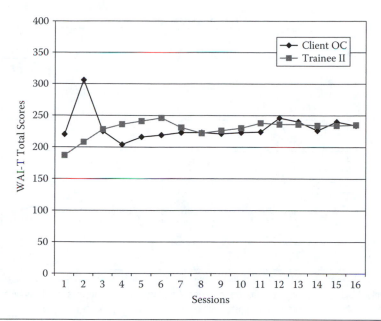

Figure 2.3 Example #3: Client and Trainee Working Alliance Scores Across Sessions. (Note: Greater scores indicate a stronger working alliance.)

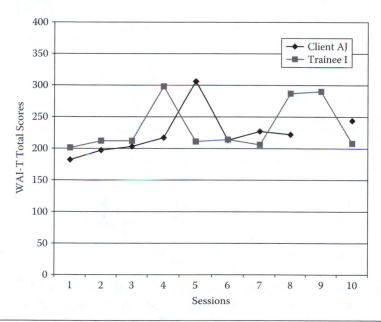

Figure 2.4 Example #4: Client and Trainee Working Alliance Scores Across Sessions. (Note: Greater scores indicate a stronger working alliance.)

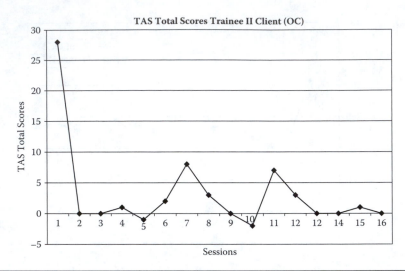

Figure 2.5 Example #1: Pre-Post Session Change in Trainee Anxiety. (Note: TAS refers to the Trainee Anxiety Scale. Scores indicate a change in anxiety from presession to postsession. Positive scores indicate a decrease in anxiety from presession to postsession assessments.)

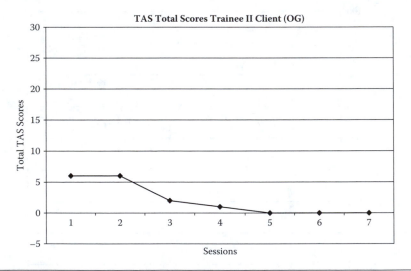

Figure 2.6 Example #2: Pre-Post Session Change in Trainee Anxiety. (Note: TAS refers to the Trainee Anxiety Scale. Scores indicate a change in anxiety from presession to postsession. Positive scores indicate a decrease in anxiety from presession to postsession assessments.)

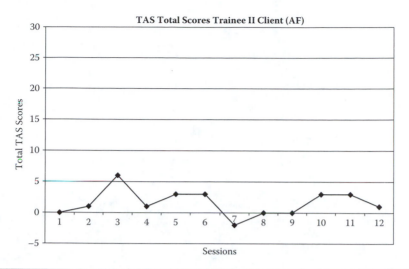

Figure 2.7 Example #3: Pre-Post Session Change in Trainee Anxiety. (Note: TAS refers to the Trainee Anxiety Scale. Scores indicate a change in anxiety from presession to postsession. Positive scores indicate a decrease in anxiety from presession to postsession assessments.)

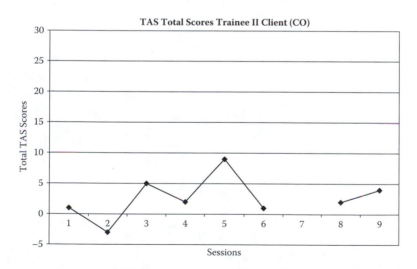

Figure 2.8 Example #4: Pre-Post Session Change in Trainee Anxiety. (Note: TAS refers to the Trainee Anxiety Scale. Scores indicate a change in anxiety from presession to postsession. Positive scores indicate a decrease in anxiety from presession to postsession assessments.)

CHAPTER 3

Understanding Your Self as a Therapist

Always acknowledge a fault. This will throw those in authority off
their guard and give you an opportunity to commit more.

—**Mark Twain**

Undoubtedly, one of the most important tasks as a therapist is to conceptualize your client. Still, a different tier of responsibilities requires you to
conceptualize yourself, as an active agent within the therapeutic session.
Although historically it has been proposed that therapists act as "blank
slates," modern theorists tend to agree that the "blank slate" exists more in
the mind of blank people than in therapy. In practice, therapists are real
people, both victims and heroes of their past experiences, and therefore
represent a rainbow of diverse opinions, values, and biases. In essence, you
will need to recognize that your role as a therapist represents a complex
integration of your personal issues (e.g., both conscious and unconscious),
family background (e.g., both positive and negative influences), demographic variables (e.g., race, gender, socioeconomic status, disability status,
age, sexual orientation, religion), and interpersonal style (e.g., extrovert,
introvert, judgmental, reflective, dominating, joyful, passive-aggressive,
inquisitive, impatient, anxious, optimistic).

Thus, the task of conceptualizing yourself involves going above and
beyond labeling your theoretical orientation or specializing in a professional domain. Rather, the responsibility involves training both inside
and outside the classroom. For instance, it includes examining your racial

identity or exploring ingrained heterosexist biases. Perhaps conceptualizing the self involves recognizing your cues to maternal and paternal countertransference or gaining insight into your unique triggers of anger or attraction. Most important, you need to be open to constructive criticism from your peers about your interpersonal style and perhaps engage in your own personal therapy.

This chapter will highlight three broad areas for therapists to consider when conceptualizing themselves: (1) countertransference issues, (2) multicultural identities, and (3) tolerance of ambiguity. These broad areas are meant to open the door to your journey of conceptualizing yourself as a therapist. They are not inclusive categories and do not address every personal issue. Therefore, this chapter is meant to provide education about options for personal growth, encourage reflection into conscious and unconscious areas, and motivate further self-exploration.

Countertransference: Definitions, Examples, and Management

By this point in your training, you have probably heard the term "countertransference," the exaggerated interfering or exaggerated facilitating thoughts, feelings, or behaviors that a therapist experiences toward a client. Maybe you have heard that a therapist is experiencing countertransference when he or she is frustrated with a client. Your experiences might have led you to believe that countertransference is always a bad thing. But what is it exactly? This section will provide (a) definitions of countertransference, (b) practical examples, and (c) knowledge about how understanding and managing your countertransference can help you become a better therapist. In the end, you will hopefully find that countertransference is not such a bad thing after all.

Imagine that a client expresses anger at the end of every therapy session, in response to unconscious feelings of abandonment established in childhood. The therapist then, instead of acting as a "blank slate," responds to the client's anger by withdrawing affection, a behavior the therapist found adaptable during her or his own upbringing. This dynamic illustrates an example of a client's transference (i.e., irrational-based anger) and the therapist's countertransference (i.e., withdrawal).

In its earliest conception, countertransference was defined by Freud as a phenomenon whereby physicians were influenced by patients' expression of unconscious feelings. Essentially, Freud described an experience where therapists felt a kind of transference (e.g., withdrawal of affection) in response to their clients' transference (e.g., expression of anger). This "countertransference" was explained to be unconscious and neurotic (Freud, 1910, 1959). Thus, Freud introduced the idea that therapists have unresolved issues, unconscious motivations, or transference problems that may be triggered by client presentation.

During the mid-1900s, the definition of countertransference continued to take shape (Benedek, 1954; Cohen, 1952; Kernberg, 1965; Little, 1951; Reich, 1951; Winnicott, 1949). Little (1951) challenged Freud's "classical view" by proposing that countertransference could be both conscious and unconscious, and could be a beneficial therapeutic tool. Essentially, she argued that countertransference, if explored and understood, could be helpful to the therapeutic context because therapists could use their own exaggerated reactions to gain insight about the client. Thus, a historical shift took place. Theorists began to hypothesize that countertransference, although detrimental if unexplored, may be beneficial if therapists were willing to validate and appreciate the origins, triggers, and manifestations of their own reactions. Hayes and Gelso (2001) may have described it best when they explained, "The carpenter has a hammer, the surgeon has a scalpel, the therapist has the self" (p. 1041). Ultimately, countertransference can be a valuable therapeutic instrument. Today, modern theorists continue to discuss and debate the concept, definitions, and essence of countertransference (Brown, 2001; Ehrlich, 2001; Ellis, 2001; Fukumoto, 2001; Gabbard, 2001; Kaslow, 2001; Kiesler, 2001; Mahrer, 2001; Suman & Brignone, 2001).

Furthermore, modern theorists recognize that countertransference does not always feel like an interfering reaction by the therapist. Therapists sometimes experience exaggerated positive reactions toward their clients (e.g., attraction; Ladany et al., 1997). Although feelings of positive countertransference are experienced as facilitating reactions by the therapist, it has been argued that detrimental effects may result from any countertransference that is not explored or understood. Thus, it is believed that positive countertransference, if not recognized or examined, also can be detrimental to the client (e.g., oversupportiveness; Friedman & Gelso, 2000).

For the purposes of the Study, we defined countertransference as those thoughts/feelings or behaviors that interfered with or facilitated the therapist's work with the client. With this definition, we attempted to account for both negative and positive countertransference, while also providing space for the different ways countertransference can be expressed (e.g., thoughts, feelings, and behaviors).

Categories and Examples of Countertransference From the Study

After interviewing beginning therapists about their countertransference, we created general themes to categorize their different reports of countertransferential experiences (see Tables 9–12 in the Appendix). These themes may represent reactions that, in the future, you will feel interfere with or facilitate your work with clients. Thus, these categories can act as a framework for you to use when conceptualizing yourself as a therapist (i.e., conceptualizing your countertransference issues with a given client). As you read through these categories, understand that you may experience these reactions with your clients. Take pause to recognize that countertransference is common and normal. Then, read on to learn how therapists can manage these reactions in a session.

Interfering Reactions to the Client's Interpersonal Style   Therapists often experience an emotional reaction to the client's presenting style (e.g., not what the client says but how the client says it). Almost 30% of therapist responses for interfering countertransferential experiences were related to the client's interpersonal style. Therapists noted they felt distracted by, curious about, frustrated with, confused by, or bothered by an aspect of the client's personality. For instance, some therapists became impatient when clients spoke in tangents without a clear focus. Other times, therapists were frustrated when clients were resistant to self-exploration, avoided questions, or did not appear motivated. At times, therapists became upset when clients reportedly were downright hypocritical or illogical.

Often, graduate training programs require novice therapists to participate in role-playing exercises to practice helping skills. However, often, role-plays focus on dealing with specific presenting issues (e.g., eating disorder), not necessarily a personality style (e.g., unwilling to talk about feelings). Thus, beginning therapists are often less prepared to deal with a client's disturbing interpersonal style, because their peers (i.e., fellow therapists in training) have role-played diagnostic criteria with generally pleasant personalities. Novice therapists are sometimes shocked or baffled by those personality styles that appear in their therapy sessions (e.g., tangential client who does not talk about problems, or an angry client who attends therapy but seems hostile toward therapist).

I remember in my (JW) experience, I once had a peer, who also was in training at the time, exclaim that she was furious at her client for not getting better. The trainee stated that she told her client how to utilize deep breathing exercises to reduce anxiety, and if the client was unwilling or unable to complete the homework assignments, then the client must be ready to terminate! It's important to remember, therapists can learn all the interventions and techniques in the world, but countertransference may interfere when our client's personality styles trigger emotional reactions in us. In this example, this trainee benefited first from acknowledging and managing her own personal reaction to the client's interpersonal style, and then was able to reassess the goals and tasks in therapy.

Therapist's Interfering Anxiety and Self-Doubt   Almost 15% of therapist responses indicated that they felt nervous, unsure, confused, or self-blaming about their lack of ability, experience or skill. One therapist noted she was thinking during a therapy session, "Holy shit, I hope my face does not read what I'm thinking because I'd be up the creek without a paddle.... I have no idea what I'm doing ... and I've felt that way before but this is the worst I have ever felt, so I'm thinking in my mind, holy shit, whattaya gonna say next?" It is only natural that new therapists would experiences anxiety, and it appears somewhat common that trainees struggle with self-doubt. We consider anxiety to be a countertransferential reaction, primarily rooted in the therapist's inexperience or inability to respond in a manner that they feel is appropriate.

Intuitively, one might assume that trainees respond to their anxiety or low self-efficacy by withdrawing, or speaking less. Interestingly, in the Study, when we asked therapists how their feelings of anxiety and self-doubt affected their behaviors in session, therapists noted they were more likely to engage in asking more questions than any other behavioral response. In other words, therapists appear to have the tendency to ask their client more questions when they are feeling inexperienced or unsure about their interventions. It is feasible that sometimes more questions are warranted if the therapist is confused. However, therapists should be cautious that asking questions does not become an interrogating behavior meant to distract the client and disguise their own discomfort and self-doubt. Inevitably, a new therapist should attempt to recognize when he or she is feeling overly nervous or self-doubting. In these insightful moments, therapists can become aware of how their behaviors may be changing in response to that anxiety. Remember that asking questions merely for the sake of asking questions is not effective therapeutic practice. Shutting down is also not helpful. When in doubt, genuinely empathize.

Interfering External Events   Therapists are often distracted by personal problems, or issues not directly related to the client. One therapist from the Study began daydreaming about his recent vacation to Arizona, whereas another therapist admitted she was overwhelmed with personal issues. Therapists mentioned thinking about the temperature of the room, their pangs of hunger, or symptoms of sickness coming over them. One therapist admitted that she was curious about how her hair looked on the video camera that day. On the surface, these distractions appear to have little or nothing to do with the client. However, we believe that all experiences of countertransference are in part relevant to the therapeutic work. For instance, if a therapist finds herself or himself "drifting off" in session, perhaps part of the experience is rooted in the boring nature of the client (e.g., client repeatedly tells tangential stories with no clear point). However, part of the experience is also likely rooted in the therapist's inability to concentrate due to an issue (conscious or unconscious) that must be resolved (e.g., therapist chooses not to confront tangents as a means to please client or therapist remains quiet to avoid the more challenging clinical tasks). It would benefit trainees to learn early on in their professional development that therapists are responsible for their countertransferential experiences, and culpable for their reactions. Therefore, therapists must take ownership for their reactions, and at the same time remain insightful about their diagnostic observations.

Sometimes clients will engage in behaviors that tempt therapists to ask, "What were you thinking?" It is not uncommon for clients to go against the advice of therapists or to make choices that therapists find ridiculous or intolerable. In our study, almost 10% of the reported interfering countertransference was a response to a client's choice or behavior. For example, one therapist had a difficult time dealing with a client who pursued an extramarital affair. Another therapist disagreed with his client's role in her marriage, "My conception of marriage and love and relationships … interfere with how she can put up with the things that she's putting up with and why she stays in her marriage, and how could she have stayed for so long … I think my own feelings of what I would expect out of a marriage are nothing like what she's getting."

The classic example of this kind of countertransference is when a therapist is counseling a woman in an abusive relationship. A therapist might ask herself or himself, "Why does she stay with him?" or "Why does she keep going back to him?" At first, the countertransference might be misinterpreted as compassion by the therapist, because the therapist cares for this client and wants her to be happy. However, sometimes the countertransference reaction leads to hostility toward the client (e.g., "Well, if you aren't going to leave him, what do you want me to do?"), a distaste for the client (e.g., therapist thinks client is stupid), and eventually a rupture in the therapeutic alliance (e.g., therapist stops displaying empathy). One of the therapists in the Study admitted, "I feel like my countertransference issues with her are just off the charts right now.… it is interfering with my therapy.… I just don't understand how she could stay with her husband!"

When a therapist is having an interfering reaction to a client's choice or behavior, the therapist may struggle with one of the basic Rogerian principles, exhibiting unconditional positive regard. Once therapeutic acceptance becomes conditional, the relationship is in jeopardy of a ruptured alliance. Therefore, it is paramount for new therapists to practice, train, and hone their skills of unconditional acceptance as part of their preparation for a practicum experience, while at the same time recognizing that attending to this skill is a lifelong endeavor.

Interfering Countertransference From the Client's Presenting Material   Sometimes a therapist will find herself or himself in session with a client who presents personal struggles that resemble the therapist's own personal problems (e.g., the client has been sexually assaulted and the therapist is a sexual assault survivor). In these situations, it is often difficult for therapists to truly engage in the absolute experience of the client. In the Study, approximately 9% of the interfering responses dealt with a therapist struggling with the nature of the topic a client presented. Specifically, one therapist was still grieving the death of a relative when a client brought up a considerable amount of grieving issues. Hence, the therapist in some ways was not entirely attentive or genuinely focused on the client's issues, because he was continuously wrapped up in his own concerns.

The topic of presenting material does not have to resonate with you personally for it to trigger interfering countertransference. Perhaps you are uncomfortable with discussions about sex, drugs, or criminal behavior. Maybe you have a hard time relating to body image issues. In these cases, the interpersonal style of the client may feel comfortable, but the presenting material becomes the active agent of countertransferential feelings. Training programs benefit from challenging their students to address many different issues within a variety of practicum settings. Exposure to a multitude of presenting topics will assist in highlighting what material might be challenging for you.

Facilitating Countertransference   Exaggerated feelings do not always seem to interfere. In the Study, therapists also reported experiencing *facilitating* thoughts and feelings, a form of positive countertransference. In general, facilitative reactions were those where therapists reported feeling sympathy for the client, relating to the client based on their own experiences, feeling as though the client was being "good" or behaving as expected, and feeling happy for or close to the client. In general, therapists noted that these feelings of positive connection were helpful to the relationship and the therapeutic process. One therapist noted that because she had suffered from depression she was better able to relate to her client experiencing depressive symptoms. Another therapist stated that he felt more motivated to work with his client when she completed her homework assignments.

Although these reactions were described as facilitative, it is important to recognize theoretically how such "positive" reactions have the potential to be detrimental. Friedman and Gelso (2000) note that it is possible to "oversupport" the client in session, and that "positive countertransference behavior is therapist behavior that seems supportive, but has a merging, enmeshed, or dependent quality to it" (p. 1230). Further research is necessary, however, to pinpoint exactly when, if ever, overattentiveness becomes antitherapeutic.

The take-home message to remember with regards to facilitating countertransference is this: Understanding what attracts you to a client is just as important as understanding what may repel you from a client. Our personal emotional reactions are relevant and present in session and can influence therapy for both the good and the bad. If you find yourself feeling particularly drawn to a client, we recommend discussing these feelings in supervision and following the five steps to managing countertransference outlined later in this chapter.

Understanding and Managing Countertransference

As a therapist, it is important to understand that your personal reaction to a client may interfere with your ability to work effectively in session. Perhaps your reaction is based on the client's annoying presenting style (e.g., narcissism, hypochondrias, histrionic), or perhaps it is based on your own anxiety (e.g., you're faced with your first client who is court-mandated). Regardless of the nature of the countertransference, it is your job to work through your exaggerated feelings so that you can connect with your client in the most appropriate and helpful way.

Several authors have addressed how countertransference may affect the therapist's ability to work with a client. From a cognitive framework, it is believed that countertransference may interfere with a therapist's ability to concentrate, conceptualize, or remember the contents of a therapy session (Cutler, 1958; Gelso, Fassinger, Gomez, & Latts, 1995). Countertransference has also been thought to affect the therapist's ability to reflect thoughtfully on client issues (Lecours, Bouchard, & Normandin, 1995). In addition, it has been suggested that countertransference reactions are related to an increase of therapist anxiety (Hayes & Gelso, 1993) and an increase of therapist avoidant behaviors during session (Peabody & Gelso, 1982; Robbins & Jolkovski, 1987; Yulis & Kiesler, 1968).

From the Study, we found a variety of ways that therapists noted their countertransferential thoughts and feelings were affecting their behaviors in session. Most often, therapists were losing focus, becoming less involved or less attentive. However, therapist responses also included becoming more focused, more proactive, asking more questions, and becoming challenging in session.

Five-step Model to Manage Countertransference

We suggest you adopt a five-step approach for countertransference management: (1) familiarize yourself with personal issues that may act as a trigger for countertransference, (2) identify cues that alarm you when countertransference may be playing out in session, (3) examine how countertransference influences the therapeutic work, (4) explore the origins of the countertransference, and (5) use supervision and consultation to develop a therapeutic plan in the best interest of the client.

First, we suggest you become familiar with personal issues that may act as a trigger for a possible countertransferential reaction. Some new therapists are unaware of their own personal issues or unique arousal triggers. Other new therapists may enter their first practicum experience with a thorough and solid understanding of their personal issues. Regardless, individual therapy is recommended as one avenue to confidentially express the feelings that might arise when clients "push your buttons." Also, it is important to utilize individual and group supervision to gain insight into your unique reactions.

Second, it is important to identify those emotional reactions or behavioral changes that can serve as cues that you may be experiencing countertransference.

Example of possible cues are

- daydreaming during session
- feeling agitated or frustrated with your client
- feeling anxious during session
- finding your client boring
- recognizing your client reminds you of your mother/father/sister/brother/spouse, and so on
- fantasizing about having a relationship with your client outside of therapy
- having dreams about your client
- utilizing every supervision hour focused exclusively on one certain client
- frequently avoiding discussing a certain client in supervision
- noticing you tend to "accidentally" come late to session
- habitually extending the session over-time
- overly self-disclosing to a client
- asking questions of your client that only serve your curiosity
- engaging in jovial exchanges instead of therapeutic interaction
- prohibiting any periods of silence in session by prompting immediate and constant dialogue

Once you become familiar with these and other cues, then you can begin to recognize when you may be experiencing countertransference during a therapy session.

Third, we suggest you challenge yourself to examine how your potential countertransferential thoughts and feelings are influencing the therapeutic work in session. Initially it is common to argue that your thoughts and feelings are completely disguised and not overtly affecting your therapeutic behaviors. We would suggest you take pause and reflect further. It is important to consider the possibility that, at the very least, exaggerated feelings may interfere with the ability to focus thoroughly on the client's presentation. On further meditation on the matter, therapists can often identify how their countertransference is represented in behaviors. Historically, the literature has assumed that countertransference is represented by withdrawal or avoidant behaviors (Peabody & Gelso, 1982; Robbins & Jolkovski, 1987; Yulis & Kiesler, 1968). However, recently there has been evidence that countertransferential behaviors are expressed through a variety of ways, including asking more questions and becoming more authoritative in session (Walker, 2003).

Fourth, it is helpful to explore the possible origins of the countertransference (Hayes et al., 1998). We again suggest utilizing self-reflection, supervision, or personal therapy as areas to process this step. Discovering origins of countertransference can sometimes be obvious and overt. For example, a therapist may have been raised in a religious faith and believes that abortion is a sin. Hence, the therapist feels discomfort with a client who seeks an abortion. This may be an example where the therapist can readily recognize that the origin of countertransference lies in a conflict of values. However, other times the origins of exaggerated feelings are less obvious, understandable, or clear. A therapist may be plagued with the realization that for the first time he has an unexplainable inability to feel empathy for one particular client. Another therapist may be resistant to exploring why she engages in nervous laughter with her male clients, but not with her female clients. Understanding our countertransference is oftentimes a painful inspection of ourselves. Yet, therapists in training must be willing to explore their reactions if they are truly dedicated to maximizing their ability to help others.

Fifth, we recommend that you and your supervisor discuss steps 1 through 4 as a way to develop a plan of effective therapy and continued empathy for your client. There are several questions for discussion that may be appropriate to ask during this step. Most important, how adept is the therapist in recognizing countertransference during the moment it is happening? If not adept, supervision can be used to discuss ways for the therapist to stop and acknowledge those moments when countertransferential feelings are aroused. Next, what is the most helpful behavior for which the therapist should engage in those moments? Supervision can be used as a time to brainstorm outcomes and decide how the therapist could best respond when countertransference is evoked. Also, where can the therapist find empathy for the client (e.g., how can the therapist see the client's pain)? If countertransference is interfering with the therapist's ability to empathize, supervision may be best spent talking about ways the therapist can try to connect on an emotional level with the client. Finally, should the therapist's internal reaction be disclosed to the client? Supervision can be used to process the pros and cons of such a self-disclosure. Moreover, when the countertransference is identified as "significant enough," then personal therapy for the therapist may be in order.

In addition to processing countertransference with your immediate supervisor, we also suggest you utilize your practicum colleaguesand group supervision moments in your training program to process these issues. As an aside, remember that you are responsible not only to explore your personal countertransference but also to hold your colleagues accountable when you notice their emotional issues interfering with therapeutic work.

Multicultural Identities

The realm of multicultural competency is built on a cornerstone of under-standing, and a shedding of stereotypes and one-size-fits-all therapy. As clinicians, we must understand and acknowledge who our clients are in order to have a chance at a successful therapeutic work. Multicultural competence can roughly be divided into three elements: knowledge, self-awareness, and skills (Constantine & Ladany, 2001). Multicultural knowl-edge consists of general knowledge about sociocultural and psychological issues related to living in a multicultural society gleaned from the liter-ature and experience. Skills pertains to responding and interacting in a multiculturally sensitive and deft manner with clients (e.g., discussing dif-ference in the session). For the purposes of this section, we focus on multi-cultural self-awareness, perhaps the most difficult and necessary condition of multicultural competence.

Multicultural self-awareness is critical to understanding oneself in relation to a client (Sue, Carter, Casas, Fouad, Ivey, Jensen, LaFromboise, Manese, Ponterotto, & Vazquez-Nutall, 1998). Multicultural self-awareness has been defined as therapists' "ability to understand their own multiple cultural identities as well as how their personal biases about others influ-ence their ways of being and operating in a wide range of interpersonal situations. Self-awareness also involves understanding how socialization processes have impacted the development of counselors' (therapists') values and attitudes. Self-awareness is typically achieved through various forms of self exploration, such as experiential and didactic activities, consultation, supervision, and personal therapy. Self-awareness is also believed to be beneficial to counselors (therapists) in using themselves as therapeutic change agents" (Constantine & Ladany, 2001, p. 491).

Multicultural self-awareness has been encapsulated in the literature in terms of multicultural identities. The basis for this work has been the understanding that simple nominal or demographic variables such as biological sex or race are less adequate at describing and predicting beliefs and behaviors than psychological variables such as gender identity or racial identity. To that end, a variety of multicultural identity models have been developed for variables including gender identity (e.g., Downing & Roush, 1985; Ossana, Helms, & Leonard, 1992); racial identity (e.g., Helms, 1994; Helms & Cook, 1999), sexual orientation identity (e.g., McCarn & Fassinger, 1996), ethnic identity (e.g., Sodowsky, Kwan, & Pannu, 1995), and spiritual or religious identities (West, 2004).

A common theme among these identity models is that people progress through stages of identity development, typically from a less developed stage to a more advanced stage. In order to manage these multiple identity models, Ancis and Ladany (2001) created the Heuristic Model of Nonoppressive Interpersonal Development. The model is intended to help therapists conceptualize themselves and their clients as well as challenge therapists about their own identity development, with the ultimate goal of facilitating more positive outcomes in therapy.

There are a series of assumptions on which the model is based. First, as already mentioned, it is presumed that identity variables are better predictors than simple demographic variables. Second, for any demographic factor (e.g., gender, race, sexual orientation, etc.), people belong to either a socially oppressed group (SOG) or socially privileged group (SPG). Because this model was developed and is most applicable to people in the United States, people in socially oppressed groups include women, people of color, people who are lesbian/gay/bisexual/transgendered/queer (LGBTQ), people with disabilities, working-class individuals, and non-Christians. Socially privileged groups include men, people who are White, European Americans, physically abled people, middle- and upper-class individuals, and Christians. Therefore, each person can have identities that are based on being a member of a socially oppressed and/or socially privileged group (e.g., a gay, white, Jewish, working-class man who is physically abled).

Ancis and Ladany (2001) indicate that people move through phases or stages called Means of Interpersonal Functioning (MIF) that include thoughts, feelings, and behaviors that are in relation to their identified groups. For example, a woman will have a different understanding and emotional reaction to what it means to be a woman at various points in her life. The model presumes that people progress though similar phases of MIF for each demographic factor, although there are also unique features depending on whether the factor is reflective of a SOG or SPG. For example, in less developed stages of MIF, both women and men will be apathetic about societal influences on gender; however, women will feel uniquely disempowered whereas men will experience greater entitlement. In addition, identities within a single person can reflect differential development. For example, a woman may understand gender oppression but not be as aware of white privilege.

The MIF stages represent a spectrum from one who is complacent and possesses a limited awareness regarding cultural differences and oppression, to someone who has an increased awareness of multicultural issues, cognitive complexity, and a genuine commitment to cultural competence. *Adaptation* is the first stage of MIF. SOG and SPG members in this stage both experience (1) complacency and apathy toward the socially oppressive environment, (2) a surface comprehension of individual differences, (3) cultural stereotypes, (4) minimal conscious awareness of oppression, and (5) a restricted emotional awareness (Ancis & Ladany, 2001). Denial and resistance are their primary defense mechanisms. Both the SOG and the SPG have particular features when a part of Adaptation. The SOG tends to idealize characteristics of the SPG, to possess a restricted awareness of personal oppression, to have a lack of motivation to alter their own circumstance, and to engage in a shedding of the features associated with the SOG of which they are a part. By contrast, the SPG during Adaptation tend to be oblivious to differences, feel that all people are the same and experience things similarly, tend to marginalize those in the SOG, and fail to possess an awareness of their privilege. People in this stage tend to see themselves as "color-blind" when it comes to race. Or, they have a perception that "homosexuality is a sin." Both examples illustrate an underdeveloped cognitive-intellectual state and minimize the implications of having such beliefs on the therapy work.

Incongruence is the second stage of MIF. This is a stage of cognitive conflict and congruence. People from both SOG and SPG tend to experience their previous beliefs of privilege and oppression as inconsistent with information with which they are coming in contact. This is the point where a woman may learn of salary differences between men and women. As a matter of fact, women mental health practitioners earn 80% of what their male counterparts make (Psychotherapy Finances Survey, 2000). Knowledge such as this creates an internal dissonance that challenges previously held beliefs about equality. At the same time, this stage finds people outside the realm of advocacy. The defense mechanisms shift to minimization and rationalization, and passive oppression continues.

Exploration is the third stage. Common features for both group members include active exploration of what it means to be a member of their respective groups. Anger is a prominent emotion fueled by shame, guilt, and the presence of current oppressive situations. This anger can be seen as insightful, and individuals may begin to consider their role in continuing the oppressive environment. People in the Exploration stage may even seek out "encounter-like events" and therapy. Members of an SOG may submerge themselves in a specific culture, whereas members of an SPG may seek to discover what it means that they are a member of an SPG and the inherent privileges therein. For example, a lesbian may march in a "Pride Parade" or an undergraduate student who is Asian American may join the Asian Student Union on campus. During this stage, what begins as an awareness of oppressive events may develop into hypervigilance or hyperawareness.

Integration is the fourth stage and is seen as the most enlightened stage. This is the time of higher processes: multicultural integrity, integrative awareness, proficiency in associating with SOG groups, recognition of oppressive occurrences, insight into oppressive interactions, and accurate feelings. People in this last stage are committed to non-oppression and the ability to genuinely empathize with members of both SOGs and SPGs. Defense mechanisms shift in this stage to conceptualizing what their environment could be like versus becoming overwhelmed. Privilege is used to promote equality and to change infrastructure within the environment. For example, a person who is White may advocate for racial equality in her or his workplace. Therapists are better able to integrate multicultural issues into conceptualizations and are more proficient in terms of their multicultural skills.

Ancis and Ladany (2001), basing their model on the work of Helms (1995), expanded up what would happen when clients and therapists come together with their myriad of multicultural identities. Specifically, they identified four types of relationship interactions: (1) progressive, which results when the therapist is at a more advanced MIF stage for a particular demographic factor than the client; (2) parallel-advanced, which occurs when the therapist and client are at comparable advanced MIF stages (i.e., exploration, integration) for a particular demographic factor; (3) parallel-delayed, which happens when the therapist and client are at comparable delayed MIF stages (i.e., adaptation, incongruence) for a particular demographic factor; and (4) regressive, which results when the therapist is at a less advanced MIF stage for a particular demographic variable.

Perhaps the best way to understand the model at work is through an illustrative example. Ruben, a therapist in training, was a 24-year-old able-bodied African-American male who identified as heterosexual and Baptist. He was very excited to learn that he had been accepted for his first practicum experience at the University Counseling Center. Ruben had been a graduate student for 2 years on the predominately White campus, and after experiencing discrimination and oppression in both overt and covert ways (e.g., hearing racial slurs, being overlooked for assistantship positions, experiencing a lack of African-American role models on the faculty) he was motivated to provide support to others in the relatively small African-American community on campus. Ruben began a support group for African-American males, and the group took off with great success. Now, in his fourth month into the practicum experience, Ruben was feeling fairly confident.

Leonard, a 19-year-old able-bodied African-American first-year student, visited the University Counseling Center. He reported feeling isolated, uncomfortable around peers, and confused about who he is and where he belongs. He also reported several depressive symptoms (e.g., trouble sleeping, low mood, loss of pleasure in things), an increase in drug and alcohol abuse, and occasional thoughts of suicide. In an attempt to ease the pain of his symptoms, Leonard decided to participate in Fraternity Rush, a collection of group organizations that were mainly White, with the hope that the process would help him feel "at home" somewhere.

Ruben conceptualized the case of Leonard and considered the significance of his client being an African-American man on a predominately White campus. Over their sessions together, the therapeutic alliance grew strong, as Ruben could passionately validate the experience of feeling "out of place" in the campus environment. To Ruben's surprise, during their fifth therapy session together, Leonard disclosed that he struggled with his sexual identity, and openly questioned his sexual orientation. Leonard's ability to come "out of the closet" to Ruben by the seventh session was a true testament to the therapeutic trust and bond they had created together. However, Ruben felt uncomfortable with Leonard's disclosure.

Ruben encouraged Leonard to reconsider the origin of his identity confusion. Ruben suggested the feelings of isolation were more a product of racial segregation. Ruben further cautioned Leonard against pursuing sexual identity exploration, in a time when the African-American men's support group needed Leonard's commitment and dedication to their Baptist principles. After all, Leonard's therapeutic goal was to feel like he fit into a niche, and Ruben had provided that for him.

As sessions continued, Leonard decided that he wanted to announce his sexual identity to both his family and his fraternity. Ruben aggressively disagreed with making decisions that could have "damaging consequences." Ruben asked Leonard to think about the guilt and shame that

Leonard may needlessly feel if he disclosed this information to others, only later to realize that he indeed was not gay. Following these sessions, Leonard did not show up for therapy and Ruben was not able to reach him to have a final session.

In the previous vignette, Ruben's personal attitudes, values, and biases prevented Ruben from connecting on a more meaningful level with Leonard. Although Ruben initially provided support and empathy for Leonard, the acceptance became conditional when Leonard considered making choices that went against Ruben's beliefs about people who are gay. Although Ruben had been educated about issues surrounding gay and lesbian development, his personal attitudes and biases kept him from utilizing that knowledge to effectively support and empower his client.

Ruben's identity reflected a complex combination of being at different MIF stages for different demographic factors. Ruben was experiencing the Exploration stage of his African-American identity, characterized by his submergence in the culture, and acute awareness of oppressive events. Although Ruben was in the Exploration stage of his Socially Oppressed Group (SOG) African-American status, he remained in only the first stage, Adaptation, with respect to his Socially Privileged Group (SPG) heterosexual status. Unfortunately, his Adaptation stage was characterized by his minimal conscious awareness of gay oppression and surface comprehension of individual differences between himself and Leonard. In sum, the racial identity interaction could be characterized as progressive; however, the sexual orientation identity interaction could be characterized as regressive. In the end, Leonard prematurely terminated therapy and the therapy work was compromised based largely on the multicultural identity interactions.

Ultimately, the task of the therapist is to continuously challenge herself or himself in relation to multicultural identities, with the goal of striving for advanced stages for each demographic factor. Of course, the work is never over. We are often reminded of the "work not being over" just when we think we have it together. I (NL) still remember a vivid example of thinking of myself as fairly knowledgeable about disability issues, having come from a family with people who are disabled. I was giving a talk to a group of mental health practitioners who were deaf and/or worked with the deaf population. In the course of the lecture I referred to deafness as a disability. Well, for anyone who knows deaf culture (which I clearly did not!), deafness is not seen at all as a disability and to classify it as such is not culturally sensitive. My insensitivity was kindly pointed out to me and it was a valuable lesson learned. All this to say, striving for multicultural competence is a life-long journey!

Tolerance of Ambiguity

Naturally, new therapists anticipate the chance to help clients. Unfortunately, new therapists sometimes anticipate that their training programs will provide them with many of the answers, the exact answers, they need. Similarly, clients frequently anticipate that therapists will be able to deliver concrete and undisputed and correct advice to solve their daily problems. Contrary to such anticipation, psychotherapy requires a high tolerance of ambiguity, because there are no clear and exact answers. Friedlander, Dye, Costello, and Kobos (1984) proposed that the first crisis in learning psychotherapy is the demand for tolerance of ambiguity. But, what does tolerance of ambiguity mean? Why is it so important? This section will outline (a) the definitions for tolerance of ambiguity and (b) why it is important to recognize your personal tolerance levels.

What Is Tolerance of Ambiguity?

Tolerance of ambiguity has been considered the way an individual perceives and processes information about ambiguous situations when he or she is confronted by an array of unfamiliar, complex, or incongruent cues (Furnham, 1994). For example, if a person has a low tolerance for ambiguity, he or she may prefer to have clear, distinct, and exact answers for questions. Someone with a high tolerance for ambiguity might enjoy recognizing abstract, indefinite, or multiple answers for questions. When presented with a situation where stimuli are incongruent, conflicting, unclear, or unfamiliar, a person with low tolerance for ambiguity will experience stress and react in a way to avoid, deny, or distort the ambiguous stimuli. A person with a high tolerance for ambiguity would perceive the incongruent unfamiliar stimuli as desirable, challenging, and interesting (Furnham, 1994). We believe that therapists are neither tolerant nor intolerant, but rather, each therapist may have the tendency to tolerate the ambiguity of some client situations (e.g., client does not know which job to pursue) but not posses the ability to tolerate other ambiguous client presentations (e.g., client mourning the death of his mother, pleading with a therapist to take the pain away).

Furthermore, each therapist's personal countertransference issues may play a role in what ambiguous situations he or she has an easier time tolerating. Imagine a therapist who spent a 2-year journey of self-reflection before discovering that she identified as bisexual. This therapist may posses a great deal of patience with a client who is struggling with issues of identity, orientation, or affectional confusion. The therapist may feel comfortable exercising a high tolerance for the ambiguity of the situation as the client, over time, experiences a range of varied emotions, attempts a list of failed solutions, and identifies with a series of different labels. This therapist may understand that the emotions, labels, confusion are all inevitably "part of the process." A therapist with a lower tolerance of ambiguity may become frustrated or impatient with the client's inability to "chose one or the other." This therapist may describe the client as fickle or histrionic in nature after cognitive-behavioral tasks and solution focused interventions do not prove effective.

Why Is It Important to Understand Our Tolerance of Ambiguity?

Friedlander et al. (1984) noted that to learn psychotherapy, there is a demand for wide-ranging tolerance of ambiguity. There are risks to face if a therapist has a low tolerance of ambiguity. The therapist may

> retreat from ambiguity into the shelter of a constricted façade of authority, knowledgeability, and pseudo-expertise. The result, which can be observed with depressing frequency in fully-trained professionals, is a therapist who cannot relax and who consequently cannot allow the patient to deal with the ambiguity and anxiety that he or she experience in life and in therapy. In such an event there lies the essential defeat of psychotherapy. (p. 194)

Clients may experience their own low tolerance of ambiguity during the therapy session. If they are met by a therapist who also cannot manage the anxiety of the unknown, then the therapist does not provide a coping method that the clients can model. Rather, the therapist may model avoidance, defensiveness, disingenuineness, or rigidity. Furthermore, the therapist may provide inaccurate answers for the sake of having answers, or deliver interventions with a false sense of certainty, for the sake of feeling certain.

I (JW) remember as a beginning therapist having a supervisor disclose that he once answered a client's question of "what should I do" with "I don't know." I remember initially feeling very uncomfortable with the blatant presence of ambiguity in that moment. How dare he? The poor client! However later, I remember feeling extremely relieved and empowered, as if I could be more genuine and curious as a therapist. It was as if, for the first time, I realized that I didn't have to *have* all the answers. Better still, I didn't have to *pretend* to know the answers.

Ambiguity tolerance has been considered a skill characteristic of master therapists (Jennings & Skovholt, 1999). They posit that when therapists are attempting to understand human life, they are likely to encounter complexity and the unknown. In these moments, master therapists do not seek to merely tolerate complexity, but they seek it out and welcome the ambiguity because it excites them. Jennings and Skovholt (1999) also note that one aspect of having a high tolerance of ambiguity in therapy may include using multiple complex criteria for judging therapeutic outcomes. The authors propose that master therapists utilize their high tolerance of ambiguity to assist them in utilizing a number of "sophisticated and somewhat idiosyncratic methods for judging effective outcomes" (p. 6).

As a beginning therapist, you might find yourself struggling with ambiguity tolerance. It is perfectly normal to experience frustration and confusion as you learn that there are no clear answers or absolutes. We noticed the trainees in the Study sometimes expressed anger and resentment toward clients as well as supervisors (and even researchers) when answers were not immediately available. For instance, one trainee snapped at her supervisor asking how to cure procrastination. Another trainee was livid at her client for not doing homework assignments and chose to respond by "throwing her hands in the air" rather than becoming curious about the possible resistance issues at play.

As you continue to grow into a mature professional, perhaps you will notice a change in your appreciation of the abstract and unknown. It isn't odd to hear supervisors reassure "that's all part of the process" or "that's all grist for the mill." These comments, in part, serve to remind trainees that clients are complex beings who may not respond immediately and consistently. These insights serve to reiterate that therapy requires a high tolerance of ambiguity for both you and your client.

Conclusion

Although conceptualizing your client is of utmost importance, hopefully you agree that conceptualization of yourself as a therapist is also paramount. Whether it is managing your countertransference, understanding your multicultural identities, or tolerating therapeutic ambiguity, all aspects of self-awareness play a role in your therapeutic presentation. Thus, as a carpenter perfects the use of a hammer, or as a doctor masters the use of a scalpel, so too should you hone the use of your *self* as the ultimate therapy tool (Hayes & Gelso, 2001).

Discussion Questions and Exercises

Discussion Questions

- What would you do if you noticed that a peer in your practicum class was allowing her or his countertransference to negatively affect the therapy? What would you like for your colleagues to do if they believe your countertransference is a problem?

- In which socially oppressed groups and in which socially privileged groups do you belong? How does this affect your work in therapy? Can you identify any demographic characteristics/populations that may be personally challenging for you to work with?
- How do you tend to act when you are feeling unsure or nervous? How might this play out in therapy? Would you ever consider telling your client that you felt unsure or nervous?
- What kind of answers (if any) should therapists always provide? What kind of questions (if any) should therapists never answer?
- Does countertransference really exist?
- Is it ever possible to be fully multiculturally competent?
- Why do some experienced therapists seem to have no doubt about what they do?
- Is multicultural self-awareness a type of countertransference? If so, then is there still a value in separating it out?

Exercises

Exercise 3.1: Countertransference Reflection

Choose a personal issue that you feel could have a bearing on your performance as a therapist. Your task is to (a) thoroughly describe the issue; (b) discuss the types of clients who may make this issue salient and why; (c) describe how the issue might play out in your therapy both consciously and unconsciously (e.g., hostility toward client); and (d) discuss how you would handle the situation if this issue were to arise with a particular client (e.g., supervision; note what you would talk about with your supervisor and how the issue may play out in supervision).

Exercise 3.2: Conceptualize Your Own Multicultural Identities

Pick a demographic factor and consider what stage of Means of Interpersonal Functioning you are at. Consider how you got there. Who were your multicultural influences? Next, consider what it would take to move you further along in terms of your multicultural identity development for that demographic factor. How likely is it that you will engage in these activities that you identify? What might it take to motivate you?

Exercise 3.3: Age as a Multicultural Identity

One demographic factor the Heuristic Model of Nonoppressive Development does not explicitly address is age as a multicultural variable. Your task is to conceptualize age as a multicultural identity and the specifics for age for each of the MIF stages.

Exercise 3.4: A Look at the Countertransference Data

Tables 9–12 in the Appendix list a variety of countertransference reactions that trainees in the Study experienced. Review the categories and think of an example in your life that may fit into one or more of the categories.

Exercise 3.5: Read About Privilege

Pick at least one of the books from this list and read it.

A Race is a Nice Thing to Have, by Janet Helms (1992)

Overcoming Our Racism, by Derald W. Sue (2003)

Exercise 3.6: Practice Tolerating Ambiguity

Over the next week, keep a journal documenting the times you feel uneasy about the unknown or those things outside of your control (e.g., not knowing all the answers). Pause and be mindful of how you tend to respond when you are faced with ambiguous circumstances. At the end of the week, reflect on your journal entries to increase self-awareness. How might these responses play out in therapy?

CHAPTER 4

Conceptualizing and Understanding the Client

Human beings, who are almost unique in having the ability to learn from the experience of others, are also remarkable for their apparent disinclination to do so.

—Douglas Adams and Mark Carwardine, *Last Chance to See*

Coupled with the beginning of any relationship is the element of the unknown. The evolution within an interpersonal relationship allows us to discover more about the person with whom we share time. Whether that person is a partner, friend, or client, the discovery of information within the relationship is crucial to its continued development. Obviously, there are multiple aspects of the client-therapist relationship differentiating it from other interpersonal relationships, such as romantic involvements and friendships (the former involves a professional contract and the latter is a personal endeavor). Nevertheless, the process of discovering and further understanding what makes the client unique is ongoing within the therapy hour and throughout the therapeutic work. The process of understanding the client, often called conceptualization, will be addressed in this chapter by identifying the various individual aspects of the client that are understood as making up a larger whole. The primary purpose of this chapter is to bring into focus the aspects of your client of which you should be aware and how to communicate what you have learned about the client to others.

Reflect back on Chapter 3, and remember all of the experiences and identities that make up who you are. You may be a student, romantic partner, parent, child, racquetball player, musician, and, of course, therapist. The range is most certainly overwhelming and at the same time makes you unique. Now consider that the client sitting in front of you has an equally complex life story. Your ability to recognize, appreciate, and empathize with the aspects of her or his life story emerges as the first step in developing a full client conceptualization. You must learn not only to recognize the individual aspects that make up who the client is, but you must also understand how to merge and integrate those aspects into a global picture—a conceptualization of the client. That global picture is not static, but it is instead a fluid process. It does not benefit our clients if we have one conceptualization and stubbornly stick to it. One aspect of a good conceptualization is reevaluation to see if the current framework still fits. Now, this is not to say that you might not have to make a conceptualization more concrete, for example, by composing a written "case conceptualization" for a clinical class or for a clinical presentation. However, as a therapist, you should always be open to new facts or insights gained from interacting with your client.

For the purpose of illustration, a written case conceptualization will be introduced and then referenced throughout the remainder of the chapter. The case is based, in part, on the actual events and information provided to us for a client-therapist pair in the Study. However, because a case conceptualization was not a requirement of the Study, the therapist did not write up this case. Rather, using the data from the sessions, and supplementing the case with information for illustrative purposes, we wrote up this case example.

Sample Client Case Conceptualization

Intake Summary

Joe is a 52-year-old White man who recently lost his job as a factory worker after 25 years as a result of the company downsizing. He has worked in temporary positions for the past 6 months but finds none of them fulfilling. He currently has an associate's degree in computer technology.

He identified three primary presenting concerns. First, he indicates that he is "searching for motivation and direction" in relation to his career status. The temporary work position he has had lately has not been fulfilling and he reports being uncomfortable with himself because he is used to being productive. A second presenting concern has to do with difficulties related to interpersonal relationships with his family. Specifically, his elderly mother desires to live with him and his wife, which Joe believes will create a number of stressful experiences. Finally, Joe indicated that he has been feeling "down" about his current job situation and would like to feel better (e.g., more like his "old self").

Joe was self-referred to therapy after believing he came to the point at which he was tired of not doing more productive things with his life. His partner also strongly encouraged him to seek help.

Background Information

History Relevant to Treatment   Six months ago, Joe was laid off from his job of 25 years where he worked in an automobile factory. He has been working in a variety of temporary positions, but none of them have been satisfying. Up until the last 6 months, he never recalled having difficulties with depression.

Family Background   Joe is currently married to Julie, and lately there have been some mild tensions in their relationship. Julie has taken a job to supplement the family income and Joe does not like the idea of his wife working. They met in high school and married soon after. Joe reports that although Julie had wanted to have children, their choice of being child-free was Joe's. Joe's mother, Dora, lives in Ohio and has had health problems for years. She asked Joe if she could move in with him and Julie, which created much tension both between Joe and Julie, and between Joe and his mother. Joe's father is deceased. Joe reported that his father and both grandfather's were alcoholics. Beyond that, however, he did not recall any history of mental health issues in his family.

Work History   As indicated previously, Joe is no longer working in a job that's satisfying. He has expressed interest in looking for a new career so that he no longer must work temporary positions.

Education History   Joe received an associate's degree in computer technology 10 years ago as part of an educational enhancement program at his work. He never enjoyed school and is not inclined toward getting another degree. He likes particular classes, such as computer classes, and might be interested in taking these types of courses.

Medical History   Joe reported that he has been "healthy as a horse" all his life. He eschews the notion of going to a physician because, as he puts it, "if it's not broke, why fix it?" He had his appendix removed about 20 years ago and realizes that he could have died because he waited so long to get help. He currently does not take any medications.

Substance Use History   Joe reported that on average he drinks about four beers on Friday and Saturday nights. He drinks when out with his buddies from the factory. He has noticed that over the past few months he has started to drink some during the week, something he only rarely did in the past. He does not believe he drinks to excess and finds that the four beers will give him a "mild buzz." Joe denied use of any other substances.

Previous Mental Health Treatment   Joe saw a "job counselor" for one session about a month before the layoffs and found this experience unhelpful.

Clinical Impressions

DSM Diagnosis

AXIS I	309.0—Adjustment Disorder with Depressed Mood (acute)
AXIS II	None
AXIS III	None
AXIS IV	Occupational Problems
AXIS V	GAF: 68 (current)

Description of Client Functioning   Joe seems to be of average intelligence and is able to problem-solve across a variety of life situations. Occasionally, he exhibits all-or-nothing thinking, particularly in relation to his quest to find another job (e.g., "I need to find a job by Labor Day or I will never find one"). Joe is able to display a range of emotions and exhibits some mild depression that has been ongoing for the past few months. His depression does not seem to prevent him from engaging in behaviors that indicate functioning across a number of social realms. He has denied any suicidal ideation or intent. His physical appearance is unremarkable and consistent with appropriate functioning.

Joe has a number of strengths, including a resiliency to overcoming obstacles. In the past he has met obstacles related to job status and been able to move through them. He also does not believe he gives up easily and is willing to do what it takes to get him out of his current situation. Because of the aforementioned strengths, Joe's prognosis is good. His depression is not severe and does not seem to be holding him back from completing tasks related to finding a new job. His environment may be somewhat prohibitive because the job market in his preferred areas is limited. However,

Joe is open to expanding his job options, some which should make reaching his goal manageable.

Client-Therapist Match

Multicultural Identities   The primary identity variable that seems to be operating for this dyad is gender identity. In terms of gender identity, Joe seems to be at a less developed stage, most likely the adaptation phase. His views about gender are quite traditional and tensions related to his marital relationship are likely a result of his beliefs. The therapist's gender identity is likely in the integration phase, in which he is able to understand gender dynamics from multiple perspectives and is able to self-reflect on the privileges that men are afforded in our culture, while simultaneously seeing how oppression toward women operates. Because the therapist is at a higher stage of gender identity than the client, therapy is more likely to be enhanced rather than inhibited due to gender dynamics. Their gender identity interaction is seen as progressive.

Conflicts   There are no current conflicts that have come to light.

Countertransference   The therapist expressed some concern that the nearly 20-year age difference between the two of them felt a little intimidating. There was some concern about whether the client would be as responsive to suggestions.

Treatment

Etiology of Client's Difficulties   An external event triggered the client's primary presenting concerns. Specifically, he was laid off of his job when the company he worked for over the past 25 years decided to downsize their number of employees. Since the loss of his job, Joe has struggled to find satisfactory work. The loss of his job also has changed the system of functioning in his marriage; now, his wife is the primary breadwinner and their roles have been altered. In addition, Joe has been feeling mildly depressed, which, is to be expected; however, the depression may be sustained by some irrational thoughts (i.e., all-or-nothing thinking).

Client's Progress to Date   To date, four therapy sessions have taken place. The primary therapeutic task has been to strengthen the working alliance, specifically attending to the bond component through reflecting, empathizing, and listening, and the agreement on goals and tasks components by discussing Joe's expectations for therapy, prioritizing goals (career), and deciding which tasks will address these goals (i.e., examining vocational interests and aspirations). The initial goals identified in the first session continue to be the goals for therapy and no new goals have emerged. The validation of his situation and the building of the alliance has seemed to help Joe feel less depressed.

Proposed Treatment Strategy   Because Joe would like to first focus on his career concerns, continued exploration of his vocational interests, work values, skills, decision making, and identity will take place. Primarily, a client-centered approach will be taken; however, at times a cognitive approach will be taken and some of Joe's dysfunctional thinking will be challenged. Holland's career theory will be used to explore the match between his interests and desired occupational setting. In addition, he has agreed to take the Strong Interest Inventory to formally assess his vocational interests and skills. Because the working alliance seems strong, it will likely be able to move to the "ground," whereas the exploratory work will be able to be prominent in the "figure."

Unanswered Questions
- Is the depression deeper than what he is reporting? What signs/ symptoms would indicate that Joe is under- or overreporting?
- How will his relationship(s) be influenced if he obtains a job?
- What are the affects of his mother's request to live with Joe and Julie?
- How does the therapist manage any countertransference that emerges?
- What are the therapist's cultural factors (e.g., race, age) as well as cultural views about the client's situation? For instance, what opinion does the therapist have about living with one's in-laws?
- Is substance use a concern of focus of counseling?

Conceptualizing a Client

No matter what your theoretical orientation, at the most basic level, your task as a therapist is to understand the client well enough to aid her or him in enacting change. In therapy, this understanding comes in the form of empathy. However, outside therapy, it is often the task of a therapist-in-training to provide a thorough case conceptualization of a client. The case conceptualization works not only as a means to present what is known about the client but also can be telling in terms of what has yet to be learned about a client. For example, there may be rich information a therapist has about the client's current functioning; however, there may be gaps in information about the client's family-of-origin.

Creating a client conceptualization is not a static endeavor; just as therapy continues to develop, so must the client conceptualization. Imagine if you sat down to write a client conceptualization after the initial encounter. Now imagine all the added information you would have to incorporate after six sessions. Twelve sessions. Fifty sessions. Oftentimes, client conceptualizations are the vehicle by which you describe the client to others around you. You may find yourself creating a client conceptualization for a practicum class, for your colleagues at your internship, for medical doctors with whom you work, or as part of a testing protocol to be used for client placement. As you imagine all the audiences for whom a client conceptualization may be written, keep in mind the paramount facet of a client conceptualization: communication. How will it be communicated who the client is? So what does a client conceptualization look like? Depending on for what purpose the conceptualization is written, the conceptualization may take many forms, but we have provided a basic outline that should prove helpful as you begin to develop your own style (see Table 4.1).

In this section, we will begin to discuss aspects of the client that need to be pulled together in order to develop a complete conceptualization. There are four basic components to a client case conceptualization: (1) Intake Summary, (2) Background Information, (3) Clinical Impressions, and (4) Treatment. Of course, a case conceptualization is never complete, and it should not be surprising to find that a case conceptualization based on the first three sessions of therapy is much less complete than one done after six months of therapy. That said, they both can provide important information about what is known and unknown about the client. So, in our opinion, a case conceptualization can be completed as soon as even the first session (sometimes called the intake session). However, it always should be seen as a work in progress.

Intake Summary

Depending on your training site, the intake session can take on a very formal tone that includes specific questions about the presenting concerns, family background, scales, and so on, or could be a very informal session that may look very much like any therapy session. Our preference is somewhere in the middle. That is, we differentiate the first session or two from subsequent sessions because they are a bit more structured, with the intent to gather basic information about the presenting concerns, as well as take into account potential crises (see Chapter 2 for more information about the elements of a first session). It is in this semistructured first session in which we gather what is typically found in the Intake Summary of the conceptualization. The intake summary contains three sections: (a) demographic description, (b) presenting concerns, and (c) the circumstances leading to treatment.

Demographic Description   Demographic description is pretty straight-forward and should include information such as gender, race, age, education level, marital/relationship status, and present occupation. Much of this information can come from an intake sheet that the client completes before the intake session.

Presenting Concerns   Presenting concerns include the primary present-ing issues that the client provides in the initial session. Oftentimes, there are two to three overarching concerns. An example may be that the client comes to therapy looking for assistance with decreasing her depression, troubles at work, or dissatisfaction with romantic relationships. The key in the presenting concerns section is to first identify the concerns and then offer a description of each concern, some of which may include quotes from the client. Be careful when working with children to differentiate concerns brought forward by the parents and those believed to be of importance to the child or adolescent. Sometimes, these concerns can be quite different.

The process of identifying the client's presenting concern in the intake or initial session becomes the building block for future explorations within the therapy hour. A note of caution: The presenting issue should not be seen as carved in stone, but instead it should be viewed as a plant that is newly potted. Just as the plant will set down new roots and send out leafy, green tendrils, so, too, does the presenting issue blossom. A client who ini-tially states that she is dealing with financial difficulties might link those difficulties to a partner with whom she has a hard time communicating.

Clients for the Study were people dealing with adjustment problems, mild to moderate depression, and mild to moderate anxiety. However, each of them brought their own unique issues to the therapy session. Some clients labeled their presenting concerns as dealing with interper-sonal relationship issues (e.g., marital problems, issues with adult children, and triangulation between adolescent children and a spouse); others dis-closed intrapersonal concerns (e.g., trouble losing weight and issues about obtaining steady employment). Through the process of therapy, each of the therapist-client pairings became more and more unique as the presenting issues were explored and expanded.

Circumstances Leading to Admission   Useful information also can be found in knowing how the client ended up coming to therapy. Was it a parent's or roommate's recommendation? Was the client self-referred? Was the client referred by another mental health practitioner? Answers to these types of questions can provide a glimpse into the client's motivation for therapy. In addition, it would be useful to know if there was a particular event that took place that prompted the client to seek treatment. As can be seen in the example, Joe's job loss was a trigger that led to his presenting concerns, but his partner is the one who prompted him to seek therapy.

Background Information

Just as we asked the clients participating in the study, "Who are you?" by way of a demographic sheet, you also will benefit from an understanding of how the client views herself or himself. Depending on where you engage in therapy, the client might be asked to fill out a demographic form before intake (or the initial therapy session), the intake specialist may have asked pointed questions about the client's background, or the client might be seen for the first session without formally divulging any personal information. Regardless of the case, it is important to understand the background information of the client. Background information might include history relevant to treatment, family background, work history, educational history, substance use and abuse history, medical history, and previous mental health history. Like the client's presenting issues, gathering information about her or his background will be an ongoing process throughout the therapeutic relationship.

History Relevant to Treatment   Although a client's history is likely quite broad, it's important to pick out the formative and salient experiences that are believed to be related to the primary presenting concerns. Some good questions to elicit this type of information are things such as:

- When did you first notice this concern?
- What were some events that took place in your life around this time?
- Who in your life do you remember first reacting this way to?

Following each of these questions, it is often illustrative to explore the answers using minimal encouragers and comments meant to continue the exploration (e.g., "Tell me more about that"). Through this exploration, the origins of the concerns can come to light and sometimes offer insight into the client's presenting problems. In the case of Joe, it seems pretty clear that his primary issues were triggered by his layoff. However, important information can be garnered by examining how he has responded to obstacles in his life previously. For example, is feeling depressed a reaction that he has experienced before and how has he pulled himself out of it in the past? Answers to these questions may provide a key to finding solutions for his current difficulties.

Family Background   Family history provides a rich source of information about the client. The relationships that we have had with family members can predict quite well how we will interact with others in our life, whether we like it or not! Oftentimes, therapy can be a means of breaking maladaptive patterns of interaction based on these previous experiences; however, without intervention, these patterns are likely to play out in romantic relationships, friendships, work relationships, and so on. Therefore, assessing family patterns can be a useful source of conceptualization material. One way to layout family patterns is through what is called a genogram. Trainees typically learn about genograms in a family therapy class, but the basic approach is rather straightforward. Generally, you can begin with a large piece of paper and essentially start drawing a family tree, using circles for women and squares for men (circles and squares have been the traditional shapes used but there is nothing to say this can't be changed). An example of an abbreviated family genogram for a 5-year-old client can be seen in Figure 4.1. There are many things that can be included in a genogram but some of the richest information about people in the genogram include gender, race, ethnicity, sexual orientation, socioeconomic status, disability, career, education, age, birth dates, death dates, marriages, divorces, separations, emotional alliances, cutoffs, illnesses, triangles, values, gender roles, substance abuse and dependence, physical abuse, sexual abuse, mental illness, conflicts, critical family events, and societal events. As part of the process, the task is to look for patterns in the family (e.g., substance abuse) and work with the client to facilitate any new insights into their life. In relation to the conceptualization, information from the genogram can offer you insights into how the client became who he or she is.

Work History   Work history offers information about the clients' career and vocational development. Important things to look for here include types of jobs, number of jobs, satisfaction with work, career decision making, and vocational interests. For children and adolescents, work history may seem less relevant; however, information about family chores and part-time jobs often can provide insights into how clients respond to work-related activities and give a measure of strengths and weaknesses about their ability to integrate work in their lives.

Educational History   Similar to work history, educational history can provide information about the client's vocational interests in relation to her or his academic interests. If there is a mismatch between educational pursuits and interests and a current work situation, then it is likely the case that the client will not be satisfied with his or her work. However, clients often find themselves unhappily stuck in work because they do not comprehend this disconnect.

Medical History   An understanding of health-related concerns, including physical problems and medication, provides the therapist with a couple of important pieces of information. First, mental health problems can be exacerbated by physical concerns and physical concerns can be exacerbated by mental health problems. The interplay between the two is important to know about when assessing change in the client's functioning. Second, medication can influence mental health, and it's important to know the types of medication that a client is taking in order to determine some of the potential ways that it may be influencing presenting concerns. Of course, when medication and physical health issues are at play, it's important to work with your client to manage and monitor these conditions with a physician, with whom you may choose to be in contact.

Previous Mental Health Treatment   The extent to which clients have seen therapists previously can offer insight into how they might handle the current treatment. For example, it's often good to ask a client what worked and what didn't work in his or her previous treatment. You may choose to have the client's records sent from his or her previous therapist. But a note of caution comes with this process. Specifically, it behooves the therapist to examine previous reports about a client with a critical eye and not wholeheartedly accept diagnoses and treatment efficacy without substantiating these issues yourself. Unfortunately, too frequently, there are mental health practitioners who are not good clinicians and clients don't get better because of the therapist, rather than something in the client. Therefore, all information should be seen as hypotheses that need to be tested.

Clinical Impressions

Although background information focuses on primarily what the client can tell you, clinical impressions come from those external of the client … namely, you, the therapist! This is the point at which your clinical training comes into play. In the next section, various aspects of your clinical impressions, which includes your inferences and hypotheses about the client, will be defined. The vernacular for clinical impressions ties you together with your colleagues, and the common language makes communicating about a client that much easier.

The common terms for diagnosing a client are typically derived from the *Diagnostic and Statistical Manual of Disorders IV* (or *DSM-IV*) currently used in version TR (or "Text Revision"; American Psychiatric Association, 2000). Although not all clinicians choose to use the *DSM-IV*, it is important to be familiar with the five-axis system for diagnosing.

DSM *Diagnosis* To diagnose or not to diagnose, that is the question. Diagnosing has a long and sordid history and although there may be many good reasons for diagnosing, there are equally compelling reasons that diagnosing is better left out of a conceptualization. Our belief is that diagnosing can be done well under certain conditions. First, there has to be an explicit recognition that traditional diagnosing models such as the *DSM* have inherent biases. These biases include gender bias, such as the slanted nature of gender-based personality disorders; racial bias, such as the predominantly White populations from which diagnostic categories have been developed and empirically supported; sexual orientation bias related to the history of heterosexist-based diagnosing and limited samples of people who are not heterosexual in the empirically supported diagnostic groups; and bias related to changing one's mind once a diagnosis has been pronounced (Cosgrove & Riddle, 2004; Davison, 2005; Garb, 2005; Javed, 2004; Kupers, Ross, Frances, & Widiger, 2005; Metcalfe & Caplan, 2004; Peltzer, 2003; Richard, 2001). This last sort of bias is something therapists should pay attention to as clients are conceptualized over time. Presumably, as clients get better, their diagnosis should change, and perhaps disappear.

The other thing about diagnosing is that clients are not their diagnoses; they are people who experience disorders. All too often, we have seen clinicians refer to their "borderline client," a term that dehumanizes a person. This is why we prefer to refer to clients as having a diagnosis (i.e., my client who has a borderline personality disorder) rather than indicating that they *are* their diagnosis.

All that said, there can be clinical and therapeutic benefits to the process of diagnosing. One advantage to diagnosing is that it offers a shortcut for therapists who can speak to one another and understand the symptomatology. Again, a note of caution is in order. Diagnosing typically speaks to the client's symptoms, but not necessarily the cause or etiology of the symptoms. These causes may be a target of intervention and hence should also be considered when making diagnoses.

Another advantage of diagnosing is that it helps new clinicians learn about clusters of symptoms that are likely to be present when seeing a client. For example, is may be helpful to assess the extent of a client's depression by learning about a multitude of symptoms related to depression, rather than just a few. It's typically known that depression is exhibited when clients report depressed mood, sadness, and loss of appetite, but some other less well-known symptoms include overeating, hypersomnia, and adhedonia.

Finally, diagnosing can help because the reality is that clients often need to be diagnosed in order to be reimbursed by their insurance carrier should they be using their insurance. Typically, clients seen by trainees are not in a position to use their insurance; however, invariably therapists have to make diagnoses once they are practicing professionals. So, it's probably a good idea to learn the system, warts and all, during one's training.

One other thing of note in relation to the example: Depending on the report (e.g., educational purposes for you), you may want to list the criteria that fits or does not fit after the diagnosis given. For example, for Joe's diagnosis of Adjustment Disorder With Depressed Mood, you could identify how well each of the criteria, from A-E, fits for a particular client. This is particularly useful when learning how to differentiate diagnoses as well as how to know when a diagnosis is provisional or not.

Description of Client Functioning   Oftentimes, this is the section in which the therapist can report on a mental status exam. A mental status exam is a profile of a series of the client's psychic functions (e.g., appearance, attention, intelligence, etc.; Othmer & Othmer, 2002). A mental status exam is a cross-sectional look at the client that comes about through observation, conversation, exploration, and testing. In contrast, a diagnosis is a longitudinal view of the client. A formal and comprehensive mental status exam can identify more than 20 psychic functions. Although a comprehensive mental status exam can be quite useful for clients with more severe psychopathology, most clients seen do not have the level of psychopathology that would require such a comprehensive approach. As such, we recommend attending to seven aspects of functioning: cognitive, affective, behavioral, physical appearance, suicidal risk, strengths, and prognosis.

How would you describe your client in terms of cognition, affect, behavior, and physical appearance? Cognition refers to the thought processes of the client. Affect is defined as the emotional processes. Behaviors are the external manifestations of both cognition and affect. Physical appearance is how the client looks to you. Look back at the conceptualization of Joe. What does the clinician tell us about his cognitions, affect, behaviors, and physical appearance? Imagine that you are a colleague of the clinician treating Joe. What types of clinical impressions have you received from the current case conceptualization? What types of clinical impressions do you feel your colleague has failed to provide? What makes the missing clinical impressions important in your opinion?

One heuristic way of distinguishing the Background Information from the Clinical Impressions is what we call the difference between "reports and states" versus "seems and appears." What is discussed in the Background Information section pertains to things the client reported or stated (e.g., the client reported experiencing bad for the past 4 days). They are primarily the client's perspective and are based on observations made by the therapist. Conversely, the Clinical Impressions section contains hypotheses that the therapist makes based on the aforementioned observations; hence, they are speculative and are typically preceded with seems and appears (e.g., the client appeared angry, as evidenced by loud volume of voice and striking table with clenched fists when discussing painful topics).

A Quick Note About Progress Notes   We also use the aforementioned formula for progress notes, which we typically break into three sections: Observation, Assessment, Plan. The observation section is the *reports and states* section. The Assessment section is the *seems and appears* section. And the plan is the proposed treatment plan.

As discussed in Chapter 2, assessing *suicidal risk* is a critical aspect of conceptualizing a client and therefore that assessment should be included in the case conceptualization. One aspect of client functioning that is easily overlooked is the client's *strengths.* This is not just an attempt to "be nice" to people. Rather, understanding how a client has persevered and overcome obstacles, as well as aspects of his or her life in which they are quite functional, can be clinically useful. Acknowledging that a client has a borderline personality disorder as a result of serious childhood sexual abuse provides a different perspective than seeing the same client who has a borderline personality disorder, which makes her or him someone who is just a difficult person to be around. In the former case, the client's interpersonal style may have been adaptive and used as a form of survival (a type of strength), even though it may not be working as well in the client's present life. In the latter case, the client's disorder is seen as wholly dysfunctional. In the case of Joe, we learn that he has been able to overcome obstacles in the past, and therefore has skills that he may be able to access in his current life circumstance. In addition, his strengths are what allow us to offer a *prognosis* that is favorable. A prognosis is a clinical impression of the client's ability to function in the future that can be short term or long term. In Joe's case, a combination of clinical impressions affords us to give a favorable prognosis.

Like diagnosing, *testing* can be fraught with bias. One type of bias is the population on which the test has been developed and subsequently normed and validated. Many common measures were created based on a White cultural norm and subsequently normed and validated on predominately White populations, creating a "white-out" effect for other populations in the sample. The results of tests also have had a tricky past. Test results are often criticized for producing statements that are not very helpful, which were originally termed "Aunt Fanny" statements, ostensibly because it's something that even my Aunt Fanny would know (Tallent, 1958). In a similar vein, therapists should be cautious about statements that sound more like something that would come from a horoscope rather than a psychological instrument. These statements have been referred to as "Barnum effect" statements, after P. T. Barnum the circus master, who coined the phrase, "There's a sucker born every minute." These types of statements are ones that are generic and tend to fit most people—for example, you like to be liked by others (Meehl, 1956).

All that said, testing can be helpful in providing information about a client that is not readily available, can offer hypotheses that have not been considered, and can quite often be gathered relatively more quickly than a clinical interview. In addition, testing can be used to demonstrate changes over time and can alert the therapist to a deterioration in functioning. To that end, we believe under certain circumstances testing can serve the therapist and client well.

In addition, the approach to testing can distinguish how well testing can be effective. Duckworth (1985) offered a series of guidelines for approaching assessment with clients. To begin with, it's important to recognize that the client should be an active participant in the assessment process. This coincides with our belief of the importance of the working alliance. The use of particular tests should be a task that is mutually agreed upon and discussed. Testing also should be for the benefit of, and provide information to, the client and therapist. When giving feedback, appropriate, nonpejorative language should be used. The last thing a client needs is too much jargon, or, as clients are likely to call it, "psychobabble." Be sure to include both the strengths and weaknesses in any interpretation. Even a client who has a Borderline Personality Disorder and demonstrates many interpersonal difficulties has strengths (i.e., they have learned to get their needs met). Strengths become important because often it is from where therapists can build.

In a similar vein, it's important to recognize the normal functioning of a client, and not exclusively focus on psychopathology. Many dysfunctional patterns originate from adaptive mechanisms initially aimed at functioning in a dysfunctional environment. An implicit assumption is that testing should be with the knowledge that a client can change. (Or why else would the client be receiving treatment?) One type of testing that often gets overlooked is vocational testing, which we believe can be very useful for clients. Work dissatisfaction, as in the case with Joe, can lead to many kinds of concerns and symptoms and should not be overlooked. After all, work is what most people spend a third of their life doing, and shouldn't go unnoticed by therapists. Finally, the ultimate goal of testing should be for the empowerment of clients by increasing their knowledge about themselves, which in turn should lead to better interpersonal functioning.

When reporting test information in a conceptualization, one approach we have found effective is to include the test data (i.e., graphs, charts, etc.) as well as an overview of the findings, including aspects of the testing that fit, those that didn't fit with therapy observations and hypotheses. Before giving an assessment instrument, it's important to have a clear rationale and hypotheses about what questions the test will hopefully answer. In Chapter 5, we talk about outcome in relation to the results of the OQ45, a measure that assesses client functioning and level of distress. In the case of Joe, it is pretty clear that over time he shows improvement, such that by the end of treatment, as well as follow-up, he has improved substantially (see Figure 4.2).

Client-Therapist Match

Multicultural Identity Interactions   As we discussed more thoroughly in Chapter 3, we each bring a set of multicultural variables (e.g., gender, race, sexual orientation, etc.) that define who we are (i.e., our identity). The task in this section of the conceptualization is to present information about the client's multicultural identities, your own multicultural identities as a therapist, and the resulting multicultural identity interaction. Although it would be cumbersome to list each multicultural identity (although it may be a task worth trying at least once!), our approach is to pick out the most salient multicultural identities based on what is known about the client and the therapist. In the case of Joe, it was determined that gender identity was the most salient, given Joe's beliefs about his marital "contract" (used to hypothesize a less-developed stage of gender identity) as well as the therapist's gender identity (based on the therapist's self-reported ideas of his own gender identity development). Using the Heuristic Model of Nonoppressive Development, we can roughly classify Joe as in the adaptation stage and the therapist in the exploration stage. The resulting gender identity interaction is, therefore, deemed to be progressive. In essence, because the therapist is at a more advanced stage than the client, the gender issues that emerge are likely to be handled fairly well. The one caveat to this is if the therapist can't resist an inclination to move the client quickly to a more advanced stage of gender identity development, something that would likely be met with resistance on the part of the client. In addition, for gender identity work to occur, there has to be some agreement on the part of the client about this goal. It's possible that the client sees this work would be useful to explore. For example, Joe may indicate that he in fact likes some things about his partner working but isn't sure how to make that fit with the way he was raised. In this case, the therapist may be able to assist the client in looking at gender from a new and more enlightened perspective.

Conflicts   Just as in everyday life, conflicts occur in therapy. In the case of Joe, no conflicts had occurred and the therapy was progressing smoothly. However, even when conflicts occur in therapy, they are not necessarily problematic. In fact, the working through of a conflict between a therapist and a client can prove quite powerful. The key is not to avoid conflicts but, rather, to embrace the conflict with the goal of providing the client with a corrective emotional experience. These conflicts sometimes result from misunderstandings (Rhodes, Hill, and Thompson, & Elliot, 1994) that in turn may lead to a rupture in the working alliance (Safran & Muran, 2000). One thing to consider is how you typically deal with conflicts. Perhaps managing conflicts is a form of countertransference worth exploring.

Countertransference   As you remember from Chapter 3, countertransference can be broadly defined as how our biases may influence our work in therapy. Suffice it to say, however, that all therapists have countertransference with every client. The key is to accept this notion, identify what the countertransference may be, and consider how it may be influencing the therapeutic work. The clearest sign that countertransference is operating is when a therapist says "I don't have any."

Treatment

Etiology of Client's Difficulties   Earlier in the case conceptualization write-up, a discussion ensued about situational events that may have led to the client's difficulties. In Joe's case, his layoff from work seemed to be a primary precipitating event. However, along with the situational events, it is often useful to offer a conceptual understanding that includes theoretical constructs, with the hope that a more complete picture is presented. Because the differential efficacy of theoretical approaches has not been empirically supported, we do not believe espousing only one particular theory is prudent. In fact, our belief is that constructs from multiple theories offer the most bang for your buck. There are a host of integrative psychotherapy models from which to choose (e.g., Norcross & Goldfried, 2005) that do a nice job of allowing for a multi-theoretical approach. As a general rule, we think it's important to at least look at multiple types of theoretical models that range from the intrapsychic to societal, thereby encompassing a relatively comprehensive view of the client's psychological functioning.

The etiology of the client's difficulties can begin with a psychodynamic-based perspective, which would include aspects such as the notion of true self versus false self and defense mechanisms (e.g., repression, projection, displacement, reaction formation, regression, rationalization, and identification). For example, you may encounter a client who chronically explains away certain unhealthy behaviors. Knowing about rationalization as a defense mechanism can help you more readily identify when the client is engaging in this defense, and in turn, help the client gain insight into how the defense is working, or not working, for her or him.

From an alternative lens, you could turn to a humanistic understanding of the client. Concepts such as previous experiences with positive regard and a client's state of incongruence can be useful in understanding how clients' life experiences influence their current functioning. From a cognitive-behavioral perspective, types of cognitive distortions (e.g., dichotomous thinking, selective abstraction, arbitrary inference, catastrophizing, over-generalization, labeling and mislabeling, magnification or minimization, and personalization) can be helpful in identifying point of intervention.

Finally, we believe that it's important to understand the client from a perspective of the social systems in which a client lives. These systemic approaches can include family systems theory that is useful to understand the family structure from which the client lives. In addition, feminist conceptualizations provide a societal understanding of how the client may be influenced from the culture in which he or she lives, as well as approaches to better empower the client. Together, these various theories can be pieced together to produce a more holistic picture of a client. One criticism of cobbling together multiple perspectives is that we do not stay true to a particular theory. This is accurate. We don't. We believe that because there are significant gaps in the theoretical models of explanation for every theory, we should not rely on a sole theory to understanding our clients. It would be analogous to painting a picture by limiting yourself to only one color. How boring!

Client's Progress to Date   In this section of a conceptualization, an overview of the therapeutic work that has taken place is described. Although a simple session-by-session summary may be used, it is often a more proficient approach to summarize major themes that have taken place. This is especially a prudent approach when there is a great deal of sessions to review. As can be seen in the conceptualization of Joe, four sessions have taken place, and the three primary areas that have been attended to include the working alliance, Joe's goal for finding new work, and a validation of Joe's experience.

We believe that the alliance is one aspect that should be addressed whenever the client's progress is discussed. The reason for this is that the alliance can make or break the therapeutic work and can be pointed to when things get rough in therapy or things are moving along as expected. It is also helpful to include things that haven't worked to date in therapy. I (NL) can remember back to one of my first clients with whom I engaged in a two-chair technique. This client was profoundly stuck in a life decision. The technique worked quite well, so well in fact that my supervisor encouraged me to do it again the following week so that my peers could see the work from behind the one-way mirror. Unfortunately, the experience of trying the two-chair technique again could not have been more disappointing to me, my peers, my supervisor, and, perhaps most important, to my client. In short, it bombed. In reviewing what had happened, what became clear is that what I thought the task should be (i.e., the technique) was not something the client really wanted again. So, in essence, our agreement on tasks component of the alliance was weak, and as a result, the technique was not effective. The lesson learned was to pay more attention to the task component of the alliance throughout the rest of our work together, something that would have naturally fit into a conceptualization.

Along with the alliance, the progress to date can point to the current state of the client's initial presenting concerns. Moreover, new issues that have emerged as salient to therapy should be mentioned. Also, it is important to consider which interventions worked and which didn't work to assist with future therapy sessions.

Proposed Treatment Strategy   In this section, the case conceptualization can again turn back toward integrating theory. We recommend that, as in the Progress to Date section, the working alliance is assessed and discussed. Ways to describe the alliance include very strong, moderately strong, solid, weak, or very weak. The strength of the alliance will, in turn, direct the therapist to what types of interventions the client can handle. For example, if there is a weak alliance, it may not serve the client well to start engaging in deep insight-oriented work. Conversely, if the alliance is strong, the therapist is afforded more intervention options because the client is likely to be able to tolerate more what the therapist can throw the client's way.

As before, we recommend multiple theoretical perspectives that range from intrapsychic to socially based models. This section is also a good section for the therapist to indicate potential interventions that could take place at a later point in time. For example, the therapist could state that if continued insight-exploration does not alter the client's struggle with her or his life decision, then a two-chair technique may prove useful to help unstick the client.

Unanswered Questions   After all that's been said about conceptualizing a client, what could possibly be left? Of course, probably more is left to say than has been said. If there were answers to all of the questions, then the therapeutic work would be finished. Invariably, there are many questions that need to be discussed. In a case consultation format, in which a group of trainees meet, unanswered questions can steer the group and attend best to the therapist's needs. Our preference is to spend very little time during a case conference literally reviewing the written conceptualization. Because we believe everyone should have read it before the meeting, we believe the time could best be served answering these unanswered questions.

The initial step in creating questions is to self-reflect on stuck-points in relation to the work that is taking place in therapy. Of course, the questions range from skills and techniques that would best serve the client to an exploration of countertransference issues of the therapist. Sometimes, a conceptualization meeting, or case conference, takes place after the client has terminated. The conference can still be useful inasmuch as the case is reviewed as a treatment autopsy, examining what went well and didn't go so well in therapy. It's never all the client's fault or all the therapist's fault when things don't go well. It's a matter of figuring out what can be learned from the interaction. Therapist learning should always be a goal for every therapy interaction, and is ultimately why the work in therapy is referred to as a "practice."

Conclusion

You may have noticed that we did not focus exclusively on theoretical orientation throughout this chapter. Rather, it is our hope that you learn to move beyond picking one perspective, and instead appreciate your client's multidimensionality by stepping back and acknowledging the "big picture" of conceptualization. Once you have this flexible framework, you'll likely notice other factors falling into place. You also may observe that you learn by referring to your original conceptualization, as much as you learn by disputing your own original ideas! Ultimately, we hope that you share our experience—that the task of conceptualizing a client is as interesting, thought-provoking, humbling, and challenging as therapy itself.

Discussion Questions and Exercises

Discussion Questions
- Which questions would you add to the intake outline presented? Which do you feel is the most important? Which questions would you leave out if you didn't have time to ask them all? Why?
- What if society influenced our behavior more than who we are as a person?
- What are the pros and cons of being an eclectic therapist?
- Is it possible to keep bias out of diagnosing?

- In what ways can we minimize bias when diagnosing?
- What are the benefits and problems associated with including sexual abuse history in an intake session?
- Would it ever be therapeutic for the therapist to initiate a discussion of gender roles in order to move Joe to a more advanced stage of gender identity development?
- What conflicts might arise between a therapist and client? In what ways might a client display or communicate conflict?

Exercises

Exercise 4.1: Person on the Street

Stop for a moment, and think about someone you just met. What did you find yourself noticing first? Her hair? His clothes? Tone of voice? This is the initial way most of us develop the way we view someone in the beginning of a relationship; we take in bits of information and create a whole. We know, however, that first impressions do not always tell the entire story.

Now reflect back when you first met a good friend or partner. Conduct the same exercise. What changed since your first encounter? What stayed the same? What does this tell you about first impressions of clients?

Exercise 4.2: Case Conceptualization

Below is an example of a conceptualization of a woman who has been seen in therapy for four sessions and whose treatment may be continued for up to 6 months on a weekly basis while she is being treated in a residential program.

Yolanda Stevens is a 32-year-old single, Caribbean-American woman who currently resides in the Horizon Residential Program. Before her most recent hospital admission, records indicate that she was admitted to Harpers Psychiatric Inpatient Unit for "bizarre behavior and destruction of property." Yolanda reports no history of drug or alcohol dependence; she further denies instances of suicidal ideation, plan, or intent. Records indicate a history of auditory hallucinations (at ages 19 and 24), although Yolanda denies current hallucinations or delusions. She is currently being prescribed Risperidone, Zyprexa, medications for oral care, and a multivitamin. She reports taking her medications as they are prescribed to her, and the nurses at the program confirm this report.

Yolanda was born on Grand Cayman Island. Her mother left Grand Cayman for the United States when Yolanda was an infant; her paternal grandparents, who she described as "strict and firm," raised Yolanda. When Yolanda was 14 years old, her grandparents left for the United States, and Yolanda was sent to live with an aunt. At age 16, Yolanda came to the United States and began living with her paternal grandfather in Newark, New Jersey. At times, her biological father also would live in the house. Yolanda reported that although she is the only child of her father and mother, her father has a son and two daughters, and her mother has three other sons and a daughter. Yolanda stated that she does not know her mother's other children well and that she only began having a relationship with her mother when Yolanda came to the United States. (Her mother lives in Connecticut, about 2 hours away by car.) Yolanda stated that her father "does not have a good job" and works as a "janitor in a hotel"; she reported that her mother works as a bookkeeper for a small export company. Before her admission to Horizon, Yolanda reported that she was living with her grandfather. She stated that because she did not have much money, she was not taking many baths and was using a candle for light (to save money on the water and electric bills).

Yolanda denied any physical or sexual abuse, but described behaviors by her grandfather (e.g., yelling and degradation) that appear to constitute emotional or verbal abuse. When asked about discipline in the family, she gave as an example being "slapped on the butt with a belt when [she] did not tell [her] grandparents where [she] was going."

Yolanda stated that she finished high school after moving to the United States. She reported that she was a B or C student. After high school, she completed one year of an associate's degree in accounting. She disclosed that a poor grade average led to her leaving the accounting program. Yolanda reported that she has worked as a bookkeeper and a bookstore manager. Records indicate and Yolanda confirmed that she has not been employed in 2 years.

Yolanda stated that she has not had many boyfriends. She disclosed that she was with a man after her time in the accountancy program, but stated that they broke up after she asked him for more of a commitment in their relationship. Yolanda stated that she is not currently romantically involved with anyone.

Yolanda has been offered weekly therapy while in the Horizons Program. It had been explained to her that this therapy is voluntary, but that the therapy is recommended as part of her treatment in the program. The boundaries of confidentiality also have been explained to Yolanda.

So now that you know a little bit about Yolanda, we will explore the different aspects of client conceptualization. But, before we go any further, take the time to reflect on the case conceptualization that you just read. What general types of information have been included (e.g., education, family background, and current prescribed medications)? Knowing that this conceptualization was written after the fourth session with the client, what more would you hope to learn in the subsequent four sessions with her? What do wish you already knew after the fourth session? What questions are coming up for you as a clinician with regard to treatment, interpersonal dynamics, and intrapersonal characteristics of the client? Take a minute and read back over the conceptualization; make a list of information you would like to see included. Divide your list into information (1) that you would have liked to see gathered by the fourth session and (2) that you would want to find out in subsequent sessions. Remember that clinicians often have stylistic differences when composing a client conceptualization, but clear and concise information is crucial. You will start to develop your own style as you see clients and construct case conceptualizations from your work with them.

Exercise 4.3: Genogram

Put together a genogram based on your family. Be as specific as possible and include as much information as possible about people in the genogram including gender, race, ethnicity, sexual orientation, socioeconomic status, disability, career, education, age, birth dates, death dates, marriages, divorces, separations, emotional alliances, cutoffs, illnesses, triangles, values, gender roles, substance abuse and dependence, physical abuse, sexual abuse, mental illness, conflicts, critical family events, and societal events.

You may have to talk with family members to find some of the information. Keep a diary of your reactions to creating the genogram, as well as your family interviews. See if you can identify any family patterns or insights into how you became who you are.

Table 4.1 Case Conceptualization Outline

Intake Summary
> Demographic Description
> Presenting Problems (include client perceptions)
> Circumstances Leading to Admission

Background Information
> History Relevant to Treatment
> Family Background (salient issues, genogram)
> Work History
> Education History
> Medical History
> Substance Use History
> Previous Mental Health Treatment

Clinical Impressions
> *DSM* Diagnosis (full diagnosis; include specific criteria met and not met)
> Description of Client Functioning
>> Cognitive
>> Affective
>> Behavioral
>> Suicidal Risk
>> Physical Appearance
>> Strengths
>> Prognosis
> Client-Therapist Match
>> Multicultural Identity Interactions
>> Conflicts
>> Countertransference issues (always have them!)

Treatment
> Etiology of Client's Difficulties (be sure to integrate theory, i.e., use theoretical constructs and support with examples from the case)
> Client's Progress to Date [include number of sessions, summary of sessions over time (can group sessions), integrate theory, mutually agreed-on treatment goals, interventions that were effective/ineffective, etc.]
> Proposed Treatment Strategy (integrate theory, i.e., use theoretical constructs and support with examples from the case)
> Unanswered Questions (rank order most salient first)

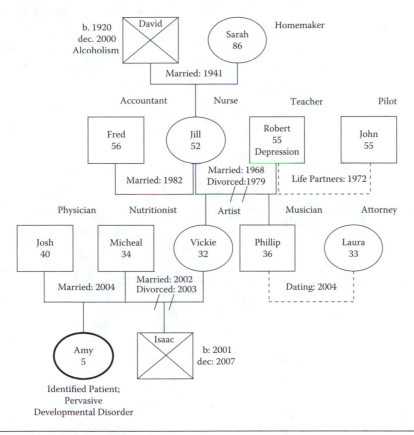

Figure 4.1 Sample Genogram.

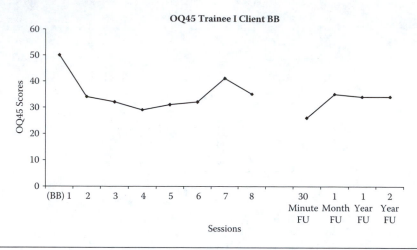

Figure 4.2 Joe's Overall Level of Distress Across Sessions and at Follow-Up.

CHAPTER 5

Therapy Outcome

Things do not change, we change.

—Henry David Thoreau

In Chapter 2, we focused on therapy process, that is, what happens *in* therapy sessions. The present chapter will focus on therapy outcome, which is what therapy *does* (Orlinsky et al., 1994). Therapy outcome can be determined by examining multiple perspectives at various levels of session analysis. One can assess outcome from the client's perspective, the therapist's perspective, and the perspective of an impartial other (i.e., clinical supervisor or researcher). Treatment outcome also can be measured at various levels of analysis, both subjective and objective, including the impact of critical session experiences, post session changes in mood (i.e., symptoms of anxiety and depression), and changes in functioning in the general spheres of living (i.e., interpersonal, social, academic, work, etc.).

In addition to the traditional definition of outcome, we attend to some nontraditional outcome variables in this chapter: external events that influence the therapy work, client no-shows and unilateral termination, client and therapist regrets, and the learning that takes place as therapists engage in therapy. Throughout, we refer to examples from the Study, in which we chose to assess outcome from multiple perspectives and at various stages of analysis. We end the chapter with a discussion of an often overlooked aspect of therapy, the point at which much of the effectiveness of therapy can be evaluated and reviewed, the termination of treatment.

Session by Session Outcome

Despite the fact that clients come in looking for the cure to something, and therapists want to provide the cure for something, these large "somethings" tend to be the thing that are least directly influenced by therapy. For example, a client may come into therapy to decrease her or his daily feelings of anxiety. As pointed out in Chapter 2, the therapist will engage in a variety of nonverbal and verbal responses that, in turn, could help the client explore the issue, gain insight into the issue, or behaviorally attend to the issue. These end result events (e.g., change in insight) may occur as part of a session, at the end of the session, or after a number of sessions. Rarely does change come in a nice package, in which change is a result of a linear series of interventions as proposed by many theoretical approaches. Instead, experienced therapists learn over time that therapy is really a series of chunks or events rather than a myriad of theoretical propositions and uncohesive facts. In sum, experienced therapists generally look at particular change events (Greenberg, 1986; Warwar & Greenberg, 2000) for a particular type or types of concern.

One way of capturing these events is to have each person in the therapeutic dyad indicate what has been most helpful and unhelpful about each session, a qualitative methodology that has had a long history within psychotherapy research (Elliot & Shapiro, 1992; Morrow & Smith, 2000). Conversely, a quantitative methodology for assessing symptom outcome, typically following each session, has provided insights into therapy outcome (Lambert & Hill, 1994). This section attends to the session events and is divided into these quantitative and qualitative aspects of therapy outcome: (a) outcome measurement and (b) session events perceived as helpful and hindering. Although helpful and hindering session events also can be seen as a kind of process, we include these events in the therapy outcome chapter because they reflect something that happened that changed the client in some fashion.

Quantitative Measurement-Based Outcomes

One of the most common ways to assess therapy outcome is using a measure of symptoms that could be displayed by a client (e.g., SCL-90, Beck Depression Inventory, Hamilton Rating Scale for Depression). The advantage of these measures is that they provide a relatively valid and reliable way to measure client symptom change that can be communicated in a standardized way across many therapists. In addition, guidelines are usually available that can provide therapists with information about how their client is doing relative to the general population. One measure that is proving quite useful for clinicians and methodology sound is the Outcome Questionnaire 45 (OQ-45). The developers of the OQ-45 set out to design a brief measure that was cost-effective in assessing patient change session by session and outcome over time (Lambert, Hansen, et al., 1996; Lambert, Okiishi, Finch, & Johnson, 1998). They designed the OQ-45 to measure both changes in clients' emotional states as well as in their level of functioning in their everyday lives. The test assesses the three primary areas that therapists most commonly assess in their clients. The first area is symptomatic distress to understand the overall emotional state. The second area is interpersonal problems to assess clients' satisfaction with their interpersonal relationships. The third area is social role adjustment, which assesses client adequacy in managing their lives. Not only does the OQ-45 assess the intensity of difficulty in the above areas, it also measures aspects of well-being with reference to positive mental health characteristics (e.g., exercise, nutrition).

For illustration purposes, we decided to use the OQ-45 for our Study over other outcome measures because of its psychometric qualities, brevity, ability to assess general functioning, sensitivity to change over time, and suitability for repeated use on a weekly basis. As a result of questions raised regarding the construct validity of the OQ-45 subscales when examined independently (Mueller, Lambert, & Burlingame, 1998), we chose to use the global score of all scales in our analysis of session outcome.

There are multiple ways in which to use the outcome data from the Study to illustrate how therapy outcome data can be used to determine therapeutic effectiveness and ineffectiveness. Of the 18 clients in the Study, two-thirds (n = 12) showed an improvement in symptom distress levels, interpersonal problems, and social role adjustment as assessed by the OQ-45, whereas one-third showed no change and one client showed a deterioration in functioning (see Table 13 in the Appendix for a breakdown of results by trainee and Table 14 in the Appendix for a breakdown of results by outcome status). Such results indicate that the treatment provided by the therapist trainees in the Study was effective for most of the clients. This is an important finding, given that they were all seeing clients for the first time.

A closer look at the overall outcome results shows a relationship between treatment length and outcome. The clients who improved (mean number of sessions = 13.2) or showed a full recovery (mean number of sessions = 12.4) had on average 3 to 4 more sessions than clients who showed no change (mean number of sessions = 9.4). Additionally, there appeared to be little difference in pretreatment OQ-45 scores in the recovered, improved, and no change groups, suggesting that there were few differences in client symptom levels. What we do not know is why the no-change group selected to end treatment earlier than the improved and recovered groups. Interestingly, the one client who showed a deterioration had a lower pretreatment score than most client participants and had fewer than average sessions (n = 5).

One can view a breakdown of individual client outcome session by session in Figures A.1 through A.18 in the Appendix. An important point for beginning trainees to note is that clients often fluctuate in functioning over the course of treatment and some clients actually experience an increase in symptoms before they get better. An examination of client progression session by session shows that client symptoms levels rose and fell over the course of treatment, even for those who showed improvement or full recovery. A possible explanation of this phenomenon could be explained by clients' responses in the post session interviews. One of the categories that emerged from the Hindering Critical Incident data was Pursuing Painful Topics. For the most part, the clients who reported that pursuing painful areas in therapy was immediately hindering to them during the session also noted that they realized doing so was an important component of treatment and likely would lead to positive treatment outcome. What therapists in training can take from these data is an understanding that clients do not need to show gains every session in order for treatment to be effective. In fact, it might serve their work with clients to let their clients know that at times they might feel worse before they begin to feel better. Sometimes, normalizing for their clients that treatment progress can be gradual with fluctuation can be beneficial so that they do not become discouraged along the way. A common analogy that can be used with clients is what happens when someone has surgery. The pain of the surgery often can be worse than the physical impairment that is treated, and recovery time has its ups and downs.

Helpful and Hindering Critical Events in Psychotherapy

Another manner in which to look at therapy outcome is via qualitative means, and is perhaps closer to what professional therapists do, albeit more infrequently than after every session. The basic paradigm is to ask clients what they experienced as most helpful or hindering from a particular session. Investigations of critical incidents of therapy have identified helpful therapy moments as including therapist interpretation and advisement (Elliot, Barker, Caskey, & Pistrang, 1982), reassurance, problem solving (Llewelyn, 1988), exploration of feelings, avoided issues, insight, the therapeutic relationship, and new ways of being (Mahrer & Nadler, 1986); and have identified hindering events that include therapist mistakes, client interpersonal difficulties (Hill, Nutt-Williams, Heaton, Thompson, & Rhodes, 1996), client disappointments, confrontation, therapist misdirection (Llewelyn, 1988), poor therapeutic relationships, lack of therapist acknowledgment of client negative feelings (Rhodes, Hill, Thompson, & Elliot, 1994), and therapist questions (Elliot et al., 1982). These studies illuminate what many therapists anticipate, that is, events in therapy that can be helpful or hindering to clients based on differing levels of therapist responsiveness to client needs (Stiles, Honos-Webb, & Surko, 1998). However, virtually no research has identified the specific types of critical incidents from the perspective of both clients and therapists at the same time.

In the Study, we asked clients and their therapists to describe what they thought were the most helpful and the most hindering aspects of the therapy sessions for the clients. Our hope was to find particularly salient events that either helped or hindered treatment that was witnessed by both members of the dyad. From the data, we developed four groups of categories: (1) client helpful incidents and their associated thoughts and feelings, (2) client hindering incidents and their associated thoughts and feelings, (3) trainee perceived helpful incidents for their clients and their associated thoughts and feelings, and (4) trainee perceived hindering incidents for their clients and their associated thoughts and feelings.

Clients identified 364 helpful and hindering critical events and 471 associated thoughts and feelings (see Tables 15–17 in the Appendix). Overwhelmingly, the clients in the Study reported receiving "Therapist Guidance" as the most helpful aspect of their therapy sessions. "Therapist Guidance" consisted of the therapist providing something that was helpful to the client and included clinical interventions such as offering explanations, suggestions, alternative perspectives, information, feedback, and advice. The next most frequently identified helpful event was receiving "Progress/Goal Orientation" interventions from the trainee. In such sessions, the therapists helped the clients to focus on their treatment progression and progress by either helping the client to work toward goals and skills sets or by helping the client to see progress and lessons learned. Clients also found therapy to be particularly helpful when they experienced "Gained Deeper Understanding or Insight" from their work in session. For example, clients described processing issues on a deeper level helped them to develop insight into their issues and integrate such learning into a better understanding of themselves and others. The next most frequent category of "Catharsis" suggests that just having an emotionally safe and confidential outlet to talk about issues and vent feelings provided clients with a sense of release. The category of "Therapist Attentive to the Therapeutic Process" consisted of instances in which the clients experienced the therapists as attentive and competent such that they felt heard and received meaningful help. Receiving "Clarification" of goals, issues, or problems also helped clients to identify core issues and focus their session work. The hallmark characteristic of the next category of "Received Support/Validation" (7.7%) was that the clients received support, validation, or reassurance, which helped them to feel accepted and not judged, and which helped them to feel encouraged to move forward. As can be seen, each of the categories generally fall under one of the three stages of helping: exploration, insight, and action.

The clients experienced multiple emotions in response to the helpful incidents, ranging from positive to negative. Most frequently, they identified feeling "Good/Uplifted," followed by feeling "Goal Oriented," feeling a sense of "Relief," having thoughts about "New Insights," feeling "Anxious/Apprehensive," feeling "Vulnerable/Painful," feeling "Validated/Supported," having thoughts about a "Positive Self-Concept," feeling "Positive About Trainee," and feeling "Anger/Frustration."

The clients also provided a range of hindering events from reporting that nothing was hindering to describing aspects of their therapy trainee's clinical skills, their own behavior, or external issues. Interestingly, clients reported "Nothing Was Hindering" (61.5%) in over half of their therapy sessions. In part, this may reflect that clients tend to want to be nice to their therapists, as it isn't easy to be critical of someone who is there to help you. However, it also likely indicates that these beginning therapists were indeed helpful to clients, something we find that beginning therapists often are. In fact, it's probably the case that for most clients, therapist experience matters only a marginal amount. Our own sense is that experience alone is a poor predictor of therapeutic outcome. As we will talk about in Chapter 8, there are a host of factors that separate the most effective from the least effective therapists and amount of experience alone contributes very little to the equation.

When the clients reported a hindering event, the most frequent category endorsed was the trainee's "Lack of Finesse/Skill" (9.3%). Examples of such events included the therapist rushing the client through issues, being defensive, or asking questions in a judgmental way. The clients also attributed the hindering events to "Client Behaviors" (8.8%) in the form of defenses such as avoidance, rambling speech, or being reluctant to work in session or complete assigned homework. So, in essence, clients seem to have an awareness of when to attribute problems in therapy to the therapist or to themselves. As with the helpful events, the clients experienced a range of thoughts and feelings in response to the hindering events including pain, anxiety, anger, and positive reactions.

Therapists identified 364 critical events and 1,057 associated thoughts and feelings (see Tables 18–21 in the Appendix). As can be seen, there are similarities to what the clients identified as helpful and hindering. When we asked the therapists what they thought was the most helpful aspect of the therapy session for their clients, they identified "Catharsis" most frequently, which they described as talking about issues or venting that allowed the clients to process feelings and gain release. The next most frequently endorsed helpful event category was receiving "Trainee Guidance." Such helpful incidents consisted of the therapy trainee providing the client with direction, feedback, suggestions, information, or alternative perspectives. The trainees identified the category "Gained Deeper Understanding or Insight" (17.6%) more frequently than the clients did (12.1%), which indicates that perhaps trainees value it more, or could be related to the psychological mindedness of the trainee. The next most frequently identified helpful event of "Trainee Attentive to Relationship/Supportive" consisted of the trainee being attentive, invested, supportive, or encouraging. The trainees identified the provision of interventions with a "Progress/Goal Orientation" as helpful, in that they helped the clients to focus on their progress by either helping the client to work on goals, integrate lessons learned, or celebrate progress. The trainees also identified aspects of the clients' behavior as helpful "Client Motivated/Invested" (3.8%), which they defined as displaying commitment to treatment by working on issues in and out of sessions.

When asked to speculate as to what they thought their clients thought or felt at the time of the helpful event, the trainees identified many of the things clients identified as well (e.g., relief, anxiety, etc.). This indicates that the trainees were pretty good at picking up what the clients were experiencing.

The trainees also identified a range of thoughts and feelings that they experienced during the helpful events. Most often, they reported feeling "Positive About Client/Relationship" followed by "Positive About Self/ Work." The therapists also reported feelings associated with the desire to "Validate/Support" their clients, followed by feeling "Positive About Progress/Goals," having thoughts of "What to do" next, feeling "Relieved/ Relaxed," and having "Concerns About Self/Work." Additionally, the therapists reported thoughts associated with "Insights/Conceptualizations" about their clients, feeling "Frustrated/Disappointed," having "Concerns About Progress/Goals," feeling "Nervous/Anxious," and thoughts associated with "Session Lack of Depth." We present these reactions as a way to normalize what you may experience as a beginning therapist. As can be seen, there are a range of positive and negative reactions.

When we asked the trainees to describe the most hindering aspect of the therapy session for their clients, most frequently they identified their own "Lack of Finesse/Skill." Examples of such events included the therapist having no idea what to say, not connecting with the client, or talking too much. This finding is typical for beginning trainees and to some extent may reflect the reality of the situation; that is, there will be times as a beginning therapist that the response modes will not be as smooth as hoped. The important thing to know is that even very seasoned therapists experience these things, probably at some point during every session. Like an actor in a play, the key task is for the show to go on, for the therapist to continue. There are always multiple opportunities to demonstrate a skill that can help a client. The next most frequently endorsed category was that of "Client Behaviors," which consisted of client defenses or motivation issues that hindered their work in sessions, such as avoidance, rambling, and resistance to interventions. The therapist also attributed the clients' experience of hindering incidents to circumstances contributing to leaving the "Client's Needs Unmet." For example, such events consisted of the trainee not providing direction, feedback, or enough structure (regardless of clinical appropriateness of doing so).

As with all of the helpful critical incidents, the therapist trainees identified a wide range of client thoughts and feelings in response to the hindering events, many of which were on target with what the client was experiencing. The trainees also were able to identify a range of thoughts and feelings that they experienced during the hindering events including negative reactions about one's self, frustration, disappointment, and concerns about what to do next. Again, these examples are provided for illustrative and normative purposes in relation to what we anticipate you will experience as a newer therapist. The last internal reaction, concerns about what to do next, is a common reaction of beginning therapists.

Outcomes Should Be Linked to Goals of Therapy

One of the helpful events identified was a discussion of progress on the therapy goals. In the formation of the therapeutic alliance, a negotiation of the goals of therapy was discussed as a critical process. In addition, it is anticipated that the goals of therapy will be modified over time, and new ones may arise throughout the course of treatment. It's important for therapists to keep the goals in mind when working with a client and periodically check in on the progress made on these goals. When clients seem unsure what to do next in therapy, one thing that's helpful is to ask them what they would like to work and on and help prioritize the next goal on which to attend. One important process in the creation and discussion of goals is to specify the goals as much as possible. Sometimes that's easy for the client and sometimes the client isn't ready to specify a goal. However, most of the time it takes some work, which includes asking what the goal is and how things would look different in the client's life if the goal is met. In addition, it's often quite useful to create mini-goals, or steps along the way that must be taken before a final goal is reached. The journey of 1,000 miles does indeed begin with the first step! Finally, as we will discuss shortly, in the context of termination, it's important to review the progress on the various goals that have come about during therapy.

Regrets in Therapy

Throughout the course of our training and postdegree therapy work, we have all had regrets about what happened during our therapy sessions. Even to this day, we ask ourselves how we could have done some things differently during our sessions with clients. When we have been clients, we, too, have asked ourselves a similar question. Interestingly, until now there appears to be no literature about such session dynamics. Believing that such information might help beginning trainees, we decided to ask the clients and their therapists in the Study to describe what, if anything, they wished that they or their client/therapist had done differently during the therapy session (see Tables 22–25 in the Appendix). We divided the responses to the therapy session regrets questions into four groups of categories: (1) client regrets of their own behavior in therapy, (2) client regrets of their therapist's behavior in therapy, (3) therapist regrets of their own behavior in therapy, and (4) therapist regrets of their client's behavior in therapy.

Across the board, clients indicated they had no regrets about how they worked in their therapy sessions. They frequently clarified their lack of regrets by saying that they had worked hard, made progress, or addressed what they intended, many stating that it could not have gone better. When the clients wished they had done something differently, they most frequently wished they were "More Prepared, Motivated, or Focused" during the session. This finding is particularly illuminating because it demonstrates that clients are aware that their motivation fluctuates through the course of treatment. Clients also identified that they wished they had been "More Insightful or Expressive of Here and Now Feelings" during the session (e.g., comments about dynamics occurring in the present moment in the room between the therapist and client). The skill of immediacy is one that seems to take longer to demonstrate particularly for beginning therapists. Our experience is that as the other skills fall into place, here-and-now comments are useful to try and can prove quite powerful.

When asked about what clients wished their therapists would have done differently, they mostly indicated no regrets, which appears to indicate that clients generally had positive reactions to the therapist and felt grateful for the help offered to them. That said, at times some clients displayed protectiveness toward their therapists. For example, some noted that they knew their therapists were in training, wanted to help them, and expressed concern that if they said anything negative that it might harm the therapist in some way (i.e., program evaluation). When such issues arose during the interviews, the researchers assured the clients that all interview responses were confidential and would not be detrimental to the therapists in any way. However, it is likely that a number of clients had similar sentiments that went unreported. When they identified what they wished their therapists had done differently, the clients most frequently said "Provide More Guidance and Direction in Session." One thing this finding points toward is that, occasionally, it becomes a challenge to structure a session for a client. In other words, some clients need extra structure in a session to help guide them on the type of work that may prove useful. The task for the therapist is to offer suggestions about how the work may proceed while also trying to empower the client to make this decision. One useful way that we have found is to review with a client the goals to date and ask them which goals they would like to work on next. Another way is to offer a here-and-now statement such as, "How are things going so far in today's session?" A question such as this one can be very useful to ensure that the work in therapy is fitting with the client's needs.

In terms of therapist regrets, in over one-quarter of the therapy sessions they wished they had "Better Management of the Session." A common example of this regret was the wish that they had a better grasp of the flow of the session and how to use the session time effectively. As just mentioned, a way to handle this is to consider the goals and tasks of the alliance to make sure the therapist is in sync with the client. Another regret was the therapists' wish that they were "More Prepared, Skilled, or Invested." In some cases, such regrets were a function of wanting to be experienced therapists instantly and in some cases the trainees expressed not preparing for or investing themselves in the session as they thought they should have been. Therapists also wished they had used opportunities to "Elicit a Deeper Focus" on the session content, for example, wishing that the session had been at a less superficial level or that they had not missed opportunities to move from the manifest to the latent content. Deeper focus can often be attained though further exploration of a client concern. The task here is to be patient as a therapist and allow the client to reflect on events in their past through thoughtful self-discovery.

In relation to what therapists wished their clients had done differently, one finding that is common for therapists of all levels of training is the desire for clients to demonstrate more motivation or be more committed to the treatment process. This can prove frustrating at times but the key is to consider why this may be happening. Of course the inclination is to kick the client along to get to the next step in the process; however, therapists must resist this urge. Instead, an examination of how it serves the client to be unmotivated should be considered as well as accept the client for where he or she is at. Sometimes the client isn't ready to move forward. That's probably true of all of us at points in our lives. In addition, sometimes clients are stuck because of a fear of proceeding further. It behooves the therapist to explore and normalize this fear. In that way, the client can more readily move to the next level of work.

No-Shows

Some clients fail to show for a session for various reasons. They might forget about the appointment or deliberately not attend. Clients might forget if the session time and day varies from week to week. However, they also might subconsciously avoid the therapist or the work in sessions for a variety of reasons, for example, the work in therapy surrounds a painful issue, as in the case of abuse histories, or the client might be upset with the therapist for perceived or actual invalidations. Although clients might genuinely forget about an appointment at times, therapists cannot rule out subconscious or deliberate motivations for client no-shows. As such, we recommend that therapists examine content and dynamics from previous sessions as well as the progression of treatment for possible treatment issues that have been unaddressed. The results of the Study suggest that clients are reluctant to address unmet needs or dissatisfactions directly with their therapists. Such unexamined dynamics likely contribute to premature or unilateral client terminations, in which the client fails to show for sessions without informing the therapist of their intent to end treatment.

A qualitative review of the client no-shows during our study revealed some interesting trends. Eleven of the 18 clients attended every scheduled session, meaning they did not have any no-shows. Of the 11 clients who attended regularly, 3 recovered, 6 improved, and 2 showed no change in OQ-45 outcome scores from pretreatment to post treatment assessment periods. However, of the seven clients who had at least one no-show during the course of treatment, only two recovered, one showed improvement, three experienced no change, and one deteriorated as measured by pre- and post treatment OQ-45 scores. A closer examination of the sessions and outcome data of such clients revealed that four of the seven who no-showed experienced an increase in problematic symptoms in the session immediately following the session no-show, suggesting a possible relationship between session no-shows and deterioration. One explanation might be that the clients felt worse as a result of not receiving treatment the previous week. However, the clients also might have failed to show as a result of feeling worse and possibly discouraged by feeling that treatment was not helping, at least at that time. Interestingly, two of the no-show clients had missed a total of three sessions each. Of those two, one had experienced no change in outcome scores post treatment, whereas the other actually had deteriorated and prematurely terminated treatment. One cannot conclude the exact cause for the lack of symptom improvement with the no-show clients without more intensive follow up to assess what contributed to their poorer outcome data. However, our descriptive look at the no-show data suggests that therapists in training as well as experienced practitioners might serve their clients well if they spend time in sessions following no-shows openly exploring with clients possible reasons for the no-show, especially reasons associated with therapist behaviors and treatment progress.

An interesting note in reference to the no-show data is that one therapist trainee failed to show for a client session. As one would expect, in the session immediately following the therapist's no-show, the client reported a worsening of symptoms. Although we do not have other data to support this finding, it suggests that unexpected therapist absences or cancellations likely have a negative effect on clients. Consequently, we recommend that therapists plan absences in advance whenever possible so that clients can prepare for a break in treatment and possibly make arrangements for assistance when their therapists are not available.

One other thing about no-shows that is important to note is that occasionally a client will no-show and the reaction of the therapist is relief or even happiness! This may be caused by a number of factors including wanting more time to work on an academic assignment, to not feeling ready to handle the client's interpersonal style that day. The important thing to consider is the operating countertransference when a no-show occurs. It can be quite illuminating to discover, not just what seems obvious, but underlying reasons as well. If you find yourself feeling excitement when a client does not attend session without reason, we would encourage you to discuss this in supervision. In the end, these types of reflections allow for us to provide better treatment to our clients.

Trainee Learning

Without a doubt, one of the best ways of learning how to do therapy is by having tried it. There's nothing like having experience as a teacher, that is, as long as we listen to that teacher! See Tables 26 and 27 in the Appendix that include positive and negative things the beginning therapists in the Study believed they learned from conducting therapy (Spradlin, Ladany, & Schutt, 2003). One of the most striking findings is that for nearly half of the identified learnings, the therapists gained confidence in their work. This finding fits with what we know about self-efficacy (Bandura, 1977, 1982, 2000), that is, performing the behavior enhances confidence in demonstrating the behavior. This finding also goes along with our own experience of developing confidence in our skills over time. We find that usually by a month or so into the work, therapists develop a reasonable amount of confidence in their work such that their lack of confidence (uncertainty about what is about to take place in therapy) gets in the way only minimally. During this time of enhanced learning, therapists also tend to have a better sense about how clients are going to behave and how to react to clients in therapy. In all, the therapy work begins to fall into a comfort zone similar to how you may have experienced any number of jobs you have done in your life, whether it be baby-sitting, delivering newspapers, waiting tables, or being a student.

External Events: Sometimes What Happens Outside of Therapy Is More Important Than What Happens in Therapy

At some point, all therapists realize that we are only with our clients for 50 minutes a week, which means that clients spend less than 1% of their week in therapy. So a reasonable question that follows is: "How do things that happen to clients away from the therapy session influence their presenting problems?" In fact, even the way this question is asked indicates a therapy-narcissism, if you will. It assumes that therapy is the center of a client's life. This may be true for some clients. However, therapy is just one aspect of a pretty full life for most folks. Quite understandably, many things occur outside of the therapeutic hour that can be more influential to the client's presenting concerns than what happens inside the therapeutic hour. Hence, as therapists and researchers we believe that we must honor these external events and take them into account when considering client change and therapy outcome.

In the Study, we asked clients about events outside their therapy that made them feel better or worse. The data proved somewhat sparse and not as coherent as other data that we gathered, perhaps because of the way we asked the questions. However, some interesting things were discovered and we offer them here as stimuli for further thought.

One area that was noted was that there were things that happened that were out of the client's control but influenced his or her mood. For example, events such as going to his daughter's wedding was an uplifting experience for one client, whereas having a relative develop a heart problem that required surgery negatively influenced another client's mood. In another case, a client developed a cold that made her feel worse about things and more vulnerable. In these cases, through no action of the client, her or his mood was affected by some external event. In other cases, the client was an active participant in positively affecting his or her mood such as finding pleasure in exercise.

Another area of influence was the client's network of social support. In some instances his or her support network played a key role in uplifting the client's spirits. In other cases, the client's social support was not so social (e.g., fight with a family member). A common stressor for clients was financial stress. Many clients have legitimate financial needs that are not being met. For others, financial concerns may be directly linked to therapy issues (e.g., spending money as a way to fulfill unmet personal needs). In all of these instances, as well as many others, we need to be aware that external events can play a significant role in how clients feel.

Termination Is Not the Time to Become Jaded

During my (NL) training, one of the worst suggestions I ever received from a supervisor was that therapists needed to become more "jaded" during termination. Given this supervisor's issues with loss and intense feelings in general, this unfortunate comment was not all that surprising. Perhaps what was more surprising was that she had more than 20 years of therapy experience and was still practicing!

In any event, the termination phase cannot be underestimated in terms of its importance to the therapy. The termination work serves two purposes. First, it provides a forum to summarize the past and future work in therapy. Second, it offers the client and the therapist the opportunity to experience a positive ending of an important relationship, something many people never get to experience.

Depending on the length of the work, the final session may be considered the *termination session*. However, for clients with whom you have been working for a few years, and where loss has been a prominent theme, there may be multiple sessions that account for the termination work. Alternatively, if there have only been a few sessions of therapy, and the client announces that the current session will be the last session, then the termination may only be minutes long. Regardless of the time frame, it is important that some form of termination is conducted.

We believe there to be six key components to an effective termination. First, both the client and the therapist should come to the final session or sessions thinking about the therapeutic work. For example, the client may be encouraged to consider how he or she has changed since the first session. In addition, both could reflect on what some of the critical moments or critical incidents of therapy have been. Moreover, the client can be supported to consider what has been learned and how he or she has changed. Similar to the client, the therapist should reflect on the therapeutic work. We tend to like to review our case notes from the beginning and jot down some of the moments in therapy we thought were critical for the client. Oftentimes there is a match between what we find important and what the client finds important. However, in many instances, what the therapist finds critical, the client may not even remember! In all of these instances, mutual learning can take place.

Second, it is important that both the therapist and the client reflect on the working alliance and then consider how the work is related to the initial and subsequent therapy goals, and how the work has been generalized to the client's life outside of therapy. Both should consider the tasks that have worked, or been helpful in therapy, and what did not work as well. Our experience is that clients can teach us a lot about how we can become better therapists in these moments. If your clients should be bold enough to give you constructive criticism, you should use these moments to model how to accept feedback in a non-defensive manner. This is not a time to shift blame or make excuses. For many clients, it may be a big step to communicate their feelings, both positive and negative. As a therapist, you should be able to accept their words and thank them for taking a risk.

By contrast, frequently clients will give their therapists great compliments. Many times, therapists are uncomfortable with compliments given to them, and they respond to compliments by saying, "Aw, it was nothing," or "It wasn't me, it was you!" Instead, we want to propose a different angle. Although we believe it is important to empower clients to take ownership of their successes, it also can be important to model how to comfortably and confidently receive a compliment! Use your best judgment to find a balance of appreciating the client's hard work as well as your own.

Following a review of the work to date, the third step is to have both the client and the therapist consider the client's "growth edges," or the work that may be left to do in or out of therapy. In addition, be sure to mutually discuss the client's strengths along with his or her growth edges.

Fourth, it is important to consider the client's approach to endings (e.g., loss, death, etc.) in their life and what it means to end a relationship that may have been quite intense and intimate. In essence, we think it's important to process with the client what it means to end this relationship. Similarly, the therapist should have explored how he or she may approach endings in life and how ending with this particular client may trigger reactions that either facilitate or interfere with this ending (a form of termination countertransference!).

Fifth, it is not uncommon for clients to bring gifts to the final therapy session. In these situations, it is imperative to consider your personal and professional boundaries, the policies of your working environment, the cultural background of your client, the ethical codes of your state, and the opinion of your supervisor. For example, when I (LPC) worked at a Veteran's Administration, it was against the rules to accept any gift worth more than a dollar. When I (JW) worked in a community mental health agency servicing a primarily Hispanic population, my supervisor told me refusing gifts (usually food) would be so culturally insensitive, that it would be a reason for dismissal! I believe (NL) that for the most part, we should graciously accept the gifts clients give us, both the tangible and intangible (Knox, Hess, Williams, & Hill, 2003). Of course, be sure that the gift is one that has more meaning than cost. Although a new automobile may be nice and needed, reasonable and ethical boundaries should be kept in mind. When in doubt, we encourage discussion with your supervisor, training director, practicum cohort, or licensing board.

Finally, the last moments of the termination work should consist of a genuine exchange of any final thoughts and feelings that each member of the dyad has. For example, if it's the case, you can tell the client how much you have enjoyed working with her or him or that it's sad to say goodbye. In addition, the final moments are when the issue of touch in therapy becomes important and can be filled with anxiety about what is appropriate and what is culturally sensitive (Tune, 2001). Some suggest to extend a hand and let the client decide to shake it or offer a hug. In some environments (e.g., nursing home) hugs may be more commonplace for termination or any session. In other therapeutic environments (e.g., a prison) touching may never be an option. Again, the important part is to allow for an ending that is appropriate to your work environment, personally and professionally within your boundaries, ethical, meaningful, and fits with the client.

Conclusion

Throughout this chapter, we have explored the many facets of therapy outcome. To be sure, the amount of data we present can be experienced as overwhelming. Not to worry. It is impossible to take in all the information at once and we hope that you can go back and reflect on the discussion over time, as it fits your emerging needs as a therapist.

Discussion Questions and Exercises

Discussion Questions

- What are the ways in which, structured and unstructured, you would know whether your client was improving? What would you do if both objective measures and your clinical observation indicated a significant improvement in your client's symptoms, but your client continued to report a lack of progress? What would you do if your assessment measures and observation told you that the client was getting worse, yet your client reported feeling better?

- Think back to a time when you have been in personal therapy for yourself. If you could have changed anything about your therapist, what would it have been and why? If you have not been in personal therapy, what are the behaviors you would hope to experience from your therapist?
- What is the therapist's responsibility when a client no-shows (e.g., call the client? Send a letter? Wait for the client to call the therapist?)?
- Do all therapy experiences warrant a termination?
- Would you accept gifts from a client? What gift would you refuse?
- Do you feel comfortable hugging a client at termination? Why do you suppose some therapists believe physical touch is only appropriate in the termination session? Why do you suppose some therapists believe touch is an important part of all the therapeutic work? Does it vary from client to client? If so, how and why?

Exercises

Exercise 5.1: The Effect of Therapy

Think back to a recent day when you were in a very bad mood. List the top five events that made your mood worse that day. How do you suppose therapy would have changed your mood on that day?

Think back to a recent day when you were in a very good mood. List the top five events that lightened your mood that day. How do you suppose therapy would have changed your mood on that day?

Exercise 5.2: Therapy Outcome Interview

Find a therapist who is willing to speak with you about what it is like to be a therapist. Interview this person with the following objectives in mind: (1) how he or she perceives therapy outcome, (2) what makes therapy effective, (3) what makes therapy ineffective, (4) an example of when therapy worked great, and (5) an example when therapy did not work.

Exercise 5.3: Self-Narrative of Significant Change Events

Think back over your life to times when you experienced significant life events. Perhaps these even can be classified as big "T" or little "t" traumas. Write about one of these experiences and then consider how this experience changed you as a person, at that time, and how it perhaps remains with you to the present day.

CHAPTER **6**

Getting the Most Out of Supervision

People seldom refuse help, if one offers it in the right way.

—A.C. Benson

Psychotherapy supervision is the primary educational way in which people learn to become therapists. In all likelihood, you will have many supervisors in your lifetime, some of which will be outstanding, some of which will be benign, and some of which would have been better off working in a profession that doesn't involve live humans. The state of affairs in supervision reflects a similar state of affairs in therapy, that is, there's the good, the bad, and the ugly. The purpose of this chapter is to describe and discuss the key elements of supervision in all its glory and all its messiness. We follow a similar format to how we presented the work in therapy (e.g., supervision process and outcome); however, we approach this discussion from a trainees'-eye view. In other words, our intention is to talk about supervision in a manner that will best serve you as a trainee. That said, we believe that supervisors may benefit from what we talk about, and in fact, we hope you will find our discussion of supervision useful for when you become a supervisor. Because we are more focused, we also do not deal with each aspect of supervision in as much depth as we did in the therapy chapters. For example, we attend to supervisor variables in a more ancillary way. However, we believe the coverage will be sufficient for your purposes.

We begin the chapter talking about trainee role induction, or what a trainee needs to know about how supervision operates (i.e., structure of

101

supervision, the supervisory relationship, and ethics). We then move to the work in supervision and attend to supervision process (i.e., levels of process, parallel process, nondisclosures) and outcome (i.e., helpful and hindering events, trainee learning, regrets, external events, and evaluation), as well as address characteristics that are salient for trainees (i.e., self-conceptualization) and supervisors (i.e., supervisor style and supervisor countertransference). As in previous chapters, when possible we use quantitative and qualitative data from the Study to illustrate the concepts we present.

The Structure and Function of Individual Supervision

The process of supervision can be traced back to Freud, when he was training new psychoanalysts. However, the formalization of what takes place in supervision was a much longer time coming, up to today when there are many different ways in which supervision is manifested. Our focus will be on individual supervision of individual therapy, although, to be sure, other formats of supervision (e.g., group supervision, peer supervision, etc.) can be useful adjuncts. What we are going to describe is how supervision should be conducted in order to be most effective, although even under these conditions there is plenty of room for variability. Supervision, like therapy, typically takes place during a 45- to 50-minute block when general topics of discussion can include things about the client, the therapy work, the therapist's role in therapy, the therapist's personal issues, and the supervision work. We believe that, like therapy, the supervision hour should be sacred. That means that the time should be uninterrupted and in the service of facilitating growth in the trainee. Confidentiality limits should always be discussed.

We generally prefer to have the trainees indicate what they would like to discuss, although at times we may interject particular topics that we feel need to be addressed. Letting trainees make the primary decision of discussion topic is useful because it empowers the trainee. Similar to therapy, goals are created, modified, and reviewed throughout the supervisory work. Although we don't believe that supervision is a form of therapy, we do think that it can have the look and feel of therapy as issues are discussed, particularly those about the trainee. The more therapeutic-looking supervision should only be conducted with a strong supervisory alliance, when the trainee agrees that this work is useful, and when it's in the service of the therapy work. Even under these conditions, when the supervision work looks too much like therapy, we recommend supervisors encourage trainees to seek therapy for their personal issues. Ultimately, the supervisor must be responsible for evaluating the trainee so it behooves the trainee to get the help he or she needs to overcome any issues that are affecting the development of therapy skills.

There are three primary ways in which supervision is different than therapy. Supervision is typically involuntary, evaluative, and has education as its primary function. The involuntary nature of supervision sometimes leads trainees to think of themselves as on parole, with the supervisor as the parole officer. To some extent, this may be the case, but the mandated nature of the supervisory experience can be minimally influential if the supervisor is able to demonstrate the craft of supervision competently. Similarly, the evaluative nature of supervision can create a stumbling block for trainees because it sets them up to have an inherent role conflict: talk about your weaknesses knowing that you will be evaluated based on how well you do (Olk & Friedlander, 1992). The best supervisors know how to balance the openness of a trainee with the evaluation of her or his skills. Finally, supervision has an educative mission. The purpose of supervision is to teach the trainee how to become a more effective therapist. Therefore, the effectiveness of supervision is primarily observed in how much the trainee learns.

The Foundation of Supervision Effectiveness

Just as in therapy, the supervisory relationship is a critical component to understanding supervision process and outcome. The most common and practical manner in which the supervisory relationship has been conceptualized and studied is via Bordin's (1983) model of the supervisory working alliance. The supervisory working alliance has been shown to be predictive of supervision effectiveness across numerous studies (Ladany & Inman, in press).

Bordin (1983) conceptualized the supervisory working alliance as consisting of three inter-related elements: mutual agreement between the trainee and supervisor on the goals of supervision, mutual agreement between the trainee and supervisor on the tasks of supervision, and an emotional bond between the trainee and supervisor. The key for Bordin was that each of these elements was something that both the trainee and supervisor mutually agreed on or felt. The less the mutual agreement, the weaker the alliance. Conversely, the greater the mutual agreement, the stronger the alliance.

Goals of supervision are essentially linked to outcomes and may include things such as learning therapy skills, enhancing conceptualization ability, becoming more aware of process issues, considering how one's self influences the therapy work, and overcoming personal issues. As with the therapeutic alliance, the type of goal is less important than the agreement on the goal. Of course, in supervision, the goals should be meaningful and linked in some way to trainee learning. A mutually agreed-on goal to become a better dancer has little place in supervision, even if it would be a nice thing to learn!

Like the goals, Bordin (1983) indicated that the tasks of supervision should also be mutually agreed on. These tasks may change depending on the goals but include things such as observing tapes, having the trainee select the topics of discussion for supervision, providing alternative perspectives to the therapy work, and giving feedback on conceptualization reports. The third component of the supervisory working alliance is the emotional bond, which is a mutually caring, liking, and trusting between the trainee and supervisor. Along with the primary components, Bordin addresses other key processes that include empathy to enhance the alliance, diffusion of the hierarchical relationship inherent in supervision, and balancing critical feedback with acknowledging the strengths of the trainee.

The supervisory alliance takes about three to five sessions to develop and there is some evidence that, across trainee-supervisor dyads, the alliance strengthens over time one-third of the time, stays about the same one-third of the time, and weakens about one-third of the time (Ladany, 1993). Of course, this doesn't necessarily bode well for trainees; the odds are that you will have one that is pretty poor at her or his job. Unfortunately, this has been the case for many, and we will discuss ways to manage difficult supervisors later in this chapter.

Results of trainee and supervisor perceptions of the alliance are presented side by side in Figures 6.1–6.3. You get a sense of when the trainee and the supervisor were in sync and other times you may wonder if the trainee and supervisor were in the same room together! Of course, these data reflect what we have seen previously in the therapy relationship; that is, the members of the dyad have perceptions about the relationship that vary.

Knowing When You Are Receiving Ethical Supervision

Another way to look at the parameters of supervision is recognizing what ethical supervision looks like. Unlike the ethics for counseling, psychology, psychiatry, and social work, the ethics for supervisors of mental health practitioners has been relatively slow to develop. After reviewing and expanding on supervisor ethical guidelines for these major mental health professions, Ladany, Lehrman-Waterman, Molinaro, and Wolgast (1999) created a set of ethical guidelines for supervisors and investigated how well supervisors were adhering to these guidelines. Among the findings were that more than 50% of the trainees sampled indicated that their supervisors violated at least one ethical guideline, with *adequate evalu-*

ation as the most frequently violated guideline. These findings were, of course, disconcerting, but they shed light on what seems to be the state of affairs in the realm of supervision, that is, that many supervisors may not be doing a very good job.

In order to assist you in recognizing how well your supervisor is performing, we present the list of ethical guidelines that were developed and to varying extents have been added to professional guidelines (although there is still room for growth among all the mental health professions). Without a doubt, gross negligence on the part of the supervisor is pretty easy to spot; however, for these guidelines, we prefer to look at them as aspirational in nature, meaning that supervisors should aspire to meet the standards. Of course, ethics often fall into the gray area and we have no doubt that even the best supervisors sometimes come close to this boundary. The guidelines and their definitions are as follows:

1. *Performance Evaluation and Monitoring of Trainee Activities.* Adequate communication between supervisor and trainee concerning trainee evaluations occurs. The supervisor provides ongoing feedback, verbal and written, and works with the trainee on the establishment of goals. The supervisor reviews actual therapy sessions via recordings or live observation when possible, and reads the trainee's case notes periodically or more as indicated by state law.
2. *Confidentiality Issues in Supervision.* Confidentiality issues are handled appropriately by the supervisor (e.g., agency policy toward supervision disclosure is explained, limits of supervisory confidentiality).
3. *Able to Work With Alternative Perspectives.* Information about theory or practice presented by the supervisor is informed by current knowledge and includes alternative points of view, such as the trainee's. The supervisor clearly presents her or his theoretical orientation.
4. *Session Boundaries and Respectful Treatment.* Adequate protection of supervision session conditions and respect for trainee (e.g., privacy, scheduling, avoiding demeaning trainee) are ensured by the supervisor.
5. *Orientation to Professional Roles and Monitoring of Site Standards.* Supervisor and trainee roles and responsibilities are clearly defined. The supervisor ensures that the trainee is engaged in appropriate and relevant therapy activities.
6. *Expertise and Competency Issues.* The supervisor makes appropriate disclosure to trainee when the trainee or supervisor is not

competent to treat a particular client or condition. The supervisor ensures adequate coordination of all professionals involved in client treatment.

7. *Disclosure to Clients.* The supervisor ensures adequate disclosure to client (e.g., conditions of therapy, trainee's status, research participation, limits of confidentiality).

8. *Modeling Ethical Behavior and Responding to Ethical Concerns.* The supervisor discusses and models ethical behavior. The supervisor adequately responds to ethical violations.

9. *Crisis Coverage and Intervention.* Adequate communication between supervisor and trainee in the event of crisis, as well as the provision of appropriate supervisory backup, is ensured by supervisor. Supervisor handles situations appropriately where someone involved with the client is threatened by client's behavior or when a client is at risk for hurting herself or himself.

10. *Multicultural Sensitivity Toward Clients.* Racial, ethnic, cultural, sexual orientation, ability, age, religion, and gender issues (e.g., stereotyping, lack of sensitivity) toward clients are handled appropriately by supervisor.

11. *Multicultural Sensitivity Toward Trainee.* Racial, ethnic, cultural, sexual orientation, ability, age, religion, and gender issues are discussed appropriately and sensitively by the supervisor toward the trainee.

12. *Dual Roles.* The supervisor handles role-related conflicts appropriately (e.g., supervisor and trainee have personal relationship, advisor/advisee or administrative work relationship).

13. *Termination and Follow-up Issues.* Termination and follow-up issues are handled appropriately (e.g., supervisor assures continuity of care, prevents "abandonment" of client).

14. *Differentiating Supervision From Psychotherapy/Therapy.* The trainee's personal issues in supervision are treated appropriately (i.e., delineating therapy and supervision adequately, making appropriate referral of trainee to counseling/therapy).

15. *Sexual Issues.* The supervisor treats sexual/romantic issues appropriately (e.g., trainee-supervisor romantic relationships are not appropriate).

Just as supervisors have aspirational ethical and professional responsibilities, so do trainees (Worthington, Tan, & Poulin, 2002). We have found that the trainees that get the most out of supervision present with an interpersonal stance of openness, motivation, and "assertive deference." Openness involves having a willingness to learn and knowing that there are places for growth. As we mention throughout this book, attending to places of growth is a lifelong endeavor. In relation to motivation, we are referring to things like coming to supervision on time, prepared with an agenda, and fulfilling the responsibilities of a practicum site (e.g., paperwork). Finally, in relation to assertive deference, we believe that too much assertiveness to the point of aggressiveness can be problematic for trainees. Similarly, too much deference is equally problematic. The idea is balance. Specifically, the trainee should feel comfortable challenging or disagreeing with the supervisor, while at the same time have the ability to do so with a recognition of the power differences. This is one of the more challenging behaviors to pull off, and we believe it is the type of interaction in which the most learning can occur. Of course, using assertive deference as a skill in supervision is contingent on the supervisor indicating and demonstrating that he or she can handle it.

Supervision Process

Like therapy process, supervision process skills can be categorized into four levels, ranging from those that are directly observable to those that are highly abstract. These levels include (1) nonverbal behaviors (e.g., head nods, eye contact, etc.); (2) response modes (i.e., how and what is said); (3) covert processes (i.e., internal thoughts and feelings of the members of the dyad); and (4) therapeutic strategies and techniques (i.e., theoretically based techniques for change such as interpersonal process recall, role-playing, etc.).

Level 1: Nonverbal Behaviors

It is anticipated that supervisors will use the types of nonverbal skills they display as therapists such as head nods and a listening posture. Similarly, it is a good idea for trainees to indicate they are in supervision to learn by demonstrating appropriate nonverbal signals. As we will see in Lydia's story in the next chapter, nonverbals are the best way to show interest and disinterest. One thing that we encourage trainees to bring to supervision is a pad of paper and pen to help them keep track of questions they have and suggestions made by the supervisor. In addition, it is wise to bring a recording of the session to supervision sessions, even if you are unsure if there will be time to listen to them. Having these materials also gives the supervisor an indication that the trainee is prepared for supervision and is motivated to get something out of supervision.

Level 2: Response Modes

Although multiple response mode taxonomies have been developed for therapy, to date we know of only one developed for the purposes of supervision (Crall & Ladany, in preparation). Specifically, using data from the Study, as well as tapes from expert supervisors, a content-based interpersonal response mode system was developed (see Tables 28 and 29 in the Appendix). As can be seen, activities most represented in supervision involve information giving and gathering (along with a number of subcategories: conceptualization, hypotheses, treatment, feedback, etc.). In addition, a key activity that was identified had to do with "demonstrating understanding," a category that contains many of the aspects of empathy. Empathy is a critical skill for supervisors to use; however, many seem to forget its importance. Often, in a supervisor's zeal to provide feedback, he or she forgets to demonstrate understanding to the trainee. For reasons unexplained, many supervisors forget to use their therapy skills in supervision and hence lose opportunities to strengthen the supervisory working alliance. As can also be seen, the work in supervision involves a give and take between the trainee and supervisor. Information giving and gathering go hand in hand. One thing about information gathering we think is important is that the supervisor uses a Socratic approach (i.e., ask the trainee to hypothesize) when gathering information. Trainee learning is enhanced when supervisors explore aspects of the therapy work with the trainee without just giving answers.

Level 3: Covert Processes

Without a doubt, internal supervisor intentions and trainee reactions are a part of supervision. The one reaction that has been studied is trainee and supervisor nondisclosures (Ladany & Melincoff, 1999; Ladany, Hill, Corbett, & Nutt, 1996; Webb & Wheeler, 1998; Yourman, 2003; Yourman & Farber, 1996). A summary of this work indicates that trainees and supervisors keep many important things from one another including clinical mistakes and negative reactions to the supervisor for trainees, and positive comments about the clinical work for supervisors. For the Study, we asked trainees and their supervisors to describe what, if anything, they did not tell the other during their supervision sessions and why (Banks & Ladany, 2002; see Tables 30–33 in the Appendix). As in the previous research, there were a number of things left unsaid in supervision. For the first time, nondisclosures were looked at longitudinally, which may explain why the most frequently endorsed category was nothing, or that the members of the dyad had nothing they believed they left unsaid. As for the trainees, one interesting nondisclosure had to do with negative reactions to the supervisor. This finding is consistent with previous research and seems to be a relatively normal reaction for trainees to have. In doing so, they and their supervisors missed out on the opportunity to discuss and resolve difficulties within their relationship. However, such a pattern is consistent with anecdotal and research literature regarding the possible consequences of addressing conflict in supervision such as fear of negative evaluation from the supervisor (Gray, Ladany, Walker, & Ancis, 2001; Ladany, Hill, Corbett, & Nutt, 1996; Moskowitz & Rupert, 1983; Nelson & Friedlander, 2001). The key, of course, is the intensity of the negative reaction, how much it ruptures the alliance, and how well the supervisor is able to facilitate the repairing of this rupture. As for the supervisors, one of the more striking nondisclosures had to do with positive feedback. Presumably, positive feedback can never be a bad thing and from the looks of how some of the trainees experienced self-doubt, positive feedback from an experienced supervisor may have proven beneficial.

Level 4: Theoretical Strategies and Techniques

Comprehensive supervision-based theoretical models for supervision have been primarily created in the two last decades (Ladany & Inman, in press). To be sure, there are a number of circumscribed models that have theoretically addressed elements of supervision (e.g., Bernard, 1979; Bordin,1983; Falender & Shafranske, 2004; Gabbard, 2004; Greenwald & Young, 1998; Hogan, 1964; Kagan, 1984; Ladany & Walker, 2003; Munson, 2002; Overholser, 2004; Ward & House, 1998); however, only three models have been comprehensive in scope, have aspects that are descriptive and prescriptive, were derived specifically for the supervision context, and have been empirically founded. These models include the Integrated Developmental Model (IDM; Stoltenberg, McNeill, & Delworth, 1998), the Systems Approach to Supervision (SAS; Holloway, 1995), and the model of Critical Events in Supervision (CES; Ladany, Friedlander, & Nelson, 2005).

For the purposes of our book, we chose CES, not just because there is overlap in the authorship! We also chose it because of its practical and descriptive utility and its applicability for understanding oneself as a trainee. We also were less keen on the other models for a variety of reasons. In particular, we have not been enamored by developmental models even though they tend to be heuristically appealing to some supervisors. One of our main concerns is that developmental models tend to pigeonhole and infantilize beginning therapists as overly dependent, anxious, and lacking self-awareness. Our experience is that this supposition is generally not the case and the empirical evidence doesn't support it (Ellis & Ladany, 1997; Ladany & Inman, in press). Also, the data from the current study do not seem to demonstrate that trainees are anxious to the point of needing a great deal of continuous and exclusive structure (Pate-Carolan, Walker, & Tyson, 2002). Sure, at times, beginning therapists feel anxious and dependent, and they are in a state of learning new things, but therapeutic excellence is not contingent upon experience. Typically, we find many beginning therapists quite able to explore their countertransference reactions, manage a working anxiety, and can solve their own questions quite readily. When supervisors see beginning therapists more like colleagues-in-training than in a childlike fashion, trainees respond immeasurably. And, speaking of measure, as we will see in the evaluation section, supervisors are notoriously poor at evaluating trainees using a developmental structure.

We also chose the CES because the *Level 2* supervision response modes theoretically and practically fit nicely within its conceptualization. The basic premise of the CES is that the most meaningful aspects of supervision involve critical events of learning. A series of events have been identified that can take place within a session to across multiple sessions: (a) remediating skill difficulties and deficits, (b) heightening multicultural awareness, (c) negotiating role conflicts, (d) working through countertransference, (e) managing sexual attraction, (f) repairing gender-related misunderstandings, and (g) addressing problematic trainee emotions and behaviors. It is believed that these events characterize much of the important work in supervision.

For any event, the supervision work is seen to occur in three phases: (1) the marker, (2) the task environment, and (3) the resolution. In addition, this work takes place in the context of the supervisory working alliance. The supervisory alliance is primarily based on Bordin's (1983) model and like in therapy, acts as a figure or the ground.

Once an alliance is strong enough, the first phase of the critical event is the marker, which is a statement or behavior made by the trainee that indicates a new event is occurring. These statements may be as simple as the trainee saying something like, "I need help learning how to use a cognitive restructuring technique with my client" but can also be less clear concerns such as feeling particularly stuck with a client or noticing an uneasiness during a session. Sometimes it's the supervisor's job to identify a potential marker such as when he or she notices a skill that needs to be attended to after listening to a trainee recording.

Following the marker, the supervision enters into the task environment phase, where the supervisor attends to a series of interaction sequences that may include focus on the supervisory alliance, focus on the therapeutic process, exploration of feelings, focus on countertransference, attend to parallel processes, focus on self-efficacy, normalizing experience, focus on skill, assess knowledge, focus on multicultural awareness, and/or focus on evaluation. Although the supervisor is primarily responsible for demonstrating skill at performing these interaction sequences, the trainee too must respond through a willingness to explore and be open to this exploration. The trainee, too, may request certain interaction sequences take place such as when the trainee indicates that the issue has to do with her or his countertransference.

The final phase is the resolution, which involves an increase or decrease in self-awareness, knowledge, skills, or the supervisory alliance. As can be seen, both positive and negative consequences can occur as a result of supervision experience; hopefully, the former occurs more often than the latter. An example of the model in operation can be seen in Figure 6.4. In this example, the trainee feels stuck with a particular client. This "stuckness" is the marker. During the task environment, the supervisor helps the trainee explore her or his feelings, while at the same time normalizing the reaction of feeling stuck. This initial exploration leads to a focus on the trainee's countertransference. Here, the discussion may turn to how the client reminds the trainee of someone in her or his life. Because countertransference can be quite personal, the supervisor checks in with the trainee about how he or she is doing with this more intense work in supervision. At the end of this work, there is an enhancement of the trainee's self-awareness. Of course, things in supervision don't always go this smoothly; however, the model hopefully allows you to see what things are possible in supervision. It is also our hope that you will have a supervisor as good as the one in this example!

Parallel Process

One concept that is wholly unique to, and a consequence of, supervision is parallel process (Bernard & Goodyear, 2004; Ekstein & Wallerstein, 1958, 1972; Gray, 2005; McNeill & Worthen, 1989; Walker, 2003). Perhaps the best way to think of parallel process is as the ways in which the therapy experience is mimicked in the supervision experience. In other words, the aspects of the interactions between the client and therapist are experienced similarly between the trainee and the supervisor. Moreover, the parallel process can go upward from the therapy relationship to the supervisory relationship, or downward from the supervision relationship to the therapy relationship (Doehrman, 1976). Parallel process also can be proximal, meaning that it occurs from a therapy session to the next supervision session (or vice versa), or distal, in which the parallel process occurs following a number of therapy or supervision sessions (Walker, 2003).

For the Study, we asked trainees and their supervisors about experiences of parallel process and combined their data into one data set (see Table 34 in the Appendix). Interesting examples of parallel process that were highlighted include acting in a collaborative fashion, taking a didactic approach, and deferring to authority. First, it was interesting to find that, when queried, trainees and their supervisors were able to identify parallels, something that has been more reclusive in the literature. Also, the data seem to show that there are many ways in which therapy and supervision parallel one another in both positive and negative ways. For example, when the supervisor empowered the trainee, the trainee seemed more likely to empower the client. Alternatively, when the client demonstrated resistance in therapy, the trainee would be guarded or resistant in supervision. Because the number of therapy and supervision dyads we had for the study were relatively small, it's difficult to know how generalizable these findings are. That said, they point to places that supervisors and trainees may want to explore in their own work to consider how supervision and therapy influence one another in more subtle ways.

Supervision Outcome

Often from the perspectives of educators and supervisors, the ultimate supervision outcome is therapy effectiveness, or client outcome. The problem with adhering closely with this approach is that the supervisor then becomes a surrogate therapist. The therapist becomes the paperboy or papergirl of the supervisor's news. In our opinion, this approach is quite disempowering to the trainee and sets up a poor learning environment. This is not to say that trainees aren't invested in client change; it's one of the primary reasons they seek supervision. However, from a trainee's-eye view, there are a number of intermediary outcome variables between the work that takes place in supervision and client change. In fact, it could be argued that given the indirect relationship that exists between supervision and client change, it should not be surprising, therefore, that there is no clear empirical evidence linking supervision with therapy outcome (Ellis & Ladany, 1997; Ladany & Inman, in press).

We believe that supervision, indeed, influences therapy outcome. However, the variability accounted for in therapy outcome comes mostly from the therapist. Although supervision can certainly enhance what the therapist does, the therapist is the tool that does the work. The supervisor is like a blacksmith who can help shape the tool to work more efficiently, but ultimately it's the tool that makes things happen. For the purposes of discussing supervision outcome, we attend to five elements that we believe make a difference to trainees: helpful and hindering events, trainee and supervisor regrets, external events, evaluation, and termination. When applicable, we draw from the Study to illustrate the types of outcomes.

Helpful and Hindering Events

Within the context of psychotherapy training, supervision plays an integral role in trainees' acquisition and refinement of clinical skills, as well as their professional development. A relatively new area of study, a number of researchers have examined aspects of supervision that affect psychotherapy trainees' growth (Allen, Szollos, & Williams, 1986; Ellis, 1991; Gray, Ladany, Walker, & Ancis, 2001; Hutt, Scott, & King, 1983; Moskowitz & Rupert, 1983; Nelson & Friedlander, 2001; Worthen & McNeill, 1996). These researchers have studied aspects of supervision that contribute to trainees experiences of critical incidents that either help or hinder their professional development. In particular, the research indicates that trainees are more likely to have positive supervision experiences when they feel their supervisors are accepting, facilitative (Hutt et al., 1983; Worthen & McNeill, 1996), collegial, respectful (Gandolfo & Brown, 1987), supportive, interpretive, and instructive (Kennard, Stewart, & Gluck, 1987). However, trainees' report negative supervisory experiences when they feel their supervisors are critical (Allen et al., 1986; Hutt et al., 1983; Nelson, 1978), dismissive (Gray et al., 2001), demeaning, authoritative (Allen et al., 1986), rigid (Allen et al., 1986; Hutt et al., 1983; Kennard et al., 1987; Nelson, 1978), or inattentive (Chung, Baskin, & Chase, 1998; Shanfield, Matthews, & Hetherly, 1993). Such results make sense intuitively, yet recent research on supervision indicates that trainees continue to report hindering supervision events that they believe affects their professional growth negatively (Gray et al., 2001; Nelson & Friedlander, 2001).

In the Study, we asked the trainees and their supervisors to describe what they thought were the most helpful and the most hindering aspects of the supervision sessions for the trainees. The result was the development of categories (see Tables 35–41 in the Appendix). For both the trainee and the supervisor, the most common helpful event involved receiving or providing supervisor guidance on a particular issue. This finding highlights the educative aspect of supervision, and makes good sense. Interestingly, although the most common, this type of event only happened approximately 50% of the time. The rest of the helpful events involved some sort of process issue such as facilitating/gaining insight, validating, or supporting. This points to the importance of supervision having more than a simple didactic purpose. A notable aspect of the trainees' responses to the helpful event question that we found particularly encouraging was that they were able to identify a helpful aspect of each session, meaning that each supervision session brought with it an opportunity for learning. In the end, it is hoped that this type of work increased the trainees' confidence in their skills that in turn facilitated better work with their clients.

From the data on hindering events in supervision, there are at least two findings of note. First, there were a number of events involving how time was used in supervision, the supervisory alliance, or meeting trainee needs. For example, there were a number of instances when the trainees felt the supervisor's agenda did not match their needs for the session, felt too much time was spent on one issue, felt the supervisor used up too much time talking, or they wanted more time from their supervisors. This finding speaks to the agreement on the tasks of supervision component of the alliance. It is unfortunate that the trainees did not feel comfortable letting their supervisors know about these unmet needs; however, this was likely due to the trainee's status in the relationship. Second, supervisors expressed concern that at times they lacked finesse or skills as a supervisor. This finding points out that as we all gain experience, even a lot of experience, we still have doubts at times whether or not what we are doing is effective.

Trainee and Supervisor Regrets About Supervision

On reflection, trainees identified a number of things they would have preferred to have done differently in supervision (see Tables 42–43 in the Appendix). In particular, they frequently wished they had been more prepared for supervision. One thing we find helpful is to have trainees come to supervision with a list of questions about what they would like to learn that day. We find this little bit of preparation can be the difference between supervision sessions that are dull and aimless versus those that are fruitful. It also empowers the trainee in important ways, something that the trainees identified as what they wished the supervisors had done more frequently.

As can be seen in Tables 44–45 in the Appendix, supervisors indicated a number of regrets about their own behavior and their trainee's behavior. In relation to their own behavior, one striking finding is their desire to have been more prepared for supervision. This finding would perhaps be less troubling, and even normalizing, except for the fact that it occurred, in combination with the Technical Aspects finding, about one-third of the time. That's quite a lot of sessions not to be prepared as a supervisor. Supervisors also indicated what they wished their trainee had done differently. Across the findings, the clear and prominent theme for this category was wishing the trainee would adopt a more active and invested role in supervision, rather than a passive role that left the supervisor guessing as to what the trainee needed. What's uniquely interesting about this is the flip side of this statement, that is, why didn't the supervisors empower their trainees to take a more active and empowering stance in supervision?

External Events

Similar to the external events questions asked of the therapists and the clients after psychotherapy sessions, we also asked questions of the therapists about external events after supervision sessions. After all, just like therapy, supervision makes up a very small amount of the entire week for therapists. Supervision is unlikely to occur inside of a vacuum, away from other aspects in our lives. Reflecting that idea, therapists identified 8 types of external events that they felt positively and negatively influenced their development as therapists. Therapists identified (1) academic development (e.g., classes and conferences); (2) clinical development (e.g., other practica and therapy situations); (3) validation (or invalidation) and consultation by peers and colleagues; (4) interpersonal reflection and insight; (5) personal life; (6) money; (7) research-related events; and (8) other. Sometimes they replied that they could not think of anything or that there was not anything of influence that week.

One therapist said, "I spent some time … just reflecting a little bit on what I want to do for next week" (Interpersonal reflection and insight). Another felt financial pressures as influencing development: " … trying to figure out how I'm going to pay for all my summer classes" (Money). "I went on vacation …" (Personal Life) was an enviable external event (LPC)! The data were really rich in examples of the events therapists felt both positively and negatively affected their development. These data remind us that development does not stop just because the supervision hour is over.

Evaluation

Along with the involuntary nature of supervision for trainees, evaluation is a clear process that distinguishes supervision from therapy. Like it or not, most supervision contains an element of evaluation. The best supervisors know how to manage evaluation and use it in the best interests of the trainee. As we mentioned previously, because supervision contains an evaluative component, trainees are set up to be in an inherent role conflict. On the one hand, they are to disclose their weaknesses and, on the other, they are evaluated based on how well they are doing (Olk & Friedlander, 1992). Another problem with evaluation is that there are likely as many evaluation measures as there are training sites (Bernard & Goodyear, 2004) and there is little evidence to suggest that any of them are reliable or valid (Ellis & Ladany, 1997; Lambert & Ogles, 1997). Even so, they are used and can influence the professional lives of trainees. From our perspective, there are two things about evaluation that should be known: what is evaluated, determining if the evaluation measure suits the trainee's needs, and how to do it well.

In terms of what is evaluated, generally the better measures use both a qualitative and quantitative approach toward evaluation and attend to three aspects of the trainee's work: therapy skills: response modes (Level 2 therapy skills), therapy skills: strategies and techniques (Level 4–type therapy skills), assessment (Level 4–type therapy skills), supervision, and professional behavior (see Table 6.1 for an example evaluation measure). In addition, the supervisor is asked to indicate how much of the behavior has been observed by having her or him indicate the number of recordings listened to, the number of clients observed, and the number of supervision sessions. In general, the more the trainee has been seen doing therapy, the more valid the assessment. In addition, the more circumscribed the behavior (e.g., response modes), the more reliable the assessment. The strategies and techniques skills generally are broad brushstrokes of skills and more difficult to assess because they require more behavioral observation that requires more observation time. Trainees almost always benefit from listening to their own therapy recordings and can sometimes help the supervisor by pointing out moments when certain skills are demonstrated and when they believe they need help with certain skills. Both of these activities are important for the supervisor to know about.

How to determine whether or not the evaluation measure fits trainees' needs is another aspect of evaluation worth mentioning. Ladany and Muse-Burke (2001) offer a framework for assessing the adequacy of evaluation measures that involves examining a series of elements about a measure to determine the measures efficacy. These elements include (a) mode of therapy (e.g., individual, group, family, etc.); (b) domain of trainee behavior (e.g., therapy, supervision); (c) competence area (e.g., response modes, strategies and techniques, conceptualization skills, multicultural competence, supervision behaviors); (d) method (e.g., trainee self-report, case notes, audiotape); (e) proportion of case load (e.g., number of clients, one client); (f) segment of experience (e.g., one session, segment of session; (g) time period (e.g., late in client treatment, early in training experience); (h) evaluator (e.g., supervisor, trainee, client); (i) level of proficiency (e.g., demonstrated skill, cohort group); (j) reliability; (k) validity; and (l) format (e.g., structured, quantitative, qualitative). Of course, no single measure could contain all of these elements; however, the merit of an instrument can be determined based on how many, and how well, each of these elements are addressed.

With a measure in place, the next issue is how to evaluate a trainee. Evaluation can be thought of as consisting of two functional components: goal-setting and feedback. The effectiveness of goal-setting can be determined based on how well the supervisor is able to work with the trainee to develop goals that are specific, clear, feasible in relation to capacity, opportunity, and resources, related to tasks, modifiable over time, measurable, prioritized, and mutually agreed on and would require trainees to "stretch" themselves. Feedback can be broken down into two types: formative, which takes place throughout the supervision work, and summative, which usually involves a more formal review at the middle and end of a semester, using a standard measure. Each supervisor has different strengths in relation to evaluation, perhaps because it is one of the most difficult tasks for a supervisor. Ultimately, what counts is how well the trainee receives the kinds of evaluation necessary for her or his growth as a therapist.

Conceptualizing Yourself as a Trainee

Just as we can conceptualize our clients, so, too, can supervisors conceptualize trainees or trainees can conceptualize themselves. Table 6.2 provides a case conceptualization outline generally used by supervisors. However, nothing stops a trainee from considering using it as a means of self-conceptualization. Each segment can be looked at as a form of self-evaluation or self supervision. You begin with who you are in terms of your demographics and then consider the goals you have had for supervision up to that point. One good question to ask is whether or not these goals were mutually agreed upon by you and your supervisor and if not, what are the consequences of this disagreement. Next, what are your impressions of the supervisory relationship in terms of the strength of the supervisory alliance? Are each of the components reasonably strong or are some weaker than others? How would you evaluate your skills in therapy and in supervision? Ideally, try using the evaluation form for your training site. Be sure to consider the adeptness of your skills in both therapy and supervision. Along with strengths, what weakness or growth edges should we look for and look to overcome?

Then, turn to the match in supervision and consider the multicultural identity interactions (Ancis & Ladany, 2001; Cook, 1994; Ellis & Douce, 1994). There is a unique state of affairs in current training. Presently, there is typically at least some multicultural training that occurs in graduate school, but even 10 years ago it was nonexistent for the most part. Thus, trainees tend to be more multiculturally adept than supervisors. This scenario leads many trainees to be in regressive multicultural identity interactions with their supervisors (Constantine, 1999; Ladany, Brittan-Powell, & Pannu, 1997). Consider how you and your supervisor are in sync with multicultural issues. Along with multicultural issues, it's not uncommon to find conflicts in the supervisory relationship. We'll talk more about how to deal with these conflicts as well as supervisor countertransference later in this chapter.

Finally, consider the progress in supervision to date and where you would like to see yourself going in the future. What unanswered questions remain about yourself and your supervisor? Ultimately, we find this self-conceptualization useful because we believe it gets trainees in touch with what it's like to be conceptualized and what it might be like for a client. In the end, we believe, the process becomes more humanizing.

Conceptualizing Your Supervisor

Typically, therapists in training meet with supervisors for 1 hour a week. Because 1 hour is usually not enough time to review every client of a therapist's caseload in detail, the therapist and supervisor must embark on the task of prioritizing issues, delegating time, and choosing importance of some questions over others. In addition, psychotherapy supervision sessions encompass much more than just client-related updates. For instance, therapists in training use supervision time to discuss professional development issues, future career directions, agency policy, personal reactions to clients (e.g., countertransference), and dynamics in the supervisory relationship.

The relationship that a therapist shares with her or his psychotherapy supervisor is a relationship unlike any other, and it is different for every therapist-supervisor dyad. Supervision can be a casual collegial weekly caseload update. For others, it can be a personally intense and emotionally intimate experience. Still others experience supervision much like another classroom hour, with a private therapy-tutor prophesizing advice and "how-to" techniques. Furthermore, some therapists have deep meaningful relationships with supervisors that become life-time mentors. Unfortunately, some therapists are wounded by supervisors who abuse their power as an authority figure.

Psychotherapy supervision is a complex and intricate relationship that is meant to help trainees become better therapists, and ultimately more mature professionals. Now that we have discussed how to conceptualize a client, and a therapist, it is important that you become savvy at conceptualizing a supervisor. The purpose of this section is to help you recognize the variability and diversity among supervisors, and the unique dynamics between specific trainees and supervisors. In this section, we talk about (a) ways in which to understand how your supervisor approaches supervision, (b) how supervisor countertransference can influence you as the trainee, and (c) what constitutes the best and worst forms of supervision and what to do when encountering a difficult or problematic supervisor.

Supervisor Style

Supervisor style has been recognized as a primary element of the supervisor-trainee relationship (Borders, 1991; Chen & Bernstein, 2000; Friedlander & Ward, 1984; Herbert, Ward, & Hemlick, 1995; Ladany, Walker, & Melincoff, 2001; Sumerel & Borders, 1996; Usher & Borders, 1993). Friedlander and Ward (1984) defined supervisory style as the different approaches that supervisors utilize, in combination with their distinctive manner of responding to trainees. In particular, they identified three interrelated supervisor styles used by supervisors: attractive (e.g., friendly, warm, open, supportive), interpersonally sensitive (e.g., therapeutic, invested, perceptive), and task-oriented (e.g., didactic, directive, focused, goal-directed, structured). These styles correspond with Bernard's (1997) three basic supervisor roles of interacting with trainees (i.e., consultant, counselor, and teacher). The expectation of supervisors is that they congruently respond to trainees' needs and preferences with a complimentary style. Although developmental models indicate that trainees differ in their preferences based on experience level, the Study did not show this to be the case for three indicators of experience, which corresponds to research that has looked at style as a predictor of supervision process and outcome (Ladany, Ellis, & Friedlander, 1999; Ladany et al., 2001). Moreover, what seems to be critical is that supervisors are flexible in their approach to trainees and have the ability to alter their style multiple times within every supervision session, something that seemed to be the case as well for the Study (Borders, 1991; Ladany et al., 2001; Sumerel & Borders, 1996; Usher & Borders, 1993). This should not be so surprising given that, as therapists, we are expected to alter our style in multiple ways for clients. Even though supervisor style can prove illustrative for the purposes of research it is limited as a variable in that it indicates general and overall preferences in a given session and is likely not as predictive as examining response modes or interaction sequences.

Supervisor Countertransference

One of the most important tasks for a therapist is to understand the emergence and implications of countertransference. What many therapists do not realize, however, is that supervisors also experience countertransference. As a beginning trainee, it will benefit you to understand realistic expectations, limitations, and possibilities of supervisory dynamics. Furthermore, if you continue your graduate program, you will likely be a supervisor someday. This information also should be of use to beginning supervisors to gain a greater awareness of the self in their roles. The purpose of this section will be to (1) define supervisor countertransference,

(2) provide examples of supervisory countertransference based on supervisory reports, and (3) discuss implications of supervisor reactions to the supervisory relationship.

Definitions The theoretical literature has recognized that supervisors experience countertransference (Ackerman, 1953; Anastasopoulos & Tsiantis, 1999; Berman, 2000; Issacharoff, 1984; Lower, 1972; Strean, 2000; Teitelbaum, 1990; Tosone, 1997; Yerushalmi, 2000). Supervisory countertransference has been described as a reaction characterized by many influences. For instance, supervisory countertransference can originate from the supervisor's personality, or the supervisor's unresolved internal conflicts and issues. Further, supervisory countertransference can be characterized by the supervisor's transference reaction toward the trainee's material, the trainee's presentation style, or the trainee's transference. Finally, supervisory countertransference could be a product of the supervisor's reaction to the client's transference (Anastasopoulos & Tsiantis, 1999; Lower, 1972; Teitelbaum, 1990). Berman (2000) notes that "the supervisor-trainee relationship ... is always a rich and complex transference/countertransference combination, even if supervision is utterly impersonal ..." (p. 276).

Although the theoretical literature offers a variety of conceptual proposals, empirical studies operationalizing supervisory countertransference are scarce (Ladany, Constantine, Miller, Erickson, & Muse-Burke, 2000; Walker dissertation, 2003). Ladany et al. (2000) utilized Consensual Qualitative Research methods (CQR) to investigate the countertransference experiences of 11 supervisors (Hill, Thompson, & Williams, 1997). Supervisors reported a wide range of cognitions, affect, and behaviors when describing their countertransference.

For instance, one interesting finding was that supervisors reportedly typically questioned their competence when experiencing countertransference. Imagine, supervisors often share the same anxieties as their trainees! Or even clients! Another interesting finding was that supervisors typically reported feeling distressed, afraid, or uncomfortable. Variant emotions reportedly evoked in supervisors during countertransference were (a) anger, irritation, or resentfulness, (b) anxiety or nervousness, (c) negative feelings about self, or (d) surprise or confusion. Again, supervisors are not immune to emotional responses in session! Behaviorally, supervisors noted they typically discussed trainee's issues. Occasionally, supervisors reportedly became less engaged, avoidant, and distant.

Thus, both theoretically and empirically, supervisor countertransference represents a complex and intricate phenomenon that can be characterized and displayed in a variety of means. For the purposes of our Study, we defined supervisor countertransference as those thoughts, feelings, and behaviors that serve to interfere with or facilitate a supervisor's work with her or his trainee. As with therapist countertransference, we recognize the presence of both "negative" countertransference (those thoughts, feelings, and behaviors that interfere) as well as "positive" countertransference (those thoughts, feelings, and behaviors that are initially described as facilitative).

Examples of Supervisory Countertransference From the Study   After interviewing supervisors about their countertransference reactions, we created general themes to categorize their different reports of countertransferential experiences. These themes highlight the complexity of the supervisor-trainee relationship and accentuate the fact that supervisors, like therapists, can also experience countertransferential reactions (see Tables 46–49 in the Appendix).

Supervisors reported feeling distracted by issues and events outside the supervisory relationship. For example, supervisors noted that they were uncomfortable in the office, thinking about their children, wondering about personal issues, or feeling tired and worn down. Although therapists in training sometimes feel overwhelmed with personal issues or distracted during therapy, it is important to realize that supervisors also experience moments when they are not 100% present in session. Like therapists, supervisors benefit from taking pause and exploring the origins of their distractions. For instance, perhaps a supervisor is too overwhelmed with personal struggles to be an appropriate mentor. By contrast, perhaps there is a quality about the trainee that is triggering a distraction-reaction in the supervisor. Any time that a supervisor notices herself or himself "zoning out" in supervision, it is definitely worth exploring.

Supervisors also tended to have reactions about their personal contribution toward the process of the supervisory relationship. Sometimes these emotions and cognitions can interfere with the supervision work. For instance, supervisors reported feeling unsure and confused about their performance in supervision. Some supervisors began second-guessing their supervisory interventions. Furthermore, supervisors reported feeling guilty at times for their lack of investment in the supervision relationship.

Findings from the Study revealed that when supervisors were feeling countertransference about the supervisory relationship, they were more likely to behaviorally respond by becoming less authoritative in session. For instance, when supervisors were feeling unsure, confused, or second-guessing their work, they were more likely to become less didactic and less structured in their supervisory style. They may have probed less, withheld evaluative feedback, let the trainee lead the session, or become less prescriptive.

Within supervision, there is a ladder of relationships. The relationship between the supervisor and trainee represents the first rung on the ladder, and the relationship between the trainee and the client characterizes the second rung on the ladder. Interestingly, when a supervisor experiences countertransference, she or he can have a reaction to the trainee's behavior in supervision. In addition, the supervisor can have a reaction to the trainee's perceived behavior in therapy.

On the first rung of the ladder, supervisors reported feeling frustrated, curious about, or bothered by the trainee's behavior with the supervisor in session. Trainees sometimes came late to supervision without apology, or often appeared unmotivated. Trainees can act passive-aggressively toward their supervisors, or they can become more overtly hostile. Supervisors reported having a reaction to trainees' interpersonal style in the supervision session to the point at which their thoughts and feelings reportedly interfered with the supervisory work.

On the second rung, supervisors reported that they disagreed with, felt frustrated by, or were bothered by their trainee's therapy work. Specifically, supervisors recognized that trainees were projecting, resisting, judging, or acting on their own countertransference rather than being empathic or therapeutic. Supervisors sometimes recognized the biased and judgmental nature of their trainees. Often supervisors disagreed with the interventions trainees chose to implement. When supervisors disagree with or feel frustrated by a trainee's behavior, it is important that supervisors find empathic teaching moments for the trainee. Responding emotionally without educational instruction proves unproductive or counterproductive (e.g., poor trainee or client outcome).

Perhaps a third rung to supervisory countertransference may be the supervisor's exaggerated reaction to the client. For instance, if a supervisor is personally struggling with issues of sexual orientation, the supervisor may have an overly adverse or overly attentive reaction to a trainee's case presentation of a client struggling with sexual identity issues.

Supervisors may become angry at clients who wound their trainees. For example, if a client insults the therapist, overwhelms the therapist, or creates anxiety in the therapy session, a supervisor may become frustrated with the perceived damage the client is inflicting on the supervisor's protégé. Finally, supervisors may become agitated with clients that do not engage in productive improvement or successful outcomes. I (JW) have had supervisors in the past become so angry at my clients for not improving that they encourage me to abruptly terminate with the client to punish the client's "lazy and stubborn" behavior. Furthermore, supervisors may become sexually attracted to clients. Perhaps the voice of a client on a recording reminds the supervisor of an old affair. Maybe a supervisor watches a very physically attractive client during live supervision and cannot stop fantasizing about an imaginary relationship with the client.

Furthermore, perhaps the trainee's presentation of the client in supervision is sexual in nature and the trainee and supervisor collude in objectifying and sexualizing client material. Although such supervisor-to-client countertransference has not been identified in the supervision literature empirically, we propose that supervisor-client countertransference does indeed exist and deserves further exploration.

Almost 40% of supervisor responses, when asked what facilitated their work with a trainee, reported identifying and empathizing with their trainee. Supervisors appeared to connect with their trainees by drawing from their own personal experiences as novice therapists. Supervisors attempted to identify with their trainees' struggles, as well as their feelings of being new, young, and nervous (Walker, 2003).

As in Chapter 3, we again visit the notion of positive countertransference, those thoughts and feelings that facilitate (rather than interfere with) one's work in therapy or supervision. We acknowledge that most times positive countertransference can be constructive and helpful. However, similar to the idea of therapist's detrimental positive countertransference (Friedman & Gelso, 2000), we predict there is a potential for detriment with positive supervisory countertransference. Specifically, supervisors reported that when they overidentified with their trainee, they were sometimes more likely to withhold needed critical feedback. As one supervisor confessed, "It's clearly a positive transference and countertransference and I think that in some respects I suppose I don't see his flaws or problems or give him advice on where he ought to be going right now" (Walker, 2003). It seems reasonable to suspect that just as a therapist runs the risk of "oversupporting" the client (Friedman & Gelso, 2000), perhaps a supervisor is also occasionally in jeopardy of such ineffective interventions.

Implications   Supervisor countertransference can have implications for the supervisory process and outcome, as well as for the therapy process and outcome. For example, our findings showed that occasionally when a supervisor becomes uncomfortable or anxious when discussing a case with the trainee, the supervisor may be likely to withdraw in the supervision session. This supervisory countertransference may begin a chain of reactions. First, the trainee does not receive appropriate direction in supervision, and, therefore, the trainee presents as unprepared in therapy session. Thus, indirectly, the client outcome may be affected by supervisory countertransference. Other dynamics that can be affected by supervisor countertransference include (a) the supervisory relationship (e.g., the supervisor becomes frustrated with trainee and stops feeling empathic for the novice therapist); (b) the therapeutic relationship between trainee and client (e.g., the supervisor and therapist collude in being overly attracted to the client; thus, the therapist neglects appropriate confrontation that could enhance the therapeutic alliance); and (c) the therapeutic relationship between supervisor and other clients (e.g., supervisory countertransference triggered in a supervision session prompts the emergence of deep-rooted unresolved issues that play out in the supervisor's therapy with her or his caseload of clients).

Managing the Best and Worst of Supervision

Thus far, we have explored a number of things about the supervision work that leads us to the question: What makes for the best supervision and what makes for the worst? Assuming that trainees come in with an open, nondefensive, and motivated approach to supervision, the key person is the supervisor. Our belief is that the best supervisors develop and attend to the supervisory alliance, empathize with the trainee, empower the trainee, effectively utilize formative and summative evaluation procedures, observe the trainee frequently in session, use a blended style of collegial, therapeutic, and didactic supervision, constructively challenge the trainee, provide as much positive feedback as critical feedback, value supervision, attend to both client outcome and trainee outcome, use case discussion sparingly and primarily in the service of the trainee, and give trainees multiple opportunities to give evaluative feedback about the supervisor (see Table 6.3 for a sample supervisor evaluation measure). As with ethical issues, these approaches to supervision are aspirational in nature. It is a rare supervisor indeed that can hit on all these fronts. However, when a supervisor is able to demonstrate these skills, supervision can be quite the rich experience.

Unfortunately, all too frequently, there are supervisors who fall seriously short of offering the "best" supervision. Most probably fall somewhere in the middle between the best and the worst, but occasionally, when the worst does occur, it can be quite damaging to the trainee. Perhaps it goes without saying that many of the worst qualities are the opposite of the best qualities. For example, it is unhelpful when supervisors marginalize supervision, don't observe trainee work, are excessively critical, are overly didactic, do not evaluate well, provide little feedback, are not invested in the supervision experience, and can't develop a supervisory alliance for all the riches in the world! Sadly, we all have had experiences with these types of supervisors. For example, I (NL) can recall a supervisor who saw supervision as what seemed to be a deviant form of object relations therapy. Every comment I made was followed up by, "What is it about you that sees it that way?" After about 6 weeks, and noticing that my recordings were never listened to, and it became clear that the most this supervision experience was going to teach me was how not to conduct supervision. Not surprisingly, I learned that this supervisor had a history of behaving poorly toward trainees.

So what does one do when encountering a difficult or problematic supervisor? If the difficulties seem more in line with a minor conflict, then it behooves the trainee first to try to talk about it with the supervisor. It is the supervisor's responsibility to be open to hearing concerns expressed by the trainee. Of course, the supervisor is not just there to agree with whatever the trainee says. However, there should be a meeting of the minds about the issues at hand, in essence, couched within the supervisory working alliance. At times when the supervisor demonstrates incompetence or is interpersonally inappropriate, we suggest the trainee speak with the training coordinator of their program for guidance, as well as the trainee's academic advisor. In addition, although it can be quite the pain, it is important to document everything that is said and done so a record is in place. Trainees have a right and should have access to due process in their educational setting. That means that trainees have the right to ensure they are getting treated fairly and with integrity. If the situation cannot be resolved with the supervisor, it is the responsibility of the training site, along with the training program, to come up with an alternative solution for the trainee (e.g., find a new supervisor). We hope you never find yourself in such a situation, but if you do, don't forget you have rights as well.

Conclusion

The supervision relationship can provide more than just advice and guidance about therapy. Good supervision can foster a deep mentoring relationship that lasts throughout one's professional development postgraduation. Like most of the relationships we talk about in this book, nothing is simple or unidimensional. Like our growing understanding of ourselves, and our continued learning of our clients, so, too, will we gain insights over time about our supervisors. The best part about receiving supervision, good or bad, might be that you can constantly use your experiences to consider and ponder what kind of supervisor you will want to be in the future.

Discussion Questions and Exercises

Discussion Questions

- Specifically, how might evaluation influence the supervisory alliance?
- Does parallel process really exist?

- What have you chosen not to disclose to your supervisor? Why?
- How do you think your supervisor would describe you? How do you think she/he would describe how you receive feedback, both positive and negative?
- How would you describe your supervisor's style? How might this be similar or different from how you expect your own supervisor style to be?
- What do you see as the attributes that make up the most effective supervisor?
- What do you see as the attributes that make up the least effective supervisor?

Exercises

Exercise 6.1: Examining Your Experience

If you have been in supervision before (either as the supervisor or trainee), how do you feel you and your partner in supervision (either your supervisor or trainee) did with regard to Bordin's three aspects of the relationship: goals, tasks, and bond? If you have not experienced a supervisory relationship yet, how has this discussion of the roles and working alliance prepared you to enter into such a relationship?

Exercise 6.2: Better and Worse Nondisclosures

Review Tables 30–33 in the Appendix and identify the content and reasons for nondisclosures that seem reasonable to keep nondisclosed and those that would have been better to disclose.

Exercise 6.3: Critical Events

Reflect back on your supervisory experience to date and using the Critical Events in Supervision Model, identify the critical events you have covered. For each event, note what the marker was, which interaction sequences were used, and how well the event was successfully resolved.

Exercise 6.4: Find Out About Due Process

Obtain the training manual from your training site and look over the procedures for due process. Collect the same information for your academic training program. Learn who your contact person is if there has been an ethical violation. Discuss with your fellow trainees.

Table 6.1 Sample Trainee Evaluation Form

TRAINEE EVALUATION FORM

Student Name: _____

Supervisor: _____

Date: _____

Practicum Site: _____

Total number of *therapy tapes* of this therapist to which you have listened to date: _____

Number of *different clients* to which you have listened to therapy tapes to date: _____

Number of *supervision sessions* you have had with this trainee to date: _____

This evaluation is designed to provide the student with constructive feedback about her or his level of therapy skills, supervision behaviors, and professionalism.

Please complete the following items using the scale below:

1	2	3	4	5	6	7
strongly disagree			neither agree nor disagree			strongly agree

(Note: If you have no information from which to make a rating, please write N/A in the space provided)

(continued)

Table 6.1 (continued) Sample Trainee Evaluation Form

I. Therapy Skills: Response Modes

Is able to demonstrate competency in the following skills consistently, across multiple clients, and in a well-timed fashion:

_____ 1. Attending and Listening.

_____ 2. Restatements.

_____ 3. Open Questions.

_____ 4. Reflection of Feelings.

_____ 5. Challenge.

_____ 6. Interpretation.

_____ 7. Self-Disclosure.

_____ 8. Immediacy.

_____ 9. Information Giving.

_____ 10. Direct Guidance.

II. Therapy Skills: Strategies and Techniques

_____ 11. Is genuinely relaxed and comfortable in the therapy session.

_____ 12. Can express thoughts and feelings clearly in therapy.

_____ 13. Can be spontaneous in therapy, yet behavior is relevant.

_____ 14. Can differentiate process from content in therapy.

_____ 15. Is able to establish mutually agreed upon goals with clients.

_____ 16. Is able to establish mutual trust with clients.

_____ 17. Displayed competency in providing empathy, warmth, and positive regard in therapy.

_____ 18. Demonstrated ability to evaluate progress of therapy.

_____ 19. Demonstrated ability to manage own affect without compromising treatment or therapy.

_____ 20. Demonstrated knowledge of current literature with regard to treatment for specific problems.

_____ 21. Implemented treatment plan with respect to short-term goals, follow-through of plan and modification of plan when evaluation suggested it.

_____ 22. Demonstrated awareness of personal biases and their effects on therapy.

_____ 23. Is self-efficacious regarding her or his therapy skills.

_____ 24. Can critique her or his own therapy tapes.

_____ 25. Can tolerate ambiguity when working with, and understanding, clients.

_____ 26. Is able to discuss multicultural differences (e.g., gender, race, sexual orientation) with clients.

Table 6.1 (continued) Sample Trainee Evaluation Form

_____ 27. Is able to integrate multicultural issues within client conceptualizations.

_____ 28. Demonstrated competency in using the initial interview to assess client needs and status.

_____ 29. Demonstrated competency in using ongoing sessions to assess client needs and status.

_____ 30. Demonstrated ability to assess suicidal risk.

_____ 31. Demonstrated an understanding of developmental issues of clients.

_____ 32. Demonstrated ability to deal with crisis management (consult with supervisor, refer client, etc.).

III. Supervision (1 hour/week required)

_____ 33. Was on time for meetings with supervisor.

_____ 34. Videotaped and/or audiotaped sessions, and reviewed selected sessions under guidance of supervisor.

_____ 35. Was nondefensive during supervision and was able to incorporate suggestions and use feedback effectively.

_____ 36. Demonstrated awareness of how personal issues influenced the therapy process and was willing to address these issues with supervisor.

_____ 37. Acknowledged lack of experience with certain problems/clients and showed a willingness to remedy this under supervision.

_____ 38. Is open to self-examination during supervision.

_____ 39. Participates actively and willingly in supervision sessions.

_____ 40. Lacks sensitivity to dynamics of self in the supervisory relationship.

_____ 41. Provided supervisor with ongoing progress notes and termination forms for clients seen.

_____ 42. Was able to discern and discuss legal concerns as a part of supervision.

IV. Professional Behavior

_____ 43. Behaved in a professional manner with other staff members.

_____ 44. Kept ongoing time sheets and informed supervisor of therapy activities.

_____ 45. Was able to communicate in writing in a clear and concise manner initial, ongoing, and summary case notes.

_____ 46. The therapist is on time for her or his appointments with clients, peers, and supervisors.

_____ 47. Demonstrated ability to deal with conflict.

_____ 48. Demonstrated effective time management.

(Continued)

Table 6.1 (continued) Sample Trainee Evaluation Form

_____ 49. Behaved in an ethical manner.

_____ 50. Informed first interview clients of the limitations of confidentiality.

_____ 51. Informed clients of their level of training (e.g., master's trainee).

_____ 52. Demonstrated knowledge of crisis intervention procedures.

QUALITATIVE EVALUATION

A. Trainee's strengths and unique competencies:

B. Trainee's growth edges requiring further attention:

   Recommendation to trainee to correct weakness:

C. Areas the student has made progress during the period being evaluated:

_____   _____

Supervisor Signature   Date

_____   _____

Trainee Signature   Date

Table 6.2 Trainee Case Conceptualization Outline

I.   Trainee Summary
    A. Demographic Description of Supervisee (gender, race, age, experience)
    B. Mutually Agreed Upon Goals

II. Supervisor Impressions
    A. Supervisory Working Alliance
    B. Evaluation of Supervisee's Skills (Strengths and Weaknesses)
       a. Therapy
       b. Supervision
    C. Trainee-Supervisor Match
       a. Multicultural Identity Interactions
       b. Conflicts: Current or Potential
       c. Supervisor Countertransference Issues

III. Supervisory Intervention
    A. Supervisee's Progress to Date (include number of supervision sessions, summary of sessions up to the present, interventions that were effective/ineffective, her or his work with clients, assessment of client progress, etc.)
    B. Progress on Supervisory Goals
    C. Proposed Future Intervention Strategies
    D. Unanswered Questions

Table 6.3 Sample Supervisor Evaluation Form

Supervision Satisfaction Questionnaire

We are interested in your honest opinions, whether they are positive or negative. Please answer all of the questions. Thank you very much; your help is greatly appreciated.

Circle Your Answers:

1. How would you rate the quality of supervision you have received?

4	3	2	1
Excellent	Good	Fair	Poor

2. Did you get the kind of supervision you wanted?

1	2	3	4
No, definitely not	No, not really	Yes, generally	Yes, definitely

3. To what extent has this supervision fit your needs?

4	3	2	1
Almost all of my needs have been met	Most of my needs have been met	Only a few of my needs have been met	None of my needs have been met

4. If a friend were in need of supervision, would you recommend this supervisor to him or her?

1	2	3	4
No, definitely not	No, I don't think so	Yes, I think so	Yes, definitely

5. How satisfied are you with the amount of supervision you have received?

1	2	3	4
Quite dissatisfied	Indifferent or mildly dissatisfied	Mostly satisfied	Very satisfied

6. Has the supervision you received helped you to deal more effectively in your role as a counselor or therapist?

4	3	2	1
Yes, definitely	Yes, generally	No, not really	No, definitely not

7. In an overall, general sense, how satisfied are you with the supervision you have received?

4	3	2	1
Very satisfied	Mostly satisfied	Indifferent or mildly dissatisfied	Quite dissatisfied

8. If you were to seek supervision again, would you come back to this supervisor?

1	2	3	4
No, definitely not	No, I don't think so	Yes, I think so	Yes, definitely

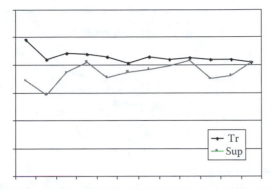

Figure 6.1 Example #1 of the Supervisory Working Alliance Over Time. (Note: Greater scores indicate a stronger working alliance.)

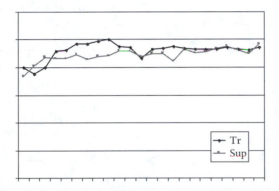

Figure 6.2 Example #2 of the Supervisory Working Alliance Over Time. (Note: Greater scores indicate a stronger working alliance.)

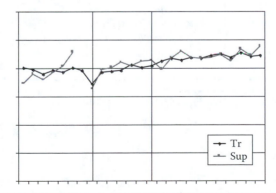

Figure 6.3 Example #3 of the Supervisory Working Alliance Over Time. (Note: Greater scores indicate a stronger working alliance.)

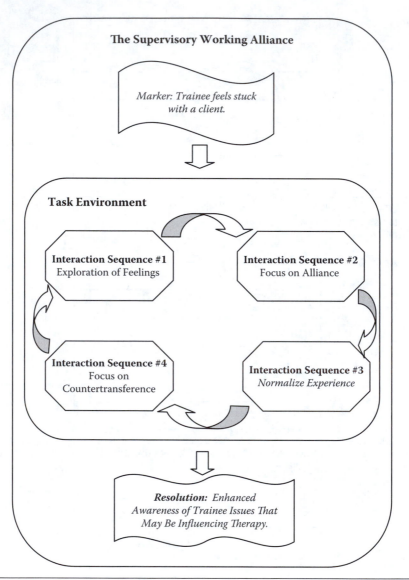

Figure 6.4 Example of a Working through Countertransference Event.

CHAPTER 7

Lydia's Story

Don't be too timid and squeamish about your actions. All life is an experiment. The more experiments you make the better.

—Ralph Waldo Emerson

Oh, the Places You'll Go!

After graduating from college last year, Lydia entered a graduate program with the hopes of becoming a therapist. Lydia was a White woman of European descent, in her early 20s, who self-identified as heterosexual and from an upper-class home. She attended her academic program as a full-time student, and also worked part time as a teacher's aid. In her spare time, she enjoyed coaching a junior league softball team.

Like most new therapists, Lydia entered her first practicum experience unable to predict the journey ahead, and uncertain where the road would lead. When asked about her expectations, she predicted that her relationships with clients would be a "constant adjustment of boundaries, roles, and understanding" and, at times, she allowed herself room to "not feel optimistic or favorable about the client and vise versa." In general, she viewed the upcoming therapy sessions as a "training camp" that would serve to increase clients' awareness, and help clients feel more competent and resourceful.

From her therapy training, Lydia knew the general rules of the therapy game. She also knew the parameters set by the Study. She was going to build a caseload of four to five clients, any of whom she could see for up to 16 sessions. She also was guaranteed weekly 50-minute supervision sessions with a primary supervisor to help her through this process. Finally, she knew this endeavor would last approximately two semesters (4–8 months). However, the rules of the game are only a framework for how the game is played. The framework doesn't tell you who will win or lose, how you will deal with disappointments, or if the outcome will be successful. In other words, just because you know the rules doesn't make you a master of the game.

It reminds us of learning the rules of softball. Think about what happens when there is a runner on first base with one out. Conventional wisdom tells us the play is at second. However, the multiple possible events that can occur after the batter steps to the plate can alter the protocol in countless ways. The end of that play may result in two runs for the opposing team, or the end of the inning after fielding a double-play. You never know what will happen until the ball is in motion. Like softball, the rules of therapy only provide a framework for how we may help our clients, but we never know what will happen until the first meeting, or until the ball is in motion. And, as a therapist, you never know if after a session you will feel more like the batter or more like the ball.

Look for the Themes

We are going to talk about Lydia's experience chronologically in the context of six themes. These themes emerged from extensive analysis of 89 therapy and supervision sessions, in addition to postsession interviews with the therapist, all clients, and the supervisors. How did we derive these themes? And, perhaps more generally, how do therapists typically identify themes in their work? Identifying themes is both an art and a science. The science part involves looking for the most common patterns of interactions that occur with the therapy trainee as the central character. Patterns can be seen with particular clients, across clients, and even across clients and supervisors, for all of the sessions. There are hundreds of potential themes that one can identify in any and all of these interactions. However, the scientific piece recognizes patterns that are the most frequent or most often repeat themselves. The artistic component involves highlighting themes that may evoke emotion, or feel the most compelling in terms of the trainee's experience.

These themes are noticed when they "pack a big punch" in terms of affect, contain multiple critical incidents and turning points, or seem most relevant to the trainee's professional growth and development. We are not going to pretend that the themes we identified are the *only* way we can narrate what happened with this trainee. In fact, in all likelihood, other clinicians could review all the sessions, as well as the qualitative (postsession interviews) and quantitative data, and come up with different patterns and different explanations. Moreover, examining other trainee cases would certainly demonstrate different, yet equally important themes to consider.

We also do not anticipate that the themes, incidents, and situations we are about to discuss will happen to all beginning trainees, and thus they are not wholly "generalizable," from a quantitative perspective. Rather, we lean toward taking a more qualitative stance, a more personalized generalizability, hoping that you will read about Lydia's experiences and take from them what fits for you, the reader. In all likelihood, we anticipate that you will resonate with many of the experiences we discuss. In other instances, you may never see yourself in those situations. Yet in still others, you may have had, or are about to have, a strikingly similar experience. In all, our hope is that you will find what follows personally and professionally meaningful.

So let's begin by setting the stage for the six themes that emerged from Lydia's work. While reading her story, we encourage you to look for these themes. We, too, will point them out as they arise. Not surprisingly, all these themes emerged in her first few supervision and therapy sessions. First, we introduce the theme of *abandonment and termination*. You will learn about how abandonment and termination issues seemed to exist in almost all of Lydia's sessions. They included supervisor abandonment, clients' experience of grief, as well as Lydia's experiences with loss in her life.

A second theme pertains to *boundary issues with time*. We will watch how Lydia struggled with ending sessions on time, having enough time in supervision, or having too much time in supervision. Third, we will follow Lydia on her journey to recognize *countertransference*. Like all trainees, Lydia had to learn what countertransference was, how to manage it, what to do with it, as well as what not to do with countertransference in both therapy and supervision. Fourth, it is said that *trainee anxiety* is a normal part of the learning process. Like Goldilocks' porridge, we will see how Lydia experienced too much anxiety, too little anxiety, and just the right amount of working anxiety during her therapy. We also will cheer Lydia's *successful moments* as a therapist, as well as discuss how to look for therapy success in places you may not expect. And, finally, we will examine what happens when clients cause the therapist pain and *when clients do not get better*. From these six themes, we were able to loosely tie together Lydia's 8 months of work.

You will now hear Lydia's story. We will take you through times when she felt confident and discouraged, empathic and bored, caring and frustrated, satisfied and disappointed, and calm and hostile. Over the course of 8 months, Lydia met with five clients (four women and one man), for as few as 3 and for as many as 17 sessions. Although Lydia began with no official practicum experience, by the time she was finished, she had worked with clients who presented with issues of anxiety, depression, grief, existential angst, a history of sexual abuse, emotional abuse, rape, and domestic violence. One client working with Lydia reported significant success, whereas another client barely improved after 12 sessions. Still another client verbally engaged in hostile and bitter duels with Lydia, before dropping out of therapy after only three sessions. In the midst of these therapeutic adventures, she had a supervisor leave their work and had to adjust to an entirely new supervision relationship (see Table 50 in the Appendix for a summary of characteristics of Lydia, her clients, and her supervisors, and Figures A.19–A.40 in the Appendix for the quantitative results to which we will be referring throughout this chapter).

Lydia engaged in a colorful range of therapeutic and supervisory experiences during her beginning training. Throughout her work, she appeared to speak candidly and genuinely about her feelings, even if that meant taking risks, becoming vulnerable, or speaking negatively about others. Lydia's genuine candor, sincere emotion, and thoughtful insight were some of her greatest strengths. It is our hope that through Lydia's successes and struggles, new therapists can learn what they may encounter, what they might expect, and what therapy and supervision can involve. Lydia represented a brave candidate, reporting her experiences so that others may learn. This is her story …

It All Starts in Supervision (Supervision Sessions 1–2)

We now introduce Tricia, Lydia's supervisor. Tricia, a heterosexual White woman of European descent, agreed to be Lydia's primary supervisor. Tricia was in her late 40s and was a master's level licensed psychologist. She had over 20 years' experience working with individual clients. Furthermore, Tricia had experience as a supervisor with six trainees in the past, all of whom she described as open to learning. Tricia described her therapy and supervisory orientation as holistic and humanistic with some cognitive influence. When asked about her expectations for supervision, Tricia predicted "mutual respect, open and honest communication, and a friendly yet professional" relationship. She hoped that her trainee would have insight into her personal therapy style. Tricia also admitted that their supervision sessions would be a learning experience for both parties.

For better and for worse, the first supervision session set the tone for the rest of Lydia's experience. Overall, the supervision session seemed to go well for Lydia and mostly well for Tricia. Tricia provided the initial structure for the session, gathered and gave contact information, and explored Lydia's initial goals for supervision. Tricia seemed helpful by letting Lydia know "you're going to make mistakes and let yourself be okay with that." In addition, she seemed to help empower Lydia by indicating that part of her job was to help Lydia develop her own style as a therapist that fits with her personality. Tricia's supervisory style seemed to favor a didactic approach, whereby she offered guidance and advice frequently. At this point in the work, it was hard to tell if this was her typical supervisory style or just her "first session" style. She also indicated that she valued honest communication and encouraged Lydia to tell her if she didn't like something she was doing so she could modify her supervisory style.

During the supervision session, Tricia proved adept at self-disclosing about her own experiences and theoretical approach, as well as exploring Lydia's thoughts about how therapy works. For example, Lydia was able to talk about how she was cognitive-behavioral, but open to learning "what that really means" before committing to it. A turning point in the session occurred when Tricia asked Lydia about her experiences as a therapist to date. To Tricia's outward surprise, she learned that Lydia had not seen anyone as a client in therapy before. Even though Tricia was informed that this was Lydia's first practicum experience, this fact seemed to have escaped her up to that point in the session. For reasons unknown, Tricia believed that Lydia would have had at least a few therapy experiences, perhaps in a pregraduate experience. Regardless of the reason, Tricia's newfound knowledge seemed to create tension in her, a tension that she transmitted to Lydia, who subsequently displayed outward nervousness. Lydia's eyes widened a bit when Tricia clarified with her that she wasn't aware that she had never seen clients before. Tricia later told us in the postsession interview that she thought to herself "holy shit!" when it became clear to her that Lydia did not have any experience. Lydia seemed to pick up on Tricia's concern, and indicated in her postsession interview that she wondered how Tricia really felt about what she was saying.

At that point in the session, Tricia's nervousness and advice-giving supervisory approach seemed to intensify. She appeared overly committed to providing Lydia with information about how to start a therapy session and what things to look for. This near-frenzied activity occurred even though they were to have another supervision session before Lydia saw her first client. Tricia, in a seeming effort to assuage her anxiety, also instructed Lydia to be sure to have writing materials in the next supervision so she could take notes.

As an aside, it seems important to us that beginning supervisors are aware that most therapists have very limited, if any, pregraduate therapy experiences. Although most programs offer some type of helping skills (e.g., Hill, 2004) training or a prepracticum, our experience has shown us that no matter the preparation, new therapists rarely feel fully ready to see their first client. So, Tricia's response seemed a bit excessive, and in fact, seemed to heighten Lydia's nervousness and fears. Tricia tried to bounce back some by reassuring Lydia that she will do fine and it's okay to be nervous, but some damage had already occurred.

The theme of *abandonment* also reared its head in the first session. As part of Lydia's openness, she revealed to Tricia that she had difficulties when people don't end relationships well with her and that "greetings and leavings" are very important to her. In a related fashion, Lydia revealed that she had a negative personal therapy experience, which Tricia left relatively unexplored. Lydia mentioned that she felt her therapist was nonresponsive, would leave her hanging, and opened her up only to walk away. Lydia drew an insightful connection between this therapy experience and the value she places on good closure, which she hoped to be able to do with her own clients. Unfortunately, Tricia did not focus on any of these points during the session. However, in her postsession interviews, Tricia questioned whether she should have delved more into these areas. There appeared to be some recognition that there were missed opportunities. Moreover, by not exploring these areas further, Tricia seemed to have indirectly indicated to Lydia that perhaps supervision should stay at a more superficial level.

In the end, though, the first session helped Lydia because she was able to derive some concrete information about how events might unfold during her first therapy session. She also seemed mostly comfortable with Tricia's style and particularly liked that Tricia seemed committed to helping Lydia develop her own style as a therapist that fit with her personality. Another helpful supervisor comment occurred when Tricia said, "it's okay if you miss something in a client; the client invariably will be sure to bring it up again and again if it's a core issue." This guidance seemed particularly reassuring to Lydia. Finally, Lydia seemed to be helped knowing that "the process of learning therapy is the process of learning about yourself."

Tricia, by contrast, revealed later that she felt pretty overwhelmed by how "green" her trainee was. It really seemed to strike home that "this is going to be a lot of work!" She also expressed concern that she didn't want to do "therapy" with Lydia.

The therapy-supervision boundary is a constant struggle for supervisors. Simply put, supervision should not function as therapy for the trainee. However, inasmuch as the trainee's interpersonal issues influence therapy work, a "therapeutic" approach in supervision may be appropriate. Oftentimes, this approach is set in the context of examining trainee countertransference, which, to us, seems a very legitimate approach to supervision. When the boundary verges too much into a therapy experience for the trainee, the supervisor needs to pull back and supportively offer the trainee referrals for personal therapy. All of this should be set within a strong supervisory working alliance where both the trainee and supervisor agree about how this will take place. In the end, Tricia's hesitancy to enter this arena in supervision, even tentatively, may have been another lost opportunity.

The second supervision session began with Tricia giving a lot of information to Lydia about what she could do in her first therapy session. Interestingly, it appeared that Lydia already knew much of what Tricia suggested to her, including specific questions she could ask her client. In the post session interview Lydia mentioned a hindering event in the session was "going over the intake interview exactly, [especially since] I had a class about doing intakes."

This state of affairs is not uncommon for beginning trainees. In fact, with a little probing, our experience is that most beginning trainees indeed know essentially what to do in a session. After all, at its core, a therapy session is simply a conversation, which most therapists-in-training have proven adept at throughout their lives. In fact, many therapists-in-training go into therapy because they find that they are the earpieces for others in their lives. We find that many new therapists have heard multiple times in their life that "you are the kind of person who is just easy to talk with."

Evidence that Lydia was more informed than perhaps Tricia was aware comes from the fact that Lydia initially didn't take notes as Tricia spoke. In fact, Lydia "forgot" to bring a pencil or pen. When she finally took notes, a quarter way into the session, it seemed clear that she only wrote down what she needed from all the information that Tricia threw at her. The key element that prevented Lydia from completely shutting down seemed to be Tricia's earnestness in trying to help Lydia. She even went so far as offering to fax Lydia additional documents.

A helpful metaphor that Tricia introduced was likening the initial phase of therapy to putting together a puzzle. Unfortunately, the way Tricia talked about the case, therapy seemed like a 10,000-piece puzzle! Not to oversimplify the work, but, in reality, each client brings in a unique and relatively circumscribed set of conditions that can be identified by a therapist. In any therapy session, a therapist would be hard pressed to attend to even more than a few of these conditions and presenting concerns. In addition, it is often difficult for supervisors to find a balance between both validating the difficulty of therapeutic technique and reassuring the trainee that sometimes things are not as complex as they seem.

Again, the theme of *abandonment* and loss was noticeably present in the second supervision session. We learned from the prescreening intakes that Lydia's first two clients had significant losses in their life. It turned out that Lydia too had experienced a number of losses in the past year, having attended four funerals and dealt with the breakup of a relationship. Unfortunately, instead of a discussion of these losses in relation to any personal concerns about working with these clients, Tricia instead chose to "teach" Lydia about how to work with a client who has experienced a death.

While somewhat helpful, it is our contention that processing this information (e.g., discussing an event and exploring personal emotions linked to the event) would have been more beneficial and would have been more generalizable to Lydia's future therapy experiences. Give a person a fish and he or she eats for a day; teach a person to fish and he or she eats for a lifetime. One of our beliefs is that trainees learn better when they discover things on their own rather than when others tell them what to do. We believe there is value in the journey of discovery itself, in which didactic shortcuts lack. Not surprisingly, Tricia revealed after the session that she regretted not having processed the loss issue further.

The *abandonment* theme was also present between Tricia and Lydia when a discussion ensued about Tricia's vacation plans for a month henceforth. A positive aspect of this discussion was that Tricia demonstrated her professionalism by planning and informing Lydia well in advance. However, given Lydia's known concern regarding people leaving her, it was surprising that Tricia did not discuss the potential feelings of abandonment that her vacation might evoke in Lydia. The lack of processing this event seemed to heighten Lydia's nervousness and lead to more discomfort about herself as a therapist.

Other than teaching, one of the best things that Tricia did was offer Lydia active and reflective listening to let her know that she was listening. So on a nonverbal level, Tricia appeared to have heard Lydia. However, toward the end of the session, Tricia seemed to blow whatever cachet she had developed when in response to Lydia's desire to "get the first session over with," Tricia said, "well let's just hope for a talker." This comment certainly seemed to undermine Lydia's emerging, albeit limited, self-efficacy. In addition, it dismissed the notion that Lydia can handle what things come her way in therapy and likely disempowered Lydia enhancing her potential dependency on Tricia. By the end of the each of the first two sessions, as seen in Figure 7.1, Lydia left supervision more anxious than when she started.

Approaching the First Therapy Session

Imagine that you are at a cocktail party, meeting someone for the first time. Regardless of your introverted or extroverted nature, imagine that you need to mingle with this person for approximately one hour. Now imagine that as a result of your mood or your personality style, you wish to do less of the talking and more of the listening during your time together. Subtract the food, drinks, and other people in the room and visualize the two of you seated, facing one another. Finally, lower the threshold of privacy, and add the element of appropriate intrusion. You have license to be nosier than the average stranger. You can appropriately ask questions that may be inappropriate to ask during the average cocktail hour. What might that hour look like?

Essentially, the parameters just described can act as a framework for an intake, or first therapy session. When you see a client for the first time, most of what you're doing involves getting to know the person, through a series of questions. Some questions will be clinical in nature (e.g., frequency and severity of symptoms) and other questions will be personal background information (e.g., do you have any brothers or sisters?). Mostly, however, the intake session purpose is to establish a relationship with the client. It may involve brief casual chat (e.g., is it still raining outside?), personal disclosure (e.g., that would stress me out also!), shared laughter, or mutually tolerated silence.

We are not suggesting that a therapeutic intake is necessarily as easy as mingling at a cocktail hour. As therapists, we use our learned skills to move things beyond a casual chat. These therapeutic skills include establishing rapport, effectively listening, reflecting feelings, empathy, creating mutual goals for the therapeutic work, collecting diagnostic information, providing psychoeducation about the limits of confidentiality, and offering the instillation of hope. Thinking about doing all this, though, can feel overwhelming when entering your first session. Try to focus on two things: gathering information and building an alliance. And, if you do nothing else, empathize.

As we've pointed out previously, something we like to tell new therapists to help alleviate their anxiety about starting therapy work is the empathy rule: "If you do nothing else, empathize." One of the few things we know about what works in therapy pertains to the formation of a positive working alliance. And what is most critical in forming this alliance is the use of empathy. One of the most difficult things to learn early on is to resist the temptation to "do something," or quickly problem-solve or take over for the client. We like to remind therapists that the working alliance takes three to five sessions to develop and it is only when the alliance has developed adequately that the action or "doing" part of therapy may come into play. Of course, there are exceptions to this such as when the client is suicidal. However, even under these conditions, the therapist must work diligently to quickly facilitate the development of an alliance while at the same time providing directed information gathering and guidance for the client.

I Survived My First Session!

Lydia's first client was Kendra, a 62-year-old heterosexual middle-class White woman of Eastern European descent. Her presenting issues included depression related to her mother's death (which occurred 6 years previously), social anxiety, and having to manage her 94-year-old father who moved in following her mother's death (which she reported changed her lifestyle considerably). She attended therapy about 15 years ago, which she found helpful. Her expectations for therapy included wanting to develop an honest relationship and hoping the therapist would help her find the help she needed within herself. Specifically, she hoped to overcome her anxieties and feelings of being inadequate.

Lydia's first session went smoothly. Lydia spent the therapy session asking a series of well-timed questions, without rushing the session or making Kendra feel interrogated. As would be expected, some of Lydia's questions were casual inquiries about background information (e.g., how did you meet your husband, when did you go to school, what are the ages of your children, is your oldest daughter married). Some questions were more personal than others (e.g., do you still keep in contact with your ex-husband). Other queries were more feeling-oriented (e.g., how was it to raise four children, were you happy you didn't go back to school). Lydia and Kendra occasionally shared laughter and seemed to establish a relaxed rapport while Lydia gathered her intake information. After collecting some background details, Lydia switched gears to collect more clinical information with the well-timed transition, "I want to know more about you feeling nervous."

From her inquiries, Lydia learned that Kendra grew up with a loving father, but with a domineering and bitter mother who was unable or unwilling to communicate affection. At a young age, in search of her mother's approval, Kendra began training to become an office assistant. Shortly after she began school, she became pregnant to her secret boyfriend, a man of whom her mother strongly disapproved. Fearing a promised disowning if she should ever come home pregnant out of wedlock, Kendra dropped out of school and eloped. Future years brought Kendra four children, one divorce, and one remarriage, all while continuing the plight to please and satisfy her mother, a woman who reportedly was cruel and cold to Kendra. As Kendra's life unfolded, she developed a strong sense of social anxiety, never feeling comfortable in crowds. By the time she came to Lydia for her therapeutic intake, Kendra was retired. Although her mother died over

6 years ago, Kendra continued to feel the self-loathing, guilt, worry, and shame her mother instilled.

Sometimes during an initial session, clients will spend the entire 50 minutes talking about nothing but their presenting issue (e.g., and another thing I'm angry about is work, and another thing I'm angry about is my husband, and another thing ...). Other times, clients will surprisingly spend very little time talking about the topic they supposedly have come in to discuss (e.g., how do you get the plants in your office to grow so beautifully?). Different theoretical orientations advise therapists to react in different ways when a client does not discuss their presenting concerns. Psychodynamic theories may instruct a therapist to patiently allow the client to "resist" the real issues while the therapist interprets her or his surface level conversation as transference. A more cognitive-behavioral approach may instruct the therapist to keep the client "on task" by redirecting the conversation back to the established short- and long-term goals. A person-centered approach would call for empathic statements that convey an unconditional acceptance of what the client presents. Along with and perhaps beyond one's theoretical orientation, we encourage therapists to consider first and foremost the working alliance (i.e., agreement on the goals and tasks, and an emotional bond). In the case of Lydia and Kendra, Lydia's information gathering questions seemed to fit with the therapy tasks Kendra had anticipated. In addition, Lydia was able to attend to the bond component of the alliance through reflecting some of Kendra's experiences. Figure 7.2 reflects the strength of their alliance.

The key for all therapists, whether beginning level or master therapist, is a continuous self-reflection about their strengths and growth edges. Not surprisingly, along with her strengths, Lydia's growth edges as a therapist started to show in this first session as well. For Lydia, one area that she could have attended to is her cognitive style, which appeared to limit her ability to use empathy, and which may have stifled the development of the alliance. In her zeal to gather information, she seemed to have forgotten to attend to empathizing with the client as often as she could have. In one striking example, at one point the client, with affect in her voice, mentioned that "my mother always kept me down." Instead of asking Kendra what that was like or how that made her feel, Lydia continued to focus on gathering more information. In this case, Lydia missed an opportunity to help Kendra go deeper in her experience. As Lydia's supervisor previously said, Lydia will have multiple opportunities to make up for any missed chances at helping a client with a core issue. Although the overall alliance was positive, we would have anticipated it would have been stronger if she had been able to empathize more, which in turn would have provided a stronger foundation for interventions in the future. In the end, though, the alliance seemed strong enough for Kendra to come back the following week.

We also learned that Kendra's mother would give her the "silent treatment" as a form of punishment. This information was something that Lydia could keep in the back of her mind as they continued to work together and when silence did or didn't occur in therapy. One other thing that Lydia did very well was a well-timed use of self-disclosure. Self-disclosure, like silence, can be a powerful, albeit infrequent, therapist tool. In this case, Kendra had mentioned that during her previous therapy work she confronted her mother, which led to her feeling more empowered but also a little bad. Lydia self-disclosed she had a similar experience confronting her mother and felt both good and bad about it. This is a good example of how Lydia and Kendra were able to make a connection that transcended their age difference. In the end, this self-disclosure likely helped strengthen the alliance.

Lydia and Kendra's session reflected a nice balance of sharing background and clinical information. In part, Lydia did a nice job asking appropriate questions. The other reason the session probably ran so smoothly is that Kendra appeared to be a reasonably socially healthy person. For instance, she generally understood social norms enough to share laughter, answer questions when asked, participate in dialogue rather than monologue, and display affect. It may sound absurd to point out such social graces as client strengths, but many individuals do not function this way. In fact, you may look around you in everyday life and begin to recognize a wide variety of sociability among friends and acquaintances, as well as peers in your graduate program! It is important to remember that clients bring both their socially appropriate and socially awkward norms into the therapy session. Hence, therapists need to be sure to attend to and recognize both of these strengths and weaknesses.

Before Lydia's training experience is over, she will encounter clients whose interpersonal styles are not as positive as Kendra's. In fact, she will at times experience clients as condescending, demeaning, and obnoxious. The task for Lydia will be to react appropriately to these problematic interpersonal styles, thereby providing a corrective emotional experience for her clients, a task that, as we will see, was not easy for her.

Following the session, Kendra indicated that she found that just talking to Lydia about things that were bothering her was helpful and she was surprised that the session went by so quickly. Lydia mentioned that she was able to resonate with the client's experiences; in particular, Kendra's experience with her mother strongly reminded Lydia of her grandmother's treatment of her own mother. In this example, Lydia was able to use her positive countertransference to help her understand her client better. Not surprisingly for a first session, Lydia wondered how she was perceived and remembered trying to come up with questions so she would look like she knew what she was doing. In the end, Lydia stated that she was pleased that "I got my first one done," and she now knew that "I can sit in front of a stranger and do it!" Figure A.19 also illustrates her relief, and you can see her anxiety decreased from the beginning of the session to the end of the session. That said, her nagging self-doubt was not all lost as she also stated "I just hope that I get better."

Losing My Husband Was Like Losing More Than Half My Body

Ruby, Lydia's second client, lost her husband of 45 years to a car accident 1 year ago, and fell into a depressed state of loneliness and sorrow. She was no stranger to therapy. Reportedly, Ruby was significantly dissatisfied with her trials from two other therapists before seeking help from Lydia. Ruby, a 68-year-old heterosexual middle-class woman, had retired from her financial advising position 10 years ago. She and her husband Ken had planned to spend a long and healthy retirement together. The grief from the loss of her husband was Ruby's presenting concern. Like many grieving individuals, she desired to "move on" but didn't know how. Here again, the issue of loss became present in Lydia's sessions. Sometimes, as therapists, it just seems like we find clients, or clients find us, who move our personal issues out of the forest and into the trees!

Lydia appeared relatively settled and relaxed in her first session with Ruby, although there were hints that she was still not yet comfortable with her therapist hat (e.g., she referred to herself as "only" a therapy student). Ironically, Lydia's supervisor's wish for a "talker" came true with Ruby. Ruby was the type of client that all therapists will work with at some point. Her interpersonal approach was one of storytelling in a relatively emotionally detached way. Her historical storytelling included meticulous details about her past, which she presented in a way that made it hard for Lydia to interrupt. Her affect was not completely flat; however, there were not many peaks and valleys, even when talking about emotionally charged topics such as her husband's death and the death of other members of her family, including the murder of her sister. Sometimes, clients like these can be frustrating for a therapist. Clients may make others in their lives feel frustrated as well. However, the challenge for the therapist is to see the client's pain and help the client move past the story-telling to the deeper issues. Lydia seemed genuinely stuck with how to move Ruby to a more meaningful level. It seemed as though Ruby's storytelling lulled Lydia. By the end of the session, when Ruby displayed emotions (slightly crying), Lydia did not respond. She seemed to use the silence to catch up with what was happening.

Where Lydia appeared to do well was showing a great deal of interest nonverbally and demonstrating good patience, which seemed appropriate for a first session. From this demeanor, she was able to learn a number of important facts about Ruby's life: her father was an alcoholic who quit drinking when she was in junior high school; she met her husband when she was 18 (first and only love); she dedicated her life to her husband, dropping out of school because "what do I want an education for? I want to get married and wash socks"; she ended up going back to school to get a master's degree; and the history of deaths in her family were sudden and unexpected (e.g., her sister was murdered).

Probably the most striking event of this session was that it exceeded its time limit by 20 minutes (the emergence of the *boundary issues with time* theme). Lydia did a nice job informing Ruby that the session time was over and it was time to stop. Ruby apologized but then asked Lydia a question about therapy that in turn led to Lydia responding to Ruby. The hook was there and the session went overtime. Instead of processing this or interrupting, Lydia hung in there and tried to end the session nonverbally, to no avail.

Interestingly, in the postsession interview, both Ruby and Lydia mentioned that the session was more of a monologue. Ruby attributed it to nervousness and Lydia believed it helped her get to know Ruby well, hearing all the stories of her life. Lydia did a very good job identifying her negative countertransference in this session. She tapped into how, during the session, she experienced feeling sad as she recalled her grandfather who recently died. She related to what it must have been like for Ruby to deal with having to visit a hospital and then later deal with the bills and associated stress of having a spouse die unexpectedly. Lydia felt that her experiences assisted her in having more empathy toward Ruby. Lydia was also able to self-reflect and identify her difficulty with focusing this client, a growth edge on which she realized that she would need to work.

Ruby began the next session by indicating that she had had a very bad week and was very depressed. Although in the phone intake Ruby reported no suicidal ideation or intent, any time a client talks about feeling "very depressed" we always encourage therapists to attend to these feelings and conduct a suicide assessment to assess suicidal risk (e.g., depressed mood, plan, means, time, place, willingness to contract that client will not hurt self; see Chapter 4) in order to ensure client safety. Unfortunately, Lydia did not attend to this. In a case of poor modeling by a supervisor, when Lydia mentioned her client in supervision, Tricia rationalized to Lydia that everything is probably okay. Even though Tricia was right, she unfortunately never requested Lydia go back and assess for suicide to be sure.

As in the first session, Ruby continued to storytell and did not respond to Lydia's attempts at focusing the session, largely because Lydia was focusing on content rather than process. We learned a lot about Ruby's life such as more of the circumstances around her husband's death, as well as about her daughter's alcoholism and difficulties in her relationship with both her daughter and her son. In addition, as in the previous session, Lydia and Ruby went overtime, this time making the session last for 90 minutes! Interestingly, at the 50-minute mark, Ruby asked if their time is almost over and Lydia responded by saying "no" it's okay if we continue on a little longer. In the post session interview, Ruby identified her talking as something she found helpful and appreciated what a good listener Lydia was. Ironically, she was concerned about going overtime and wished they hadn't. Lydia, too, was concerned about going overtime, but indicated that she "didn't want to hurt her feelings by cutting her off." Lydia identified it as an issue to talk about in her next supervision.

Looking at these time issues a different way, a legitimate question may be "Who said therapy must be 50 minutes anyway?" The answer, "Convention and tradition dictates," is certainly not sufficient, but it does provide a pathway to legitimate therapeutic reasons. Some argue that having time limits is one way that a therapist can model forming and maintaining appropriate boundaries with a client. However, more important than the actual time limit is how time is used. In other words, we can learn a lot about clients and therapists based on how they use time in their work. In Ruby's case, for example, pushing the boundaries of time may be a way to keep her connected with someone so she won't have to be alone. In Lydia's case, allowing Ruby to push the time boundaries seemed to indicate a lack of assertiveness, possibly reflecting her discomfort in the role of therapist. As with most issues in therapy, we encourage therapists to attend to what time issues represent rather than brushing time issues aside as a simple skill to learn.

Sometimes Supervision Is About Learning What Not to Do

For reasons that are not exactly clear, Lydia showed up for her next supervision session but Tricia did not. Apparently, there was a mix-up when they scheduled with one another. In any event, Lydia was quite upset to find Tricia unavailable. She was particularly disappointed that she was not able to talk about her first session with her first client and she would not be able to talk with Tricia about feeling abandoned when Tricia leaves for vacation. In an insightful manner, Lydia also had come to the conclusion that she and Tricia tend to be "surfacy" in supervision.

The next day, Lydia and Tricia were able to make up their missed supervision session. Regrettably, Tricia never processed the missed supervision session. Instead, she proceeded to make suggestions and offer advice to Lydia about her first client, Kendra. At points, Tricia did a nice job asking Socratic questions (e.g., how do you suppose that serves Kendra?) to facilitate Lydia's conceptualization about Kendra. However, the Socratic questions were few and far between a multitude of suggestions and advice, making them less powerful and less meaningful to Lydia. For the entire session, Tricia plodded along with her teachings. In a fascinating manner, Lydia looked like she couldn't be less interested. It was apparent that she was shutting down and tuning out her supervisor. Beyond her nonverbal disinterest, Lydia did not take notes for much of the session, another clear sign that Tricia's interventions were not getting through. It seemed that all it would have taken was some here-and-now processing on the part of Tricia to change the downward spiral of the session. In here-and-now processing, the supervisor discusses experiences that are happening in the moment between the trainee and supervisor. For example, Tricia could have mentioned that she noticed Lydia not taking notes and questioned what may be going on for Lydia right then and there. Because Tricia didn't do this, Lydia was able to remain defended and disinterested.

To make matters worse, on three separate occasions Tricia stated that she thought Lydia might be letting her personal biases influence therapy but then never processed these concerns. This was in response to Lydia taking a risk and disclosing her possible countertransference between her feelings about her grandparents and her clients. What Lydia seemed to need was more empathy and compassion and less education and instruction.

The next few supervision sessions proceeded in a similar fashion with Tricia assuming a very didactic approach to supervision. We should note that this approach was not entirely lost on Lydia. There were a number of times that Tricia said things that seemed to resonate with Lydia (e.g., types of structured questions to review with clients), as evidenced by her occasional note-taking. However, unfortunately but also understandably, much of it did not seem to reach Lydia.

Not coincidentally, two dynamics that occurred in supervision ended up getting mimicked in therapy (i.e., cases of parallel process). First, it was not surprising to find that Lydia had trouble ending her therapy sessions on time, when Tricia similarly had difficulty ending their supervision session on time. Tricia continued to state that the supervision hour was not enough time to discuss two clients (clearly an unusual expectation). Second, Tricia's lack of here-and-now processing with Lydia was reflected in Lydia's lack of here-and-now processing with clients. This parallel process was probably the most significant error that originated in supervision because it seemed to have an effect on how well Lydia was able to facilitate change in all her clients. Although, many times, Lydia was able to facilitate some change in her clients, it seems reasonable to suspect that more of her clients could have benefited had this processing been modeled in supervision.

Lydia Finds Her Groove

In spite of the mixed effectiveness of supervision, Lydia's work with Kendra flowed relatively smoothly from beginning to end. Kendra was very receptive to Lydia's interventions and they genuinely seemed to like and care about each other. Lydia's primary approach involved listening, reflecting, empathizing followed by challenging the client in a nonthreatening way (e.g., through humor) to consider how her negative self-talk may be causing her depression. They looked at Kendra's past experiences with her mother and how her mother's critical voice still resides in Kendra's head. In a postsession interview, Lydia remarked, "She acts like her mother is sitting on her shoulder telling her what to do and she makes her decisions based around what she thinks her mother would have said." Lydia also empowered Kendra by offering reassurance that she has many strengths and helping Kendra reconsider her negative self-beliefs. Kendra's improvement showed across a number of indices. Some examples included (a) an insight event in which she recognized how her mother's former criticisms influenced her self-esteem presently, (b) she joined a gym, (c) she started wearing clothes she had always wanted to but didn't for fear of her mother's disapproval, (d) a significant decrease in her level of distress as indicated by the OQ45 (see Figure 7.4), (e) she exercised her assertiveness by disagreeing with someone at a social event, (f) she did not take responsibility for her father's anger, (g) she chose to accept her brother's personality and no longer expected him to change, and (h) she weaned herself off of antidepressant medication she had received from her general practitioner. Moreover, the sessions seemed to be a positive experience as evidenced by their alliance and session impact ratings (Figures 7.2–7.3), albeit Kendra consistently had more favorable perceptions than Lydia.

In addition, most of Lydia's interventions worked. In one case, she did a nice job of normalizing Kendra's experiences by stating how "everyone sometimes has doubts about their relationships." Lydia also attended to Kendra's "good voice" in the service of weakening her mother's critical voice. Lydia was able to use her countertransference (such as Lydia's mother's relationship with her grandmother) to help her understand and empathize with Kendra. Lydia also did a nice job pointing out Kendra's strengths as well as making interpretations that resonated with Kendra (e.g., linking mother's and brother's controlling and critical behavior, pointing out generalizations of her new interpersonal skills).

Although early on Lydia used some dysfunctional thoughts worksheets to help structure the session, paradoxically, her abandonment of these worksheets seemed to help move things along better for their work. After one session, which typified the later work, Lydia reported, "The 50 minutes went by really fast and I thought a lot of positive things came out of it even though I went into it not knowing what I was going to do. It was positive that as a therapist I could get through the session, accomplish something and not have things written down on a piece of paper that included exactly what I wanted to cover and without a whole lot of preparation or guidance." In addition, she mentioned "I'm used to my supervisor saying, 'You know, these are the things maybe you should cover, important things you haven't touched on.' And today I didn't really do that. I wanted to kind of see where she was at and I didn't know what to do. It felt good because, I guess just gives you confidence that it's possible."

Her abandonment of her supervisor's voice, interestingly, paralleled Kendra's abandonment of her mother's voice. This is not to say that Lydia's supervisor, Tricia, presented with a harsh and critical voice. Rather, the parallel process pertained to the disempowerment that Lydia experienced from Tricia's chronic and overwhelming number of suggestions, which was similar to the disempowerment that Kendra experienced in relation to her mother's voice. Both Lydia and Kendra empowered themselves by transcending and abandoning their reliance on these "voices."

A qualitative shift occurred in the work around the eighth session. From the 8th through the 11th sessions, Lydia and Kendra attended to relapse prevention–type activities (Prochaska & Norcross, 2001). Initially, Kendra expressed concern that, without therapy, she may slip back into old patterns of thinking and not wanting to "fall 10 steps back without the support." Lydia performed well by examining things such as what Kendra might do if she started to feel depressed (e.g., reattributions of negative thoughts) and continued to encourage Kendra to put herself in positions that are at least slightly uncomfortable to continue the generalization of her newly developing interpersonal style (e.g., seek out crowds or interact with more people). The relapse prevention work seemed to take hold for Kendra. In one example, she was able to see a current down mood as only a temporary thing.

By the 11th session, it was evident that things were clearly winding down. Even though there was still some concern by Kendra that she may lose some of her recent gains, she mentioned "maybe I should try it on my own," which was a good sign that the work was headed toward closure. Initially, Lydia did a nice job beginning the termination process by asking how therapy has worked for Kendra. For example, she asked, "When you look back at your first session, what do you remember and how are things different?" However, the one skill area that Lydia had difficulty with all along, processing in the here and now, ended up affecting the termination phase. Without the here-and-now processing, Kendra found herself running out of things to talk about. In fact, they ended the 11th and final sessions early, the last session going only about 20 minutes! Thus, opportunities were lost to talk about what it was like to end the relationship.

Lydia's issues with endings also likely played into her inability to process her relationship with Kendra. In a sad and unfortunate example of fateful coincidence, Lydia revealed in a postsession interview, "I kept looking at the clock because I was thinking that my dad was probably having our cat put asleep at that time, Um, and I guess just my feelings surrounding the whole thing with our cat, I don't know. I just wasn't focused this session."

Additional termination skills became salient in these final sessions. In terms of providing closure, as mentioned earlier, Lydia did well to initiate a discussion about the gains that Kendra made in therapy; however, she did not do well when it came to processing these gains. As noted in Chapter 5, termination is a critical phase in therapy that should not be overlooked. One area that Lydia could have focused on further included processing the feelings that both of them were having in their final sessions. Both reported sadness, but only in the post session interviews, not in the therapy session; this was a lost opportunity to make a closer interpersonal connection. A few times, Kendra complimented Lydia but Lydia deflected these compliments. For example, Kendra stated, "You helped me open my eyes," to which Lydia responded, "You opened your own eyes." Although at some level this is true, it also may benefit clients at times to model how to receive a compliment and show that the therapist and client were in the process together.

Unfortunately, Lydia did not even extend her hand for a handshake at the end of their work, a skill she was actually able to demonstrate with other clients. It is imperative that therapists consider how touch can be used at the end of therapeutic work in a culturally sensitive manner (Tune, 2001). Although Lydia did not behaviorally demonstrate good therapeutic technique, she was insightful about her responses in relation to termination. In her postsession interviews, she was acutely aware of what was happening. Her comments said it all. "Like it's so weird, you see a person every week for like four or five months and all of a sudden you're not going to see them anymore. My stupid-ass comments throughout the entire session were hindering. Just stupid. Like I just didn't know what to say. And I feel like some of the stuff just didn't really fit and I, I was kind of like scraping around for something cuz I didn't know what to say. Cuz I was uncomfortable with ending the session. I think in general, I'm uncomfortable with ending relationships. Cuz I don't think I've had good experiences with like clear breaks and ah, and I was uncomfortable with ending this relationship cuz I don't know really know how to make a clean break." And although Lydia certainly was a bit hard on herself, we should not lose sight that much of this could have been avoided had "greetings and leavings" been processed in supervision.

Even though termination did not go perfectly, the overall work with Kendra seemed to be a success for both the therapist and the client. In a posttreatment interview, Lydia mentioned that she still regretted the poor ending but that Kendra taught her lots: "Before her, I didn't know I could do it!" Up to 1 year posttreatment, Kendra's level of distress was still in the healthy range (see Figure 7.4). In addition, she continued to report that "I no longer see myself as responsible for my failed relationships" and "I am very grateful for the opportunity to participate in the sessions. It's an amazing change for me to have good, pleasant, and positive thoughts and feelings."

It Was the Best of Times, It Was the Worst of Times

While all was going well with Kendra, Lydia was presented with a different challenge from Bill, a 74-year-old retired minister who had a doctoral degree in theology and a master's degree in social work. As a result of the insistence of his wife, he came to therapy "looking for insight" into his feelings of sadness related to being retired and not having anything to do, as well as serious difficulties with procrastination. It didn't take long to see that Lydia and Bill were going to have a rocky relationship. At the beginning of the session, as part of the role induction, Lydia revealed that she is a practicum student under supervision, to which Bill replied, "That's okay, I've trained therapists throughout my life." Interpersonal comments similar to this one occurred throughout their work and a battle for control in the relationship, over time, became the only dance they knew. Even so, Lydia managed to hang in there in the first session. She did a very good job listening, tracking, and reflecting Bill's comments. From this approach, Bill was able to talk about his concerns, which, in addition to feeling sad and having problems with procrastination, included existential questions related to finding worth in his life and wondering if he had made the world a better place through his previous work. We also learned that he has suffered a number of significant losses in his life, including his father and both of his sisters, and in relation to these losses, had questions about his own mortality.

Lydia's exploratory approach provided us with a good example of how one size doesn't fit all for the clients with which we work. Similar to Kendra,

Bill was depressed; however, he was less compliant or ready than Kendra was, and not as open to cognitive restructuring work with which Lydia felt comfortable. Rather, he engaged in many "yes-buts" and through much of the time, did not seem to even need Lydia in the room. Instead of pointing out the here and now process (e.g., I notice that every time I make a suggestion you say "yes-but"), Lydia tried in vain to engage Bill in a task in which he had no interest. Bill was very bright and he used his intelligence to rationalize and argue against Lydia's suggestions. In this case, rather than continue with the sparing, Lydia may have been better off taking a more nondirectional stance.

In the first session postsession interview, Bill found that the session helped him ramble and talk about lots of things. He also indicated that he had two intruding thoughts: Lydia's lack of experience and her young age. On the surface, this statement is certainly accurate. However, clients who don't want to work in therapy will invariably find something about the therapist with which they cannot connect (e.g., too young, too old, inexperienced, intimidating because of all the degrees). We have found that, in general, the reasons are more apt to be defenses used to avoid deeper exploration in therapy. The problem is, many beginning therapists have a heightened awareness about their inexperience and too readily accept the defense as a legitimate limitation. Instead, the client would be better served if the therapist were able to process the work in the session. More evidence of this contention came from other things mentioned by Bill in the post session interview. For example, he stated, "I don't expect words of wisdom from her." What became clear is that Lydia was set up to fail if she only responded to Bill's defense.

Lydia was unable to process his defensiveness, or his transference. In Lydia's postsession interview, she admitted feeling intimidated and defeated by Bill. She was able to identify some emerging countertransference, recognizing that Bill reminded her of her father. In addition, she admitted that she didn't like that Bill reported having thoughts that she considered sexist (e.g., domestic chores are not for men) and this bothered her during and after the session. Referring back to the model of nonoppressive interpersonal development in relation to gender identity, what seems to be happening here is that Bill is at a lower stage of means of interpersonal functioning (i.e., adaptation as evidenced by his sexist comments) and Lydia is at a higher stage of means of interpersonal functioning (i.e., incongruence as evidenced by her recognition of sexist comments). Although she is at a slightly higher stage, she is not at a high enough stage to understand his sexism and then work with the sexism in a productive and therapeutic fashion. Instead, their interpersonal interaction style (i.e., parallel-delayed) results in another stuck place in therapy.

The spiral down that began in the first session continued in leaps and bounds in the second session. Bill wasn't sure what to work on so Lydia chose procrastination (not a mutually agreed-on task). They soon drifted to other topics as Bill's maladaptive narcissism became more pronounced. At one point, Bill exclaimed, "A person your age could never understand what someone my age is going through." Instead of processing this reaction, Lydia valiantly tried to attend to ways in which he could solve his procrastination problem. It is clear that they were missing one another and that they disagreed with their goals and tasks for therapy (poor alliance). (As an aside, one of the things we notice when working with clients is that whenever we are not moving anywhere in therapy with a client, invariably it is because our goals and tasks are not in sync.)

In his second session postsession statements, Bill indicated that Lydia's inability to react well when he mentioned she couldn't understand someone his age made him want to reveal less in therapy (a rupture in the alliance). At the same time, Lydia was aware that the session was unhelpful to Bill. She also expressed frustration and annoyance about how he talked to her. Specifically, in relation to his query about age differences, she indicated that he made her feel "like crap," and from that point onward, she couldn't be compassionate with him, was less invested in the session, and shut down because she couldn't stand it anymore. She also was frustrated with herself for not keeping her own personal stuff out of the session.

In relation to her anxiety, Lydia consistently entered sessions with Bill with a great deal more anxiety than when she finished sessions with Bill (see Figure 7.5). It almost seemed as though she was anticipating the worst but felt relief once it was all over. The final session, in fact, showed the greatest decrease in anxiety of all Lydia's therapy and supervision sessions.

The final session was cordial and relatively superficial. Through an e-mail before the meeting, Bill had made it clear that this would be his last session. He let Lydia know that he felt better, his depression had lifted and he appreciated her willingness to let him talk, something he found most helpful. In follow-up interview, Bill continued to indicate that Lydia helped him by allowing him to talk about his life experiences. As time progressed posttreatment, though, he mentioned more of his negative reactions. By 2 years' posttreatment, he openly indicated that he felt Lydia's approach caused him to stop therapy and that she gave far too many suggestions and advice. We don't need to look far to find where suggestions and advice was modeled for Lydia.

In Search of Corrective Emotional Supervision

Tricia had played the supervisory role of advice giver and, although Lydia seemed to respond well to some of it, there came the time with Bill that Lydia had to rely on her own devices, or what she had been told up to that point. Regrettably, the advice she had been given did not fit the needs of Bill. In a bit of fortune, though, Lydia interacted with a replacement supervisor while Tricia was away on vacation.

The replacement supervisor was Julia, a White licensed psychologist in her early 40s who had over 10 years of therapy experience and had worked with more than 15 trainees in her lifetime. They had their initial session following Lydia's session with Bill, when Lydia seemed to need it the most. The issue of grief and loss came up almost immediately and Julia proved adept at processing Lydia's reactions. By the middle of the session, Julia had formed a decent alliance and was able to encourage Lydia to seek her own therapy, one of the few suggestions Julia offered. In addition, they began to examine why Lydia felt compelled to ensure that clients "feel better" every session. This supervisory session was clearly more trainee-focused than client-focused and Julia used a nice mix of therapy and collegial supervisory roles (e.g., they explored Lydia's negative reactions to Bill). It seemed equally clear that Lydia learned more about how she can work with clients from this experience than when she was told what to do by Tricia. Julia did a very nice job working with Lydia to come up with ways to work with Bill, at one point saying, "it seems you really do have some answers to your questions" (incredibly empowering!). Lydia also recognized that the harder she tried with Bill, the more she seemed to put herself in a rut. Both used the metaphor of a "tug-of-war" to conceptualize the dance in which Bill and Lydia engaged.

Julia also used the supervisory relationship as a means to teach Lydia about therapy. At one point, Lydia expressed concern that she didn't know how to slow clients down, to which Julia responded in the moment, "I did that with you." "How did I do that?" Lydia seemed to learn quite a bit from her experience with Julia. And when Julia taught, she didn't just teach or offer suggestions and then stop. Rather, when she offered suggestions, she also explored how Lydia was reacting to the suggestions. Unlike Lydia's work with Tricia, which often resulted in Lydia feeling more anxious from supervision, Lydia's work with Julia resulted in feeling less anxious after supervision (see Figure 7.6).

In the postsession interview, Lydia marveled at how "despite the fact that Julia didn't know much about my clients, we got a lot of work done in supervision." Lydia also mentioned that what was most helpful was that "She treated everything as if it was important because it was important to me."

Interestingly, both Lydia and Julia identified a similar nondisclosure regret, that is, they never told one another that they liked their work together.

Back to the Egg

Lydia came to her seventh session with Tricia (her primary supervisor) following the second session with Bill. Tricia accurately interpreted Lydia's anger as countertransference that was getting in the way with her work with Bill. However, Tricia proceeded to attempt to "teach" Lydia how to deal with countertransference. Rather than helping Lydia self-reflect and examine what makes it difficult to see the client's pain, Tricia interrupted the process and interpreted the problem as something that resides in Lydia. Lydia's response was to shut down and become defensive. At one point, Lydia angrily asked, "Well then, how are you supposed to help someone with procrastination?" Regrettably, Tricia did not attend to the affect and instead responded by telling Lydia how she can work with someone who procrastinates. As an example of continued parallel process, the supervision session went over time, lasting 80 minutes!

Lydia identified, in her postsession interview, a common reaction that most trainees go through as they learn to become therapists. She reported, "I just think when you become a therapist and you start to get insight into things, things that you might have looked at before as positive, you now see as negative. I don't know if I can really explain it. You're just not as naive I guess, as you could be if you are maybe an engineer or something (laughs). You are constantly thinking about people's emotions and analyzing everything."

And this is true. Close friends, partners, and family members may say things like "stop analyzing me!" or "don't give me all that psychobabble stuff!" One of the occupational hazards of being a therapist is that you do start seeing the world differently. You begin to see patterns of dysfunctional behavior in yourself and others more readily and it becomes harder to ignore this new-found insight. All that said, our suggestion is rather than try to ignore it, embrace it! Analyze everything and everyone. Having insight isn't a bad thing, although it certainly can cause discomfort at times. We argue, though, that the discomfort has always been there, it's just been repressed and expresses itself through neurotic anxiety. Better to be genuinely sad about a particular state of affairs than anxious over multiple trivial matters. Thus, perhaps ignorance is not truly bliss or, as Fritz Perls once said, "Understanding is the booby trap!"

In an omen of things to come, Tricia mentioned in her postsession interview that she continued to be overwhelmed in her daily life with too many obligations.

Anything You Can Do, I Can Do Better

In Lydia's most daring indirect statement yet about her displeasure with supervision, she no-showed to the next supervision session (which would have been their eighth meeting). As Tricia reflected on Lydia's absence, she expressed both disappointment and anger. She also mentioned, "I think the fact that she missed the session is not necessarily a bad thing because I think you can learn from that, because we will be able to talk about that in our next supervision session. So, I kind of accept things as they come and use them as tools for learning."

In spite of Tricia's thoughtful reflection about the no-show, and that the no-show may indicate a problem in supervision, it was never discussed in the next supervision session! Supervision, by this point in time, became primarily case discussion, in which Lydia talked about her cases and Tricia offered educational advice about how to handle cases. For example, Lydia wondered what kind of books she might recommend to a client and Tricia suggested some titles. The modus operandi continued to be primarily teaching facts with little processing of the emotions playing out in the supervision and therapy sessions.

Even in the case of suggesting books, it would have been important to explore why Lydia, and subsequently the client, would find a book helpful. Of course, bibliotherapy can be very helpful, but we caution therapists to explore and understand the reasons why bibliotherapy is used and how it can be helpful. On the helpfulness end, the client may be looking for enhanced insight into their primary concerns; however, on the end of unhelpfulness, both the therapist and client may be using bibliotherapy as a way to avoid talking about particular issues in therapy (e.g., abuse). Nothing is ever straightforward in therapy!

In addition, things began to go underground for both of them. Lydia reflected on how she wished supervision would focus on more personal issues and less on teaching, but recognized that this approach was not consistent with Tricia's style. "Having enough time" was identified as a continued hindrance by both parties. It seemed both ended up equating good supervision with covering everything that happens in therapy. Of course, this made us wonder: Is superficial coverage of every detail a way to avoid going deeper into issues and thus becoming more intimate?

Interestingly, significant reactions were left for the postsession interviews. It seemed they both more readily talked about supervisory concerns with the researchers than they did with one another. In one example, Tricia reflected on the importance of listening to Lydia's tapes and wondered why Lydia kept choosing not to bring in a tape. Yet, she never asked Lydia about it in supervision. Ironically, Lydia stated in her postsession interview that Tricia "probably wondered why I didn't bring or listen to a tape, but she never mentioned it."

Learning the Ins and Outs of Therapy Work and About What's Behind Client Symptoms

About the time that Lydia was finding her therapy groove with Kendra, she started work with Debi, a White women in her 40s from a working-class background, who was suffering from depression throughout much of her life. She also seemed to have some generalized anxiety as evidenced by her excessive worry about things. She admitted to seeing everything negatively and believed her depression began about 20 years ago when her grandparents died. Her grandparents, as it turned out, were a buffer between Debi and her dysfunctional parents.

Lydia exemplified what an effective therapist might do in a first session. She reviewed issues surrounding confidentiality and the parameters of therapy. She effectively used skills such as attending through nonverbals, tracking, listening, reflecting feelings, and restating client reactions. In addition, she explored the client's presenting concerns well and used some advanced skills such as here and now processing. For example, at one point, she mentioned to Debi, "You seem to feel frustrated when talking about that." In another instance, she was able to integrate a solution-focused therapy question when she asked Debi, "What would you like your life to be?" All together, these skills helped facilitate an early development of an alliance. Lydia ended the session with a formulation of the goals of therapy: "see life more positively, not feel so dissatisfied, enjoy life more, and be more direct and assertive." She particularly did well to bring the therapy relationship into the work when she stated, "you can start practicing being direct in here with me."

Following the session, both Lydia and Debi felt the session went well. Lydia was particularly pleased to find herself more confident and how this was her "fourth first session" and things seem to go more smoothly for her. Finally, because Debi arrived late, they had an abbreviated first session that lasted less than 30 minutes. Lydia felt particularly good about the fact that they were able to develop a preliminary alliance, even in an abbreviated session.

Therapists can perceive and work with clients who come late in a number of ways. There are two primary therapeutic issues to consider when working with a late client. First, the reason for a client's lateness should be examined, at least internally within the therapist, and then possibly interpersonally with the client. Clients come late for a variety of reasons that include fearfulness of therapy, hostility toward the therapist, being late for others is part of their interpersonal style, or because of external factors (e.g., traffic jam) that were beyond their control. Therapists should consider these and other reasons, and, inasmuch as it is related to the therapeutic work, may bring it up with the client. Contributing factors that may help determine if the therapist brings it up is if there was a particularly intense session the week before or the chronicity of the tardiness.

A second therapeutic issue relevant to clients coming in late has to do with how late can a client be before the session is canceled. We suggest that you discuss this issue with your supervisor in advance to understand the policies of your specific agency. In general, we recommend that clients may arrive as much as 30 minutes late for a session before it is canceled. Even with abbreviated sessions, as was the case with Debi, important work can be done. We also recommend that therapists call the client somewhere in the 15- to 30-minute range when the client has not arrived. If the client lives close by, calling at the 15-minute mark may give them time to make the session. Depending on your theoretical perspective, you may have been trained to "allow the client's resistance" and wait for your client to contact you. Some agencies where I (JW) have worked in the past have a "no-show policy" that does not tolerate absences if the client is seeking ongoing service. Thus, there are several factors to consider when addressing a no-show.

Although we tend to prefer to give clients the benefit of doubt when they arrive late for sessions, in general, we also recommend that therapists do not extend a session, even if they have time, when a client arrives late. This condition may be therapeutic in and of itself because it reinforces the boundaries of therapy. In addition, we do not recommend that therapists call to remind clients of upcoming sessions. The more clients are empowered to take responsibility for their therapeutic work, the more effective the treatment will be.

In Debi's case, she indicated that she was late because she had trouble finding the building. Lydia did a nice job accepting Debi's reason and then ending the session on schedule, thereby honoring the boundaries of therapy. She also did well to ponder this fact after the session was completed.

Interestingly, and perhaps not coincidently, Debi no-showed for the next therapy session. This event then provided evidence to Lydia that there may be more to Debi's tardiness than difficulty finding the building. Instead, we can again wonder whether Debi had some concerns about therapy or was questioning her commitment to treatment. We believe that therapists need to not react negatively to clients dipping their toes in the therapeutic water but instead accept their trepidation and hope that they come around to coming to therapy with the hope of positive results.

On the day that Debi did not show for therapy, Lydia reacted by indicating to the researchers that she felt relieved because Lydia was quite tired that day and was concerned that she wouldn't have been her best. On the surface, we may think, how could she feel relieved? How nontherapeutic! However, Lydia's reaction to the client no-show is not an uncommon one. It takes energy to present oneself as unconditionally accepting and empathic and there are days when all of us experience fatigue that interferes with our ability to be therapeutic. The key is to ensure that we consistently monitor how much our fatigue gets in the way of our work and we engage in self-care as therapists. There is always a balance between being there for our clients and being there for ourselves. We recommend that therapists occasionally take an inventory of how they engage in self-care, recognizing that self-care should contain both simple (e.g., a brief walk) and more complex (e.g., therapy or supervision) methods. For a good source of methods of therapist self-care, we recommend Baker's (2003) *Caring for Ourselves: A Therapist's Guide to Personal and Professional Well-Being*.

Although the judgment of talking about tardiness is one that is not so straightforward, we generally believe that bringing up a no-show is an important thing to do. However, Lydia did not mention Debi's no-show in the subsequent therapy session. When looking for reasons for the missing discussion, we only need to go to her experience in supervision. As a reminder, Tricia never discussed Lydia's supervision no-show. It seemed like another case of parallel process via supervisory modeling.

Sessions 3 and 4 moved slowly between Lydia and Debi. They talked a lot about Debi's frustration with her roommate, who seemed to take advantage of Debi, as well as discussed Debi's lack of assertiveness in multiple aspects of her life. Lydia did a very good job exploring these issues with Debi. For example, Lydia was able to help Debi see that anger is an okay emotion to have in relation to her experiences with her roommate. Lydia tended to try to move Debi into the action phase of therapy work but Debi resisted by continuing to talk in great detail about her roommate troubles. To Lydia's credit, she was able to self-reflect in the postsession interviews and recognized her desire to try to move the client in the action phase. She also did an excellent job identifying some of her countertransference, noting that at one point in the session she thought about a recent trip to the beach, then caught herself, and later felt bad for what she thought was a lack of empathy toward the client. Unfortunately, Lydia just needed to take it a step further and, instead of blaming herself, it would have been useful to explore the client's potential role in Lydia's countertransference. By the fifth session, a better understanding of the client's reluctance to move into the action phase of their work, her tardiness, and the likely source of her depression came to light.

The research indicates that it takes about three to five sessions for the working alliance to be adequately developed (Horvath & Greenberg, 1994).

Perhaps not coincidentally, the fifth session proved to be significant for Lydia and Debi. Lydia began the session with an excellent use of the immediacy skill. After the session began, she said to Debi, "You look down." From there, Debi talked about her history of feeling down and noted that it began when she was 9 years old, from which time she never had "health, happiness, and love." Lydia astutely picked up the point of time that Debi mentioned and asked what had happened at the age of 9. Debi, in turn, disclosed how her father was an alcoholic and was sexually abusive toward Debi. Debi found that she could not protest his abuse because she was afraid he wouldn't love her, not an uncommon reaction of children who were sexually abused. In addition, we learn that Debi tried to seek solace by joining a church. Sadly, though, the messages she received from her church experiences were that she was responsible for things that happened to her because she must have been sinning. In addition, she mentioned that the "church told me that God allows sexual abuse to prevent people from being promiscuous later." All of this added to her trauma.

She also reported that she had sought therapy at one point and found it not so helpful in relation to the abuse. In addition, her father tried to apologize later in her life but also told her that his psychiatrist believed that Debi probably enjoyed the abuse. All together, it was not surprising that Debi was a bit soured on therapy and therapists, and approached a new therapy experience with much trepidation. In one fell swoop of a session, Lydia learned of Debi's abuse, and her subsequent poor experiences with therapy and therapists, which brought together the three key aspects of Debi's difficulties and therapeutic work to date: her depression and her interpersonal style, reasons for coming to sessions late or not showing, and her reluctance to engage in "action-type" therapeutic work.

Unfortunately, it is all too common to work with clients who have had poor therapy experiences. Because clients seek therapy at the most vulnerable times of their life, they are also ripe for exploitation by poor or ineffectual therapists. As a result, effective therapists find themselves working with many clients who need corrective therapy experiences. Lydia's acceptance of Debi, and validation of the wrongs done to her in the past, likely provided Debi with what she needed most to continue therapy, that is, a corrective emotional experience about therapy. In fact, Debi mentioned in the postsession interview that the most helpful aspect of the session was discussing her previously poor experiences with therapy and therapists.

The fifth session was a turning point for Lydia and Debi. The sexual abuse disclosure was powerful and set them both down the path of what to do, and how to work through this trauma. In the initial sessions that followed this disclosure, Debi indicated uncertainty about how talking about the sexual abuse would be beneficial. Lydia responded by being understanding and trying to offer Debi a different therapy experience than what Debi had experienced before. One approach that seemed to work well was Lydia's use of metaphors in their work.

Metaphors can often be quite helpful to clients because it allows them to see the issues from a different and, perhaps, less threatening manner. Lydia, for example, talked about how therapy is like two people walking in a forest together, and that while they both may be lost at times, they are in it together. In another instance, Debi likened her life since the abuse to "treading on water." We encourage therapists to facilitate the creation of, and explore, metaphors with their clients. A useful question to ask a client is, "What image comes to mind when you picture that feeling/thought/reaction/etc.?" In a related fashion, having clients bring dreams into therapy can be quite powerful (Hill, 2003).

Debi revealed much in the subsequent sessions including how she was repeatedly raped and "fought off sex" from the ages of 9 to 14, and she found that food was the only thing in her life she had control over, which led her to overeat. Debi also shared that she never came to terms with her father's death, and that she had a tendency toward black-and-white thinking. Lydia, to her credit, was very focused and attended to Debi's reactions. She used silence quite well, and even though she was internally uncomfortable with crying, did very well to empathize and provide Debi a holding environment while Debi cried in therapy. Debi's crying and processing was very cathartic and one of the keys to the successful parts of their therapeutic work. In addition, the exploratory work offered Debi a mechanism to gain insight into her difficulties. For example, they discussed how Debi's current interpersonal issues related to trust were linked to the abuse. Relatedly, Debi was able to talk about how she felt good about surviving the abuse, but that she has never felt in control. Furthermore, Debi was able to link her current physical complaints and difficulties to the intensity of the therapeutic work.

There were a few other lessons that Lydia offered us when considering what effective therapy can look like. First, Lydia did well to positively reinforce and support Debi's work. In one instance, she noted that Debi was doing a wonderful job expressing herself in therapy. In another instance, Lydia did well to reframe Debi's perception about how she can't make decisions. Lydia pointed out that "not making a decision is a decision." What made this intervention powerful, however, was that Lydia acknowledged that perhaps Debi was making the best decision she could make for herself at that time. Another thing that Lydia did that was helpful to Debi was assisting her to recognize that her "experiences are normal and that what she experienced was abnormal" (a quote that came directly from supervision with Tricia). Finally, Lydia did well to periodically check in with Debi regarding Debi's suicidal ideation, and although the ideation remained vague, indicating low risk, the checking in helped Debi feel safe and cared for. Although Lydia, in general, performed quite well with Debi, at times she ran into challenges that were good examples of what not to do in therapy.

One of Lydia's challenges was that she would become visibly and inter-personally frustrated when Debi was doing more of what Lydia thought was "superficial" work. Indeed, there were times when Debi would talk at length about her roommate or work troubles; however, not coincidently, these dis-cussions frequently took place after much exploration of the sexual abuse. In all likelihood, Debi needed a break from the therapeutic intensity. Instead of honoring a healthy resistance, Lydia became frustrated and more impatient and tried to challenge Debi too much. To Debi's credit, she would provide Lydia with feedback (mention when she felt Lydia was not being fair or help-ful or validating). Lydia, in turn, did well to respond by indicating that she appreciated Debi's honesty. The conflict that was worked through in therapy seemed to be quite empowering to both Lydia and Debi. At the end of their work, Lydia in hindsight regretted and felt guilty about her frustration in previous sessions. So, the lesson, in the end, was not lost.

A second challenge for Lydia was her continued lack of self-efficacy regarding her work. Even during times when she was doing quite well, and even after she had conducted over 40 therapy sessions, she felt her inex-perience hindered her effectiveness. Additional evidence for this conten-tion can be seen in her ratings of the therapeutic working alliance. Across all of her clients, she perceived the alliance to be weaker than they did! Although her inexperience may have affected her somewhat, in all likeli-hood, her lower self-efficacy hurt her more than her actual inexperience. Unfortunately, the lack of empowerment she received in supervision was likely the culprit in relation to her low self-efficacy. In addition, we learned that Lydia's difficulties were more than just about self-efficacy.

That's the Way the Supervision Crumbles

At about the midpoint of her work with Debi, Lydia and Tricia met for what would turn out to be their final four supervision sessions. A large part of their work consisted of case review, Tricia offering her perspectives on cases, and listening to Lydia's tapes. Providing alternative perspectives and reviewing the audiotapes proved to be the most beneficial to Lydia. Again, what Lydia seemed to do best was to make the most out of super-vision. She accepted the teaching style of Tricia. Perhaps it was because that was all she knew about supervision, but, in reality, it offered her, in essence, vicarious therapy experiences such that she could hear about what could be done in therapy. In addition, Tricia continued to positively sup-port Lydia's work and demonstrated investment through her shear will to teach her everything she possibly could. To that end, the sessions continued to run over one hour and both left supervision feeling like not enough was accomplished. From an observer's point of view, we wondered how this dynamic may have served both of them. It is our contention that the dynamic prevented them from looking at their own self-doubts in relation to their work and tolerating the ambiguity that is inherent in therapy and supervision work.

The review of audiotapes by Tricia with Lydia indeed seemed to help Lydia a great deal. In some cases, Tricia would take a therapy tape with her and review it outside of supervision. At other times, they would listen to the tape together in supervision. Tricia would play, stop, and review the segments. Although clearly this process helped Lydia, we couldn't help but wonder if it would have helped even more if Lydia had been empowered to play, stop, and then process her reactions to each segment they listened to, which is more consistent with the Interpersonal Process Recall approach of reviewing tapes developed by Kagan (1997). This is another case of good work that could have been better through greater empowerment of Lydia.

Another dynamic that seemed to emerge between Lydia and Tricia was that the more Tricia told Lydia what to do, the more Lydia would behave dependently and indicate that she didn't know what she was doing. Perhaps not coincidentally, a similar dynamic was set up between Lydia and some of her clients. In fact, Lydia recognized that some of her clients asked for quick fixes in therapy, and Lydia engaged in a similar endeavor in supervision.

Things began to unravel for Lydia and Tricia in their 12th supervision session. Tricia had decided that she no longer could conduct supervision because she was overwhelmed with her other work activities. Lydia was clearly shocked to receive this news and her fears of abandonment were actualized. Sadly, Tricia never attended to Lydia's feelings of loss but instead chose to focus largely on offering advice to Lydia for how to work with her clients. Ironically, one of Lydia's clients had to have her cat euthanized but instead of processing the loss and Lydia's reaction (anger), Tricia said, "You need to separate yourself from her emotionally without losing empathy.... Don't take it personally."

We learned in this session and the final supervision session, though, that Lydia was understandably taking a lot personally, especially in relation to her clients. Lydia expressed concern about her own feelings of being overwhelmed and a number of activities in her personal life that left her overcommitted. Furthermore, she came across as a bit depressed and angry, especially in relation to her work with Kendra and Debi, who were dealing with their feelings of depression and anger. It seems reasonable to suspect that Lydia may have been experiencing vicarious traumatization from working with her clients. In vicarious traumatization, therapists experience distress as a result of repeated exposure to client descriptions and reactions to trauma (Figley, 2002). In Lydia's case, she had clients who were talking about a variety of abuse situations, and together with her feelings of abandonment in relation to supervision, it isn't surprising that Lydia experienced a marked increase in emotional turmoil. In her own words, she said that some of her clients "took joy away from her."

It seemed that Tricia recognized Lydia's pain and recommended Lydia consider personal therapy. Lydia indicated she didn't feel she had the time or money to seek help so rather than reaching out, she turned further inward. In essence, she did not respond as we would have hoped a therapist would respond, that is, engaging in self-care. We cannot say enough about the importance of therapists seeking their own therapy. It helps not only with managing day-to-day stressors or "big T" or "little t" traumas; it also serves to teach therapists how to be therapists. In fact, we all have learned a great deal about how to do therapy from being in therapy ourselves, sometimes more than what we learned from our graduate work or supervision!

Lydia and Tricia never processed their termination and Lydia admitted that the premature termination left her with a poor attitude, feeling frustrated, and let down, and likely disrupted her work with her clients. However, Lydia also felt she got a lot out of supervision. She found it particularly helpful that Tricia helped her find her personality in the context of therapy, and provided her with useful client conceptualizations. She noted that it was their positive relationship that she most remembered. Months later, in their follow-up postsession questionnaires, Lydia continued to express disappointment in relation to Tricia's departure and sadness about Tricia leaving "before the story was over."

A Role for Gender in Therapy

There were two therapeutic approaches in which Lydia engaged that related specifically to gender that warranted our attention. In the first case, Lydia successfully navigated and integrated gender-related work, and in the other case, Lydia missed the gender-related issue altogether.

The first gender-related issue with which Lydia had to contend pertained to the revelation that Debi had had an abortion when she was 16 years old. Abortion may be the most difficult countertransference issue for therapists. It is taboo to discuss in the culture of the United States and it is not likely to be discussed much in graduate training. We think it may be the biggest secret that therapists do not openly talk about. However, in 2000, more than one in five pregnancies in the United States ended in an abortion (Finer & Henshaw, 2003). That means that therapists are very likely to see a client who has had an abortion. That also means that as long as therapists want to work with women, they will have had to come to terms, or actively come to terms, with offering empathy and unconditional regard for women who have had an abortion. Lydia offered an exemplar case. In the postsession interview, Lydia noted that she had appreciated having explored pregnancy and abortion issues previously and that although Debi's revelation was a bit surprising, Lydia felt that she was able to hang in there with Debi, which seemed to be the case. What could have been a moment of judgmental behavior on the part of the therapist turned into a moment of empathy and compassion that served to strengthen the alliance and their work together.

The gender-related issue that Lydia missed had to do with concerns that Debi expressed about her body image. Debi saw herself as overweight and had been for much of her adult life. She expressed much dissatisfaction with her body, not an uncommon issue for many women who live in the United States. However, instead of considering external factors (e.g., media images) that may have influenced her body image in an effort to empower Debi, Lydia chose to attend to how Debi may diet differently and how she shouldn't be concerned with what others think. In sum, Lydia failed to understand and convey how the personal is political (Brown, 1992).

The later third of their work together proved to be the period where much of the difficult and momentous work took place. During this phase, together they read and engaged in exercises from the book *The Courage to Heal,* a book intended for clients on abuse survivors. What was particularly effective was that they did the work together, thereby strengthening the mutual agreement on tasks component of the alliance. Using the book as a stimulus for discussion, they were able to talk about Debi's feelings of being a victim, problems that she had setting boundaries, feelings of shame and difference, and her desires to run away from it all. Throughout much of this work, Lydia was able to present as patient, focused, normalizing, and caring. Lydia's compassion was exemplified in a statement she made to the researchers: "I felt really bad and inadequate. I just wish there was something I could do, like, a big Band-Aid or something. I don't know. I just, I feel really sad for her."

In the post session interview of the 15th session, Debi reported that she found it quite helpful that Lydia pointed out that Debi minimizes her pain. Debi admitted that she had been told this before by Lydia, but that on this day, it finally "clicked." Debi's report is a common therapy experience. Sometimes therapists tell clients things that don't connect right away, or not until long after the therapy has stopped. The lesson for us is that, at times, some therapy outcomes never become visible to the therapist.

The work between Lydia and Debi went for 16 sessions that took place over 5 months. Much progress was made; Debi learned to trust Lydia, which proved to be a corrective emotional therapy experience that Debi needed. Transition to group therapy was the next step for Debi. In the 2 years of follow-up research, we learned from Debi that she never quite connected with the group but was able to get back into individual therapy. She recalled how her work with Lydia resulted in her feeling less negative and more in control about life. In addition, she mentioned that therapy with Lydia helped her by talking about her problems, gave her insight, helped her face how the sexual abuse was a needed area of work, and that therapy could be helpful.

New Beginnings

Julia, who Lydia had as a one-session substitute supervisor early in her work, became her full-time supervisor after Tricia left. Julia set the tone for this new supervision experience in the first few minutes of the session when she asked, "What's up?" Lydia responded in a manner consistent with her previous supervisor, "Where do you want me to begin?" Julia's reaction to Lydia's query was, "Anything you want help with. I don't know the style of your last supervisor, but the way I work is that whatever question you have, and whatever you want to pick my brain about, it's up to you." In this brief interaction, Julia empowered Lydia and set the tone for a trainee-driven supervision experience.

Although Lydia did not readily accept her new empowered position, she was able to bring up some issues that were troubling her in relation to her clients. In particular, we saw Lydia reveal more indications that she was experiencing vicarious traumatization and perhaps burnout as a therapist. She reported experiencing Ruby, the client who storytells and who she has now seen for 10 sessions, as "sucking the life out of me" and that she found her annoying because all she seems to do is complain. Following her sessions, Lydia noted that she "feels like crap the whole week." Clearly, Lydia was suffering, a pain that was enhanced with the unresolved abandonment she felt from Tricia.

Julia succeeded where Tricia failed in relation to working with Lydia's difficult reactions. Instead of offering suggestions on how to work with clients, Julia explored with Lydia her countertransference reactions with her clients. As a result, Lydia revealed that part of her reaction was because Ruby reminded Lydia of her grandmother. Julia astutely pointed out a pattern that Lydia seemed to have. Specifically, Lydia seemed to have the most difficulty with clients who, like her grandmother, she experienced as cold, critical, or judgmental. In addition, Lydia made the connection that Ruby's personality and then her issues surrounding her husband's death were an affront to Lydia at her psychological core. She mentioned "I feel like she is a glimpse of the future and she is ruining it for me. I don't want to see. I don't want to know how painful it is to lose a husband. I'm not even married yet. I haven't even had the good stuff yet, and she's already loading me down with the ending."

Julia continued to process Lydia's reactions and did a nice job of balancing offering suggestions (e.g., Do you want to hear what I think?) and then helping her formulate how she may work with Ruby. A critical supervisory intervention occurred at this point. Julia stated to Lydia that she was working too hard in therapy, and, in fact, was working harder than Ruby.

This supervisory work directly attended to the therapeutic alliance between the client and the therapist. A common dynamic that is set up in some therapy relationships is that at times therapists will find themselves working harder than the client. When this happens, invariably it is because the alliance is not strong enough. The tasks and goals, in particular, are likely not mutually agreed on. As a result, the therapist finds herself or himself working hard to "cause insight" in the client, or get the client to complete some homework exercises. All the while, the client sits back passively and subtly, or not so subtly, becomes less and less engaged in the therapeutic work. It would be expected that the client would have similar interactions with people in their daily life. The reaction of these people, and of the therapist in therapy, is to work harder in the relationship, and then get annoyed and frustrated that they seem to be "the only one that cares about the relationship" or is the one who seems to have all the energy for the relationship. We all have these types of people in our lives! The key for the therapist is to step in and offer the client a new experience. What can be done is to reconsider the therapeutic alliance and reexamine the goals and tasks of therapy, all the while ensuring that the emotional bond is at least stable through empathic comments.

So, for example, from supervision, Lydia felt more empowered to go back to Ruby and ask her what she would like to do in therapy. In a renegotiation of therapeutic tasks and goals, Ruby could say she wants to focus on her depressive thoughts. Then, if she began to storytell, Lydia could, in a supportive tone, point out the inconsistency of what Ruby says she wants and what she does. Then they could explore why Ruby falls back into this pattern (e.g., to avoid something, it serves the client in some fashion, etc.). Even if Ruby says she just wants to storytell, that would be fine! The key is that then Lydia doesn't have to feel responsible for getting Ruby to do something Lydia wants her to do. In essence, Ruby becomes empowered for her own therapeutic work once she makes the decision about what she wants to work on. Unfortunately, though, we will learn that Lydia's empowerment in supervision did not ultimately permeate down to therapy with Ruby. The supervisory intervention was too late to have the desired impact.

Julia also did well not to feed into Lydia's negativity. At one point in their work Lydia questioned whether a few of her clients may have been "borderline." Instead of accepting Lydia's statement and proceed to offer suggestions to work with clients who have a Borderline Personality Disorder, Julia had them together review the *DSM* criteria and the extent to which characteristics fit or didn't fit. This was a superb intervention on the part of Julia. Our own experience is that some therapists like the notion of referring to clients as "borderlines." In general, we find this practice unkind and dehumanizing, and, in all likelihood, more a reflection of the therapist's experience of burnout or need for empowerment. We encourage therapists to consider when they are referring to their clients as diagnostic labels. This exploration may lead to important information related to countertransference reactions that have been left unchecked.

At the end of this supervision session, Lydia asked, "Are you sure you're in it for the long haul?" Clearly, this is a reflection of the abandonment that Lydia still experienced. Julia did well in the subsequent supervision session to explore the change in supervisors and Lydia's feelings of abandonment. Similar to Debi needing a corrective therapy experience, Lydia needed a corrective supervision experience in relation to feeling left abandoned. At points throughout the supervisory work, Lydia found herself comparing her new supervisor, Julia, with Tricia, thereby adding an element of trainee transference that needed to be managed in supervision.

Lydia's dissatisfaction with therapy led to a discussion about whether or not therapy work is in Lydia's future. Julia did well to explore Lydia's career goals, normalize her self-reflective questioning, and supported Lydia in a nonjudgmental fashion to make whatever decision was best for Lydia. A helpful intervention by Julia was to self-disclose that at times in her life, she questioned whether or not she was cut out to be a therapist, which Lydia found helpful.

In general, we wondered if supervisor self-disclosure is used frequently enough, and/or effectively, by supervisors. Supervisor self-disclosures pertaining to their own struggles as a therapist have been found to be quite powerful. By contrast, self-disclosures that are consistently irrelevant can make supervision largely a waste of time. The extent to which a supervisor self-disclosure is effective can be determined based on three factors: how discordant or congruent the self-disclosure is in relation to the trainee's need, how nonintimate to intimate the material is, and how much the self-disclosure is in the service of the supervisor versus the trainee (Ladany & Walker, 2003).

Getting Worse Before Getting Better

Right around the time that Lydia changed supervisors, we learned that Ruby is not doing better in therapy, and in fact is becoming more depressed. Through the first 10 sessions, she did a lot of storytelling but at points showed more emotion in therapy, at times crying. Although Lydia expressed concern about working with Ruby, she really excelled at being a good listener, tracking Ruby's comments, and showing tremendous patience. Although Lydia barely talked in therapy and questioned her own performance, Lydia was perceived as helpful by Ruby. However, things seemed to become problematic around the time of the anniversary of the death of Ruby's husband. Anniversaries of deaths, as well as other significant anniversaries of people who have died, are critical times for people who are bereaved. Unfortunately, Lydia did not recognize the significance of the anniversary and continued to try to engage Ruby in some activity to get her to feel better. The exact opposite, though, was what was needed. For people who are grieving, the most important thing a clinician can do is just "be there" (Yalom, 2000). In other words, patiently listening and empathizing are the critical interventions at these times. Regrettably, Lydia's frustration for lack of movement increased, thereby canceling out her generally patient stance, and she was unable to really "be there" for Ruby just when Ruby needed it the most. That said, Ruby continued to come in for the full 16 sessions, so there was some evidence that she was getting something out of therapy, and in fact, she indicated that therapy was helpful to her in posttreatment follow-ups. She indicated that she particularly liked Lydia's ability to listen and her patience.

The Lesson of Empowerment

Through much of their work in supervision, Julia expressed concern about Lydia's difficulty with empathizing with some of her more difficult clients, and Lydia's unrealistic expectations about how therapy should fix people. At the same time, Julia resisted the urge to "fix" Lydia by directly telling her what to do. Instead, she explored and processed Lydia's reactions. She worked with Lydia's tendency to ask questions and receive answers in supervision, thereby empowering Lydia to think more on her own. Additionally, she normalized Lydia's concern that she needed lots of experience to work with clients but also challenged this belief by indicating that much of therapy entails the formation of the relationship by using basic therapy skills (e.g., listening, reflections, empathy). In fact, there is much evidence to suggest that empirically supported therapy may be misguided and missing out on the most important common elements that make therapy most effective (e.g., Wampold, 2001). Julia demonstrated the therapeutic importance of patience, empathy, reflections, and well-timed self-disclosures by engaging in these interventions in supervision. At times, when Julia became more directive, she did so only with the permission of Lydia (e.g., Would you like to hear what I'm thinking?). Although this certainly can be considered a loaded question (how could Lydia say no?), it reflected another subtle way that continued to empower Lydia.

There was one area that Lydia expressed dissatisfaction about her supervision with Julia (at first she only told the researchers in her postsupervision session interviews). This was because Julia did not listen to Lydia's recordings of her therapy work. In fact, this omission was the only major problem of their supervision that we noticed. Our own experience indicates that a large part of the learning in supervision takes place when supervisors listen to the trainees' recordings. Without knowledge of the work, the supervisor has little solid ground to stand on when making evaluative comments. And, not coincidentally, Lydia had concerns that she was not receiving evaluative feedback on her tapes. To Lydia's credit, though, and likely the result of Julia's empowerment, Lydia was able to ask Julia to listen to a tape in supervision, all of which was an indication that Lydia was taking more responsibility for supervision. In addition, Lydia gave Julia feedback on termination that not listening to tapes was one area she had wished was done more often.

In the end, the supervision termination experience proved to be a very positive one for Lydia, although Lydia still harbored feelings of resentment about the abrupt way her previous supervision had ended. Julia ended supervision in an exemplar fashion. She set the stage for Lydia to receive feedback about her therapy work, and self-reflect about her strengths (e.g., gutsiness and ability to be forthcoming) and weaknesses (e.g., easily discouraged). In addition, Julia opened it up for Lydia to offer feedback about Julia's work as a supervisor, to which Lydia was again able to talk about her preference for more evaluative feedback from listening to her tapes. In the end, their last session was a model supervision termination.

A Tale of Two Supervisors

With every supervisor comes new ways of learning and new ways of not learning. Both Tricia and Julia had their strengths and weaknesses as a supervisor and these strengths and weaknesses likely influenced how and what Lydia was able to learn. Tricia, who was mostly a client-focused supervisor, demonstrated her willingness to give lots of feedback, perhaps at the expense of the supervisory alliance and the understanding of supervision and therapy processes. Julia, who was mostly a trainee-focused supervisor, demonstrated her ability to empower Lydia and let Lydia lead the supervisory work, perhaps at the expense of offering enough evaluative feedback. With Tricia, Lydia talked very little, and with Julia, Lydia talked a lot.

To us, a blending of both styles may have been ultimately what would have been most effective. However, Lydia was able to learn from both styles and perhaps she said it best when she said, "I liked having a new supervisor because every supervisor has different techniques to offer. It reminds me of when I play the guitar, if you always have the same teacher you're kind of mimicking their style and you'll never be introduced to anything else. Both supervisors widened my experience." Moreover, she said, "When I first started I was like, how do I do a first session, what do I say, very structured, and Tricia was very good at that. I needed to know what to do, and she gave me worksheets and told me what to say and I needed that. But now my question is how do I let more of me be in the session as opposed to talking book, how to be empathic," which then was the focus of Julia.

The Themes Revisited

At the end of Lydia's first practicum experience, she had much on which to reflect. Over approximately 8 months, she managed a caseload of clients (Kendra, Ruby, Bill, and Debi) and was mentored by two different supervisors (Tricia and Julia). Some clients she saw only briefly (three sessions with Bill) and other clients utilized the maximum capacity of time (17 sessions with Ruby). Lydia negotiated a variety of personalities and presentation styles, including Kendra's politeness, Ruby's uninterrupted narrative style, Bill's condescending tone, and Debi's initial guardedness. She experienced a range of personal responses including boredom, anger, and genuine empathy. She utilized a wide array of therapy techniques including cognitive-behavioral strategies, Rogerian active listening, interpersonal here-and-now processing, bibliotherapy, and solution-focused skills. Lydia balanced self-disclosure by sometimes choosing to share pieces of herself and other times remaining focused on the client.

Throughout the work, six themes emerged. First, with the themes of *abandonment and termination,* several clients brought grief issues into the therapy work and Lydia herself struggled with personal grief. In addition, her first supervisor left the practicum setting before the 8 months was over. Second, with the themes of *boundary issues with time,* Lydia had difficulty ending her therapy sessions on time, and the supervision sessions with Tricia were often extended. Third, with the theme of *countertransference,* Lydia observed her own judgmental responses to Bill's sexist comments, her frustration with Debi when she didn't focus on the task at hand, and her resistance to pursue client issues that were her personal hot-buttons. Fourth, with the theme of *trainee anxiety*, Lydia began the practicum experience with an appropriate amount of anxiety (e.g., her first session with Kendra) and learned throughout her work that she was allowed to be human, and allowed to not know all the answers. One client (Bill) specifically triggered her anxiety when he highlighted his advanced educational level in comparison to hers. Although anxiety was an occasional companion, eventually Lydia learned to replace the anxiety with an increased ability to tolerate ambiguity. Fifth, the theme of *successful moments* was perhaps the most important to Lydia's development. She witnessed Kendra reaching specific behavioral goals (attending social functions) and emotional goals (decrease in anxiety). She observed Debi taking monumental interpersonal risks (sharing a secret in therapy after having had a negative experience in previous therapy). She was able to provide corrective experiences, and she witnessed those "aha" moments. Finally, one theme was *when clients do not get better*. This was an important theme to include; we felt it was honest and candid to acknowledge that sometimes clients do not get better. Lydia learned that the process is not magic. She grew from her struggles and challenges as much as her successes.

Lydia Gets the Final Words

We hope that you have found Lydia's story meaningful professionally and, perhaps, personally. We thought it best to end our chapter in Lydia's words, which she offered postsupervision. "I think I expected to come in and get therapy experience, but what I learned was more about myself (e.g., I'm a fixer), and how other people perceive me (e.g., clients feel I'm a good listener and are really with them). I disproved my theory that they wouldn't trust me because of my age. And I learned I don't have to know everything to be able to support my clients."

Discussion Questions and Exercises

Discussion Questions

- At what point in Lydia's journey did you most relate to her? In what ways are you different from her?
- Which of Lydia's clients would you most look forward to working with and why? Which clients would you be more reluctant to work with and why?

- What parts of Tricia's supervision style would work well for you? What parts of Julia's supervision would you find helpful? How comfortable do you feel about getting your needs met in supervision?
- How might supervision of Tricia's supervision looked and might it have helped stem the difficulties that ensued?
- What was your favorite part of this story? Least favorite part? Where did you find yourself feeling resistance to the interpretation of the authors?
- What are the ethics of self-disclosure to a supervisor?
- Other than gender, what multicultural issues might have been salient in Lydia's story?

Exercises

Exercise 7.1: Yes-But

Practice role-playing with a peer in your practicum class the "yes-but" scenario. Practice what it feels like to make suggestions that your client refuses. How should you respond when you're working harder than your client? How can you focus on having a contract of tasks and goals of therapy that is mutually agreed on?

Exercise 7.2: Interrupting Storytelling

Practice role-playing the "interrupting" scenario. Practice what it feels like when you are trying to wrap up the session, and your client won't stop talking!

Exercise 7.3: Uncomfortable Questions

Practice role-playing and respond to the questions "how much experience do you have?" or "how old are you?" or "how could you possibly help me if you haven't been in my situation?"

Exercise 7.4: Breaking Up Is So Hard to Do

Practice role-playing a termination session. Explore your style of how you manage and negotiate endings. Try to role-play a therapy termination as well as a supervision termination. Be aware of how you provide feedback. How is your style different in each role-play?

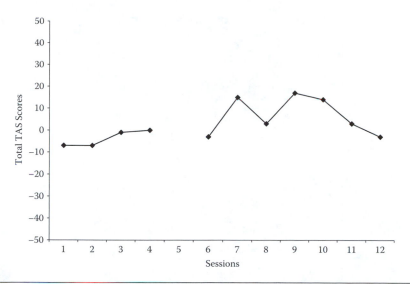

Figure 7.1 Change in Anxiety for Lydia in Supervision with Tricia. (Note: TAS refers to the Trainee Anxiety Scale. Scores indicate a change in anxiety from presession to postsession. Positive scores indicate a decrease in anxiety from presession to postsession assessments.)

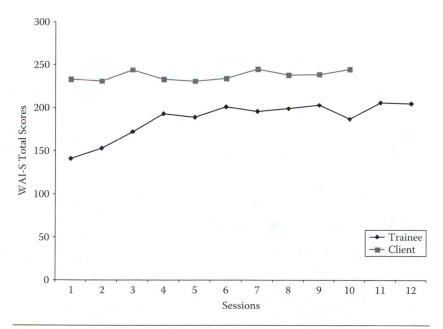

Figure 7.2 Working Alliance in Therapy Between Lydia and Kendra. (Note: Higher scores indicate perceptions of a stronger working alliance.)

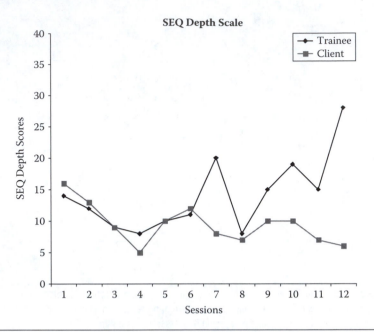

Figure 7.3a Session Impact in Therapy Between Lydia and Kendra. (Note: Higher scores indicate greater depth.)

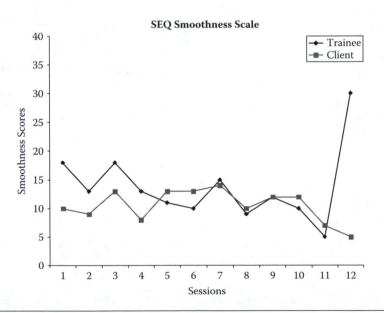

Figure 7.3b (Note: Higher scores indicate greater smoothness.)

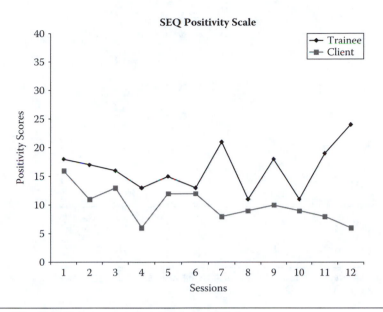

Figure 7.3c (Note: Higher scores indicate greater positivity.)

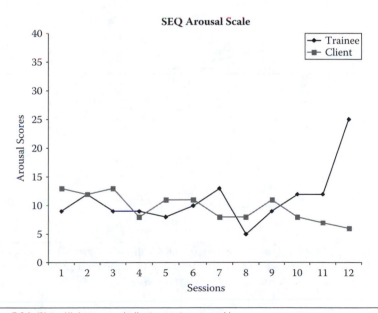

Figure 7.3d (Note: Higher scores indicate greater arousal.)

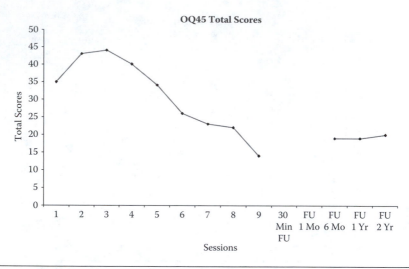

Figure 7.4 Presession Level of Client Distress for Kendra. (Note: Higher scores indicate greater client distress.)

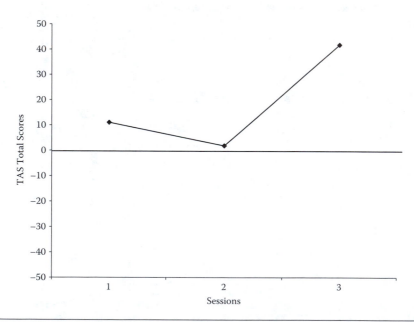

Figure 7.5 Change in Anxiety for Lydia in Therapy with Bill. (Note: TAS refers to the Trainee Anxiety Scale. Scores indicate a change in anxiety from presession to postsession. Positive scores indicate a decrease in anxiety from presession to postsession assessments.)

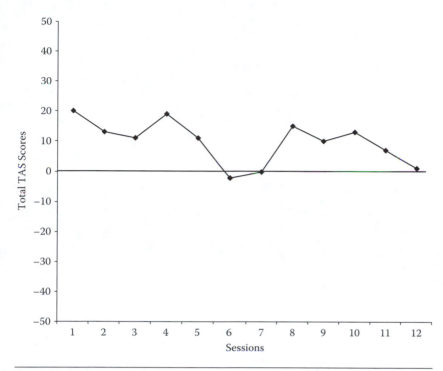

Figure 7.6 Change in Anxiety for Lydia in Supervision With Julia. (Note: TAS refers to the Trainee Anxiety Scale. Scores indicate a change in anxiety from presession to postsession. Positive scores indicate a decrease in anxiety from presession to postsession assessments.)

CHAPTER 8

The Next Steps in the Journey

A ship is safe in harbor, but that's not what ships are for.

—**William Shedd**

Guiding us throughout our book was the notion that the process of learning how to do therapy well takes a lot of hard work and emotional energy, and is vitally important in how it helps others. To be sure, learning how to do therapy is a lifelong endeavor that involves balancing continued professional growth with taking care of yourself and fostering your personal growth. For this final chapter, we thought it best to consider what experienced clinicians can tell us about what it means to be a therapist and also what it means to take care of yourself.

What the Experts Have to Say

Up to this point, we have largely relied on our collective experiences, the research literature, and findings from the Study to inform our discussion. One source we have found incredibly useful in the training of therapists comes from a meaningful study by Jennings and Skovholt (1999), who interviewed expert therapists about their work. In a clever approach to finding this sample, these researchers asked therapists in the Minneapolis, Minnesota, area for nominations of therapists who they believed were the best of the best, who they would most likely to refer a family member or friend, and who they would likely go to as a therapist. The researchers interviewed the seven women and three male *master* therapists. These therapists had a range of degrees, averaged 59 years old, and had an average of 30 years of experience. From the interviews, they identified nine things about who they were as therapists that included they (1) were voracious learners, (2) drew heavily on accumulated experiences, (3) valued cognitive complexity and ambiguity, (4) were emotionally receptive, (5) were mentally healthy and mature and attend to their own emotional well-being, (6) were aware of how their emotional health impacts their work, (7) possessed strong relationship skills, (8) believed in the working alliance, and (9) were experts at using their exceptional relational skills in therapy.

The research limitations notwithstanding, the aforementioned qualities are excellent aspirational goals for all therapists. There is something important that we would like to highlight about the majority of these competencies. One does not have to first complete multiple advanced degrees or accumulate decades of experience before cultivating these characteristics. You can begin pursuing these skills as a student, and you can continue working toward these abilities throughout graduate school and then later as a developing professional in social work, psychiatry, psychology, community mental health, or school counseling! We encourage you to consider these characteristics and their importance in the field of mental health. In addition, we believe it is important to reflect on your personal strengths and unique contributions that may or may not be represented in the aforementioned list. In other words, what things about *you* make you a good therapist?

Caring for Yourself as You Desire Others to Be Cared For

Inevitably, we come to the point as therapists at which we are so concerned about helping others that we forget about helping ourselves. We have talked a few times in the book about how we became therapists because we tended to be the ones to whom people came because they needed to be heard. Often, we also were the ones who could contain a lot of emotional angst for others, or be the emotional barometer of a family. Continuously listening to others and empathizing with their experiences can take an emotional toll on therapists if left unchecked. These experiences can lead to vicarious traumatization or compassion fatigue (Figley, 2002). Therefore, we encourage you to consider ways in which you can take care of yourself as a therapist, beginning now, while in your graduate program. In fact, we argue that therapist self-care is a skill that needs to be nurtured as part of your training repertoire (Baker, 2003).

There are multiple ways in which therapists can engage in self-care. Supervision is an obvious resource and outlet. So, too, is personal therapy.

Our sense is that the best therapists themselves have been to therapy on multiple occasions and that in many ways, along with self-care, it's one of the best places to learn therapy. Another resource includes mentors who can offer guidance and who likely have gone through what you are going through. Peers are also essential people to whom you can vent and who can understand your perspective. Other positive support systems may include family members, coworkers, and friends who are not part of your mental health community. In addition, many people find comfort in their churches, synagogues, temples, mosques, and other religious or spiritual circles. Along with socialization and sharing with others, self-care also can take the form of healthy living, which includes nutrition, exercise, and rest. We cannot overemphasize these elements! Proper nutrition (including healthy decisions regarding alcohol and other drugs), regular physical activity, and sound sleep hygiene are essential pieces to self-care and emotional health. Remember that we ask our clients about substance use, eating patterns, and sleeping routines because we know there is such a strong correlation between these wellness behaviors and mood! Imagine how unfortunate it would be to deny these factors in consideration of our own emotional management. Although we acknowledge that graduate school can sometimes be a time when students pull "all-nighters" to study, eat on a less-than-ideal budget, and don't have time for the gym, we insist on therapists making time for self-care in these areas whenever possible.

A final component to self-care includes activities and hobbies. Extracurricular activities can include participating in a political cause, listening to music, watching a favorite television show, reading a novel, playing a sport, walking a dog, gardening, martial arts, dancing, shopping, riding a motorcycle, cooking, video games, surfing the Internet, or whatever involves a different sort of experience than therapy-related work. We encourage therapists in training to budget time for hobbies just as they would budget time to read their textbooks and write papers! Imagine that! We would discourage viewing fun activities as a luxury that can only be appreciated when all academic material is done. Students who take this stance too rigidly quickly learn that in graduate school, the work is never truly done—there is always more to do! Some find themselves waiting until graduation to enjoy their hobbies. We believe this mentality can foster resentment and frustration. Self-care is an ongoing necessity and is important now as well as after graduation.

For those of you who cannot think of an activity in which you're currently engaged, remember that volunteerism can serve as a rewarding and enriching hobby. Whether it is picking up trash, building a house, recycling cans, mentoring children, distributing orange juice at a blood drive, visiting the elderly, or petting animals at a shelter, volunteerism can replenish energy and can contribute to self-care.

As with our aspirations to be like master therapists, developing a healthy lifestyle also may be an ambitious goal, but it is a worthy one nonetheless. Without a doubt, our mind can influence our body and our body can influence our mind. Thus, both our body and mind need nurturance. Ultimately, as we say to our clients, you are worth it!

Conclusion

Our students told us they wanted a "how to" book for when they see clients, based on the experiences of real people. We tried to meet that need by writing a book that was theoretically and empirically sound, but, mostly, practically driven to provide direction and validate the real experiences of first-time therapists. Your experience as a therapist will likely be a unique journey, which no book can perfectly predict or outline. However, remember to use this and other books as a roadmap. Use your peers and professors as guides. But, ultimately, remember that you are the one who gets to decide which roads to take, the pace to keep, and when to stop and take breaks. This is your path. In the end, it's a journey worth taking.

Discussion Questions and Exercise

Discussion Questions

- Do therapists really need to have experienced their own personal therapy?
- What are the obstacles to self-care that our clients are likely to tell us about?
- What are the obstacles to self-care for you?

Exercise

Exercise 8.1: Self-Care Plan

Develop a plan for self-care that includes the types of activities in which you engage, activities that you can access should you find yourself needing more self-care, and ways in which you would assess if the amount of self-care is adequate.

Appendix

Overview of the Appendix

The primary purpose of the Appendix is to offer a closer and more expansive look at the qualitative and quantitative results of the Study that were used to illustrate the topics discussed throughout the book. It is here that you will find more examples of therapist nondisclosures and countertransference, client's perceptions of helpful events, supervisor regrets, and so forth.

This Appendix begins with the protocol and methodology used for the Study and identifies the therapy and supervision variables we used in the investigation. Our research team spent over 1 year developing the protocol and narrowing the variables that we believed would best capture the interrelationships among therapy process and outcome, and supervision process and outcome, all with the intent of using what is most meaningful to therapists in training.

The table and figures in the Appendix can be seen as consisting of roughly two types of data: qualitative data in the tables and quantitative data in the figures. These data include the reactions of trainees, their clients, and their supervisors, thereby offering what we hope is a well-rounded view of therapy and supervision experience from all those involved. We believe these data also offer useful insights into the process and outcome variables and can serve as a means to further explore and discuss the implications of the findings, which ultimately will lead to more learning opportunities for you.

Table 1 Protocols and Methodology Used in the Study

Participants

Clients: 18 (all White; 12 women and 6 men) who ranged in age from 31 to 71 years. Educational level included high school graduate (n = 6), some college (n = 6), undergraduate degree (n = 2), master's degree (n = 3), and doctoral degree (n = 1). Socioeconomic status included 8 reported working class and 10 reported middle class. Fourteen had received therapy previously. As for presenting concerns, all reported mild to moderate depression or anxiety, largely as a result of any combination of issues related to family of origin problems, relational conflict, low self-esteem, and employment difficulties.

Therapy Trainees: 4 (all White; 2 women and 2 men) who ranged in age from 23 to 27 years. One had reported having engaged in personal therapy previously.

Supervisors: 6 (1 African American and 5 White; 4 women and 2 men) who ranged in age from 30 to 51 years. Three were licensed psychologists, three had Ph.D.s, one had a Psy.D., and two had master's degrees. All reported having been in personal therapy previously. One supervisor served as a substitute for another who went on vacation for a period of time and another replaced a supervisor who left the study early.

Setting: University clinic set up for working with clients from the community.

Procedure

Clients were recruited through local media advertising, and referral from local social service agencies and practicing psychologists. The advertisements offered up to 16 sessions of psychotherapy for no charge, to persons experiencing mild to moderate depression, anxiety, or adjustment difficulties. Clients were screened for suitability, and those experiencing crises or severe psychopathology were referred to alternative agencies. The four therapist trainees conducted weekly therapy sessions (Range: 2 to 16) with each of their assigned clients (n = 18; 4 to 6 clients per therapist trainee), for a total of 182 sessions. The four therapist trainees also participated in weekly supervision sessions (Range: 7 to 23) with their respective primary and substitute supervisors, for a total of 84 sessions.

Questionnaire Protocol and Variables

Pre-Therapy and Supervision Variables

- Demographics (QT)
- Client Expectations for Therapy
- Client Multicultural Identities
- Client Level of Distress (OQ-45)
- Client Tolerance for Ambiguity
- Client Social Support

- Trainee Demographic Questionnaire
- Trainee Expectations for Therapy Questionnaire
- Trainee Expectations for Supervision Questionnaire
- Trainee Self-Beliefs Questionnaire
- Trainee Ambiguity Tolerance Questionnaire
- Trainee Counseling Self-Efficacy Scale
- Supervisor Demographic Questionnaire
- Supervisor Expectations for Supervision Questionnaire
- Supervisor Self-Beliefs Questionnaire
- Supervisor Ambiguity Tolerance Questionnaire
- Supervisor Counseling Self-Efficacy Scale
- Supervisor Supervision Self-Efficacy Scale

Pre-Therapy Session Packet

- Client Level of Distress Questionnaire
- External Events Questionnaire - Client
- Trainee Anxiety Scale

Post-Therapy Session Packet

- Therapeutic Working Alliance Inventory – Client
- Therapeutic Working Alliance Inventory – Trainee
- Trainee Anxiety Scale – Trainee
- Session Evaluation Questionnaire – Client
- Session Evaluation Questionnaire – Trainee
- Post Counseling Session Qualitative Interview – Client
- Helpful Critical Incidents
- Hindering Critical Incidents
- Nondisclosures
- Regrets
- Post Counseling Session Qualitative Interview – Trainee
- Helpful Critical Incidents
- Hindering Critical Incidents
- Countertransference
- Nondisclosures
- Regrets
- Trainee Learning

Post-Therapy Treatment Packet

(30 minutes, 1 month, 6 months, 1 year, 2 years)
(same protocol given at each interval)

- Therapeutic Working Alliance Inventory – Client
- Therapeutic Working Alliance Inventory – Trainee
- Client Level of Distress Questionnaire
- Client Self-Beliefs Questionnaire

(continued)

Table 1 (continued) Protocols and Methodology Used in the Study

- Client Ambiguity Tolerance Questionnaire
- Client Social Support
- Client Satisfaction Questionnaire
- Post-Treatment Therapy Questionnaire - Client
- Post-Treatment Treatment Questionnaire - Trainee

Pre-Supervision Session Packet

- Trainee Anxiety Scale - Trainee
- Preferred Supervisor Style Inventory - Trainee

Post-Supervision Session Packet

- Supervisory Working Alliance – Trainee
- Supervisory Working Alliance – Supervisor
- Trainee Anxiety Scale – Trainee
- Supervisor Style –Trainee
- Supervisor Style – Supervisor
- Session Evaluation Questionnaire – Trainee
- Session Evaluation Questionnaire – Supervisor
- Post-Supervision Session Qualitative Interview – Trainee
  - Helpful Events
  - Hindering Events
  - Nondisclosures
  - Regrets
  - Parallel Process
  - Trainee Learning
  - External Events
- Post-Supervision Session Qualitative Interview – Supervisor
  - Helpful Events
  - Hindering Events
  - Nondisclosures
  - Regrets
  - Parallel Process
  - Countertransference
  - Trainee Learning
  - External Events

Post-Supervision Treatment Packet

(30 minutes, 1 month, 6 months, 1 year, 2 years)

- Supervisory Working Alliance – Trainee
- Supervisory Working Alliance – Supervisor
- Supervisor Style –Trainee
- Supervisor Style – Supervisor

- Trainee Self-Beliefs Questionnaire
- Trainee Ambiguity Tolerance Questionnaire
- Trainee Anxiety Scale
- Trainee Counseling Self-Efficacy Scale
- Supervisor Self-Beliefs Questionnaire
- Supervisor Ambiguity Tolerance Questionnaire
- Supervisor Counseling Self-Efficacy Scale
- Supervisor Supervision Self-Efficacy Scale
- Role Conflict & Ambiguity Scale – Trainee
- Trainee Satisfaction Questionnaire
- Post-Supervision Treatment Questionnaire – Trainee
- Post-Supervision Treatment Questionnaire - Supervisor

Data Analysis

Quantitative measures were compared using a variety of multivariate multiple regression approaches. Qualitative interviews were transcribed and analyzed using a discovery-oriented-exploratory approach (Hill, 1990; Ladany et al., 1996; Mahrer, 1988). Sample sizes that reflect the number of occurrences of a particular variable ranged between 80 and 1,057. Categories for each of the variables were created and coded via consensus with inter-rater reliabilities exceeding .80.

Limitations

Because we used a naturalistic approach, limitations included but were not restricted to the sample of participants (e.g., primarily White, beginning practicum students, etc.), the generalizability from the relatively small sample size, and the selective attention to particular variables of study.

Note: QT refers to quantitative measures and QL refers to qualitative measures; more information regarding the protocol and analyses is available by contacting the authors.

Table 2 Specific Therapy and Supervision Variables

Category	Specific Variables
Client Characteristics	Sex, race, ethnicity, sexual orientation, age, socioeconomic status, religion, multicultural identities, interpersonal style, experience as a client, expectations for therapy, presenting concerns, social support, physical health.
Therapist/Trainee Characteristics	Sex, race, ethnicity, sexual orientation, age, socioeconomic status, religion, multicultural identities, personality style, experience as a client, experience as a therapist, experience as a supervisee, therapy self-efficacy, theoretical orientation, therapy-related anxiety, expectations for therapy, expectations for supervision, tolerance of ambiguity, reflective ability, graduate training.
Therapy Process	Therapeutic working alliance, client disclosures, therapist disclosures, client nondisclosures, therapist nondisclosures, parallel process (as influenced by supervision), client transference, therapist countertransference, therapist responsiveness, therapist interventions, client-therapist response modes, trainee and client intentions, critical incidents.
Therapy Outcome	Change in client level of distress and symptomatology, session impact, client satisfaction, client regrets, therapist regrets, change in therapist skills and professional identity.
External Events Client	Environmental events that influence the therapy work (e.g., managed care, life experiences, etc.).
Supervisor Characteristics	Sex, race, ethnicity, sexual orientation, age, socioeconomic status, religion, multicultural identities, personality style, experience as a client, experience as a therapist, experience as a supervisee, experience as a supervisor, therapy self-efficacy, supervisor self-efficacy, therapy theoretical orientation, supervisor theoretical orientation, expectations for supervision, tolerance of ambiguity, reflective ability, therapy graduate and post-graduate training and supervision, supervisor graduate and post-graduate training and supervision.
Supervision Process	Supervisory working alliance, trainee disclosures, supervisor disclosures, trainee nondisclosures, supervisor nondisclosures, parallel process (as influenced by therapy), supervision role understanding, conflict, and ambiguity, trainee transference, supervisor countertransference, supervisor responsiveness, supervisor interventions, supervisor-trainee response modes, supervisor and trainee intentions, critical incidents.

(continued)

Table 2 (continued) Specific Therapy and Supervision Variables

Category	Specific Variables
Supervision Outcome	Changes in trainee self-efficacy, therapy skills, conceptualization skills, professional identity, satisfaction; trainee evaluation (supervisor, self, and other); changes in supervisor self-efficacy, supervision skills, conceptualization skills, professional identity; trainee regrets, supervisor regrets, session impact.
External Events Trainee	Environmental events that influence the therapy or supervision work (e.g., peer feedback, peer interactions, classroom work, agency rules, evaluation policies, etc.)
External Events Supervisor	Environmental events that influence the supervision work (e.g., supervision of supervision, agency rules, peer feedback, etc.)

Table 3 Interpersonal Response System for the Therapist

1. **Information Giving** [A statement used by the therapist to convey information to the client.]

   A. **Therapeutic Relationship** [A statement that defines or clarifies the interpersonal roles between the therapist and the client. Responses concerning role orientation and confidentiality would be included. Information about administrative aspects of therapy (e.g., payment and scheduling) would not be included here.]

   Examples: "My role is not to just give you advice."
   "Go ahead and start wherever you feel comfortable."

   B. **Administrative Issues** [A comment that addresses any of the "business" aspects of therapy, such as scheduling and payment. These responses are less about the interpersonal relationship and more about the management of therapy as a fee-for-service interaction.]

   Examples: "Let's meet next week at the same time."
   "You can pay at the receptionist's desk as you leave."

   C. **Client Presentation/Immediacy** [A comment that reflects how the therapist is experiencing the client currently or in-the-moment; it may involve perceptions of the client's behaviors, feelings, or thoughts.]

   Examples: "You look angry right now."
   "Your voice has gotten very loud since we began talking about your sister."

   D. **Treatment Options** [A statement that introduces a possible course of action within therapy to the client. This response type would consist of a specific treatment available to the client (e.g., role-playing, deep-muscle relaxation, hypnosis) rather than a description of the interpersonal dynamics that may occur (e.g., the therapist orienting the client to the idea that the client should begin the session).]

(continued)

Table 3 (continued) Interpersonal Response System for the Therapist

> *Examples: "We could try deep muscle relaxation as a way to alleviate your tension."*
>
> *"One technique we could incorporate into our therapy is hypnosis."*

E. **Advice/Directive** [A statement in which the therapist tells the client what she or he should do with regard to thinking, feeling, or behaving outside of the therapy session. It may act to provide the client with another course of action that may not have previously been considered.]

> *Examples: "I want you to attend an AA meeting this week."*
>
> *"You should take 10 minutes a day to clear your mind and relax."*

F. **Direct Session/Agenda** [A statement in which the therapist expresses what he or she expects to be discussed within the therapy session.]

> *Examples: "Let's pause here to really discuss your feelings about him."*
>
> *"Go back to that last point you made before we started talking about your dad."*

G. **Linking Past Relationships With Present Situation/interpretation** [A response that includes past and current instances in the client's life in order to draw a connection between them.]

> *Examples: "It sounds like she's expecting things of you the way your mother used to."*
>
> *"This current fear of abandonment might be a reaction to your mom leaving you when you were small."*

H. **Demonstrate Understanding/Restatement of Thoughts/Reflection of Feelings** [When the therapist relays to the client what she or he is hearing the client say; the statement must go beyond the client's own words (see "Minimal Encourager"). This is not simply a echoing of what the client has said but more of an elaboration of what is being heard.]

> *Examples: "So you really feel alone on the weekends your husband has the kids."*
>
> *"I'm hearing you say that you feel there's no way out."*

I. **Self-Disclosure** [A personal statement by the therapist that divulges what she or he is thinking/feeling/experiencing; the statement is something that would not be obvious to the client.]

> *Examples: "I am feeling so sad for you right now."*
>
> *"I hope that you continue to use the insights you have gained in therapy once we end our sessions."*

2. **Minimal Encouragers/Facilitative Comment/Reinforcer** [A statement that uses the client's words, but does not qualify for "Demonstrate Understanding." The response is restricted to an echoing of the exact words of the client, or some notable indication that the client should continue (e.g., "um hmm" and head nodding).]

> *Examples: "um hmmm," "…..feel used and tired" (when the client has said "I feel used and tired."), "Go on."*

(continued)

Table 3 (continued) Interpersonal Response System for the Therapist

3. **Information Gathering/Query** [An inquiry by the therapist with the goal of obtaining information from the client.]

    A. **Past** [Time frame: childhood up to and including therapy]

        1. **Client's Experience** [Queries concerning the client's personal experience.]

            Examples: *"How did it feel when your sister put you down like that?"*

            "I wonder what it felt like to be so small and all alone?"

            "What did you think about your parents getting divorced?"

        2. **Others Through Client** [A statement in which the therapist asks the client to express or postulate as to others' thoughts, feelings, and behaviors.]

            Examples: *"How do you think your mother felt when you went off to college?"*

            "What did your brother do when that happened?"

    B. **Immediacy** [Time frame: currently, here and now, in the moment]

        1. **Client's Experience** [Queries concerning the client's personal experience.]

            Examples: *"How are you feeling right now?"*

            "What's going through your mind?"

            "What do you want to do having heard me say that?"

            "Do you realize that you are biting your nails?"

        2. **Others Through Client** [A statement in which the therapist asks the client to express or postulate as to others' thoughts, feelings, and behaviors.]

            Examples: *"Where does he think that you are, if not at therapy?"*

            "What is she doing while you are here?"

    C. **Future** [Time frame: some time after the current moment, in the future]

        1. **Client's Experience** [Queries concerning the client's personal experience.]

            Examples: *"How will that make you feel?"*

            "What sorts of feelings do you think you'll have when she finally dies?"

            "What reflections do you think you'll have about the life you have led?"

            "What else might you do besides drink at the party this Friday night?"

        2. **Others Through Client** [A statement in which the therapist asks the client to express or postulate as to others' thoughts, feelings, and behaviors.]

            Examples: *"How do you think she'll react when you leave her?"*

            "What will your children do without you?"

(continued)

Table 3 (continued) Interpersonal Response System for the Therapist

D. Demographics

Examples: "How old are you?"
"What classes did you say you were taking?"

4. Other [Inaudible verbalization or incomplete phrase due to interruption]

Examples: "and so I … [pause and interruption]
"and so I [inaudible] for her"

Note: "Information Gathering" can focus on any particular issue or content including family of origin, therapeutic relationship, interpersonal relationship, romantic relationships, and self.

Table 4 Interpersonal Response System for the Client

1. Information giving [A statement used to transmit information to the therapist.]

A. Past [Time frame: childhood up to and including therapy]

1. Client's Experience [Statements given by the client pertaining to what she or he has experienced.]

Examples: "I felt really scared on that first day of school."
"I would get so anxious when I was trying to learn to swim."
"Sometimes I wished I could go to camp like everyone else."
"When I was small, I would hide under my bed 'til someone found me."

2. Others Through Client [A statement in which the client expresses or postulates others' thoughts, feelings, and behaviors.]

Examples: "My sister was always jealous of me."
"My mother felt very responsible for what happened to him."

B. Immediacy [Time frame: currently, here and now, in the moment]

1. Client's Experience [Statements given by the client pertaining to what she or he has experienced.]

Examples: "I am so tired right now."
"Talking about this makes me feel anxious."
"I'm struggling with the idea that it really may not be true."
"I'm just sitting here, doing nothing!"

2. Others Through Client [A statement in which the client expresses or postulates others' thoughts, feelings, and behaviors.]

Examples: "My kids miss their father."
"He still drinks way too much!"

(continued)

Table 4 (continued) Interpersonal Response System for the Client

  C. **Future** [Time frame: some time after the current moment, in the future]

    1. **Client's Experience** [Statements given by the client pertaining to what she or he has experienced.]

> *Examples: "I will really be sad when it's over."*
> *"If he ever says anything, I will be furious!"*
> *"I would really have to think about that!"*
> *"I don't think that I ever could get on a plane."*
> *"I wouldn't do it!"*

    2. **Others Through Client** [A statement in which the client expresses or postulates others' thoughts, feelings, and behaviors.]

> *Examples: "Oh, she'd definitely go there by herself."*
> *"He'd say that I wasn't his type."*

  D. **Demographics**

> Examples: "I am 24 years old."
> "My parents were both from Italy."

2. **Expressed Understanding/ Agreement** [A statement made by the client that conveys to the therapist a level of comprehension/understanding.]

> Examples: "Oh, I get it now."
> "Right." "Oh, I see."

3. **Information Gathering** [An inquiry made by the client with the goal of obtaining information from the therapist.]

  A. **Therapeutic Relationship** [A question by the client requesting definition or clarification as to the interpersonal roles between the therapist and the client. Questions concerning role orientation and confidentiality would be included. Questions about administrative aspects of therapy (e.g., payment and scheduling) would not be included here.]

> *Examples: "Should I start talking now?"*
> *"So is your job just to give me advice?"*

  B. **Administrative Issues** [A question that addresses any of the "business" aspects of therapy, such as scheduling and payment. These questions are less about the interpersonal relationship and more about the management of therapy as a fee-for-service interaction.]

> *Examples: "Will we meet the same time next week?"*
> *"Is there any way to get the fee reduced?"*

  C. **Client Presentation/Immediacy** [A question that requests how the therapist is experiencing the client currently or in-the-moment; the inquiry may concern perceptions of the client's behaviors, feelings, or thoughts.]

> *Examples: "Do I seem crazy to you?"*
> *"Do I look as scared as I feel?"*

(continued)

Table 4 (continued) Interpersonal Response System for the Client

D. **Treatment Options** [A question that explores a possible course of action within therapy. This response type would be an inquiry of a specific treatment available to the client (e.g., role-playing, deep-muscle relaxation, hypnosis) rather than a description of the interpersonal dynamics that may occur (e.g., the client asking the therapist if she or he should begin the session).]

> *Examples: "Do you know anything about hypnosis?"*
> *"What was that thing you mentioned before … guided imagery?"*

E. **Advice/Directive** [A question in which the client asks the therapist what she or he should do with regard to thinking, feeling, or behaving. The client may be asking about another course of action that may not have previously been considered.]

> *Examples: "Do you think that I should leave him?"*
> *"How should I feel when it happens again?"*

F. **Direct Session/Agenda** [A statement in which the client inquires as to what will be discussed.]

> *Examples: "Should we talk about my childhood?"*
> *"Do you want me to tell you about my family?"*

G. **Linking Past Relationships With Present Situation/Interpretation** [An inquiry that includes past and current instances in the client's life in order to draw a connection between them.]

> *Examples: "Do you think that my fear of heights has something to do*
> *with my vacation as a child to the Grand Canyon?"*
> *"So you think that my relationship with Fred is like the relationship I*
> *had with Phil?"*

H. **Inquiry Concerning Understanding/Restatement of Thoughts/Reflection of Feelings** [When the client asks the therapist what she or he is hearing the client say; the question must go beyond the client's initial words (see "Minimal Encourager"). This is not simply asking for an echoing of what the client has said but more of an inquiry of what is being heard.]

> *Examples: "Do you get what I mean when I say I was 'trapped'?"*
> *"Am I explaining that clearly enough?"*

I. **Self-Disclosure** [An inquiry by the client that aims to acquire personal statements by the therapist divulging what she or he is thinking/feeling/experiencing.]

> *Examples: "What do you do when you get sad?"*
> *"What would you do if you were me?"*

4. **Other** [Inaudible verbalizations or incomplete phrase due to interruption.]

> *Examples: "and so I … [pause and interruption]*
> *"and so I [inaudible] for her"*

Note: "Information Giving" can focus on any particular issue or content including family of origin, therapeutic relationship, interpersonal relationship, romantic relationships, and self.

Table 5 Trainee Nondisclosures in Psychotherapy

Content	% of Responses	Definition	Example
Thoughts or Feelings Related to the Client, Relationship, or Therapeutic Work	20.7%	Trainee thoughts or feelings in response to client during the counseling process	Frustration with client; looking forward to termination; admire client's perseverance
Thoughts or Feelings About Personal Experiences	18.3%	Trainee thoughts or feelings of their personal experiences triggered during the session	Shared similar family conflict; had a similar problem with anxiety; was worse than client's child when that age
Interpretations, Conceptualizations, or Hypotheses About Client's or Others' Behavior	14.6%	Trainee perceptions and hypotheses regarding the behavior of the client or others in the client's life	Aware that client is avoiding anger; client's family isn't as supportive as client thinks; client behaving similarly to those she/he is complaining about
Thoughts or Feelings about Therapy Process	14.6%	Trainee thoughts about interventions, process dynamics, or session goals	Client focusing on others rather than on self; awareness of client pattern of interrupting; don't think client will change much in treatment
No Nondisclosures	14.6%	Trainee did not hold back any disclosures	Trainee denied any nondisclosures or was not aware of having any during the session
Perspective or Advice on What Client Should Do	11.0%	Trainee beliefs or opinions regarding client choices for behavior outside of session	Opinion that client should leave husband; believe client should go on medication
Other	3.7%	Identified nondisclosure does not fit into a category	Client will count as a study participant if she/he comes to next session
Trainee Lack of Experience, Knowledge, or Skills	2.4%	Trainee perceptions of their lack of clinical skill	No training with sexual abuse; not comfortable with death; no idea how to help client gain closure and move on

Table 6 Trainee Reasons for Nondisclosures in Psychotherapy

Content	% of Responses	Definition	Example
Not Therapeutically Indicated	28.0%	Trainee did not believe disclosure would be therapeutically appropriate at that time	Client appeared too vulnerable to handle disclosure; would take session off current track; didn't want to increase client anxiety
Maintain Professionalism	24.4%	Not a professionally relevant or appropriate disclosure	Disclosure would be trainee's personal belief; personal self-disclosure wouldn't be appropriate; disclosure would be about trainee's issues and not client's
Empower Client	22.0%	Trainee wished to empower client	Allowing client to work at own pace; want client to come to own conclusions; didn't want client to feel pressured to change
None	14.6%	Nothing was nondisclosed or there was no reason for the nondisclosure	Don't know why
Protect Relationship	8.5%	Trainee nondisclosed to protect the therapeutic alliance	Feared disclosure might alienate; didn't know how to say it without offending client; client would think trainee was an idiot
Trainee Lack of Expertise or Training	1.2%	Trainee felt unprepared to make disclosure or a lack in skill to address issue	Didn't know how to deal with aftermath of disclosing; didn't know how to explain it to client
Other	1.2%	Identified reason for nondisclosure does not fit into a category	Can't remember why; feelings are natural and don't need to be disclosed

Table 7 Trainee Perceptions of Client Nondisclosures in Psychotherapy

Content	% of Responses	Definition	Example
No Nondisclosure	28.0%	Did not identify a client nondisclosure	Not aware of client nondisclosing; client did not hold anything back
Sensitive Feelings or Issues	18.3%	Client nondisclosed information or experiences associated with a sensitive or difficult issue	Feelings of pain, hurt, helplessness; guilt about mother's death; negative feelings about self
Thoughts or Feelings About Therapist's Interventions	18.3%	Client nondisclosed thoughts or feelings in response to therapist's intervention	Disagreement with trainee; didn't like trainee's challenges; relief about diagnosis
Thoughts or Feelings About the Treatment Process	12.2%	Client nondisclosed thoughts or feelings in response to the treatment process	Doubt about the effectiveness of therapy; feelings associated with termination
Thoughts or Feelings About the Therapist or Relationship	12.2%	Client nondisclosed thoughts or feelings about the therapist or their relationship	Client transferential feelings; frustration with trainee; concerns about trainee's age
Information About Relationships With Others	9.8%	Client nondisclosed details regarding their relationships/ interactions with others	Romantic interest in new friend; extent of boyfriend's drinking; extent of difficulties in marriage
Other	1.2%	Identified reason for nondisclosure does not fit into a category	Sure there was something but can't remember what

Table 8 Trainee Perceptions of Client Reasons for Nondisclosures in Psychotherapy Category System

Content	% of Responses	Definition	Example
None	31.7%	Trainee had no reason for why client nondisclosed	Trainee didn't know why; nothing was nondisclosed
Protect Therapist or Relationship	23.2%	Trainee believed client nondisclosed to protect her/his feelings or their relationship	Didn't want to burden trainee; didn't want to be confrontational; disclosure (criticism of trainee) would hurt relationship
Protect Self	15.9%	Client nondisclosed to protect self or self-image	Client avoiding painful, upsetting topic; Client did not want to appear needy or dependent; too embarrassed to disclose
Timing Issue	12.2%	Timing was not right for disclosure	Too early in relationship for client to trust trainee with disclosure; client not comfortable with trainee yet (i.e., first session)
Unsuitable or Irrelevant to Content or Goals of Therapy	9.8%	Disclosure perceived to be irrelevant or inappropriate to discuss in therapy at that time	Felt feelings were wrong; not relevant to discussion at the time; taboo topic
Client's Personal Style or Character	4.9%	Aspects of client's interpersonal style or character prevent disclosure	Not like client to confront; client tends to shut down
Other	2.4%	Identified reason for nondisclosure does not fit into a category	Can't remember why; trainee didn't pursue the issue further

Table 9 Therapist Countertransference: Categories of Interfering Thoughts and Feelings

Content	% of Responses	Definition	Example
Client's Interpersonal Style	29.1%	Felt distracted, curious, frustrated with, confused by, or bothered by an aspect of the client's interpersonal style	Clients talked tangentially; engaged in resistance; avoided answering questions; spoke illogically; did not appear motivated; were hypocritical
None	15.9%	Therapist reports not having any interfering thoughts/feelings	Therapist answered "none" to the question
Therapist Self-Doubt	14.3%	Felt nervous, unsure, confused, or self-blaming about their lack of ability, experience, or skills.	Unable to relate to a client's experience; never had training on how to work with sexual abuse survivors
External Events	13.2%	Distracted thoughts while attending to something outside the therapy process	Felt tired, sick, hungry, cold; distracted by personal issues; distracted by the audio/videotape
Client's Choices/Behaviors	9.9%	Emotional responses based on having a personal conflict with the client's life choices or reported behaviors	Upset by a client having a relationship outside marriage; baffled by why a client would stay married to her spouse
Client's Presenting Material	8.8%	Felt uncomfortable with the nature of the client's presenting issue or content topic	Uncomfortable talking about termination; uncomfortable talking about death issues

Table 10 Therapist Countertransference: Categories of Interfering Behaviors

Content	% of Responses	Definition	Example
Lost Focus	24.2%	Becoming less involved or less attentive	Stopped listening; spaced out; not there 100%
None	22.0%	No behavioral response	Believed their interfering thoughts/feelings did not have an effect on behavior; did not identify interfering thoughts/feelings
More Focused	13.2%	Therapist focused session or focused more attention	More attentive; more directive; moved back on track
Asked More Questions	12.1%	Frequency of questions increased	Probed more; asked more
Proactive Instruction	5.5%	Explained an idea, pointing out a concept; giving advice; offering suggestions	Showed a client what she is doing to others when she interacts with them
Challenging Behavior	4.4%	Challenging the client on a given topic	Disagreed with client and asked them to consider therapist's point of view
Empathic Intervention	4.4%	Attempted to communicate empathy	Told the client if he wants to share his feelings the therapist is there for him
More Patient	3.8%	Therapist reported being more patient	Did not push the client; did not rush the client
Other	10.4%	Responses did not fit the established categories	Vague answers; noninterpretable answers; did not fit categories

Table 11 Therapist Countertransference: Categories of Facilitating Thoughts and Feelings

Content	% of Responses	Definition	Example
Sympathized With Client	27.5%	Therapist felt compassion for client's situation	Felt sympathy for client helped enhance the connection; it increased ability to understand client because therapist cared what client was going through
Therapist Reflects on Her/His Intervention	27.5%	Therapist recognized facilitative thought/feeling emerged from her/his positive work with client	Had knowledge of how to work with client; having used a technique learned in class or supervision
Related to Client	20.9%	Understood client based on personal experiences	Related to feelings of loneliness; had also experienced depression; has been there
Good Client	15.4%	Client behaved well; became motivated; did homework; found insight; made progress as desired	Client completed a homework assignment where he documented what he ate and what emotions he felt after doing so
Felt Happy for/Close to Client	7.1%	Therapist in general felt comfortable with, happy for, excited for, or close to the client	The relationship was really good; certain amount of closeness as far as being able to share intimate feelings
None	.5%	Therapist had no facilitative thought/feeling for client	Therapist responded "none" to question

Table 12 Therapist Countertransference: Categories of Facilitating Behaviors

Content	% of Responses	Definition	Example
Provided Focus	37.9%	Facilitated insight, offered a perspective, provided structure, offered advice, suggestions, or referrals	Told client to change homework assignment; probed client to make a connection between his behaviors and his significant other
Supportive Interventions	20.9%	Became empathic, encouraging, reassuring, pointing out progress	Tried to show empathy; told client he was doing a good job
Became Relaxed and Friendly	10.4%	Became comfortable, friendly, or joked with client	Therapist warmed up to client; therapist became relaxed
More Attentive	9.9%	Therapist became more interested and involved	Paid attention more; made therapist more attentive; made therapist focus more on what client said
None	6.6%	Therapist reported no facilitative behaviors	Reportedly, thoughts/ feelings did not affect behaviors
More Patient	5.5%	Therapist became more patient	Did not push client; used silence
Self-Disclosure	3.3%	Therapist self-disclosed to client	Therapist self-disclosed to client that he understood her son's situation from personal experience
Other	5.5%	Responses did not fit the established categories	Vague answers; noninterpretable answers; did not fit categories

Table 13 OQ-45 Scores Pre- and Posttreatment Scores by Therapist

Client	Pretest	Posttest	Change	# of Sessions	Outcome
Trainee I					
OD	75	57	-18	13	Recovered
AG	104	101	-3	3	No Change
AJ	72	56	-16	9	Recovered
BB	50	26	-24	8	Improved
Trainee II					
OC	64	64	0	16	No Change
OG	83	76	-7	5	No Change
OH	61	37	-24	2	Improved
AF	116	83	-33	12	Improved
CO	76	78	+2	7	No Change
Trainee III					
OJ	50	80	+30	5	Deteriorated
AH	70	62	-8	16	No Change
BA	77	40	-37	9	Recovered
BC	110	77	-33	16	Improved
Trainee IV					
OB	35	14	-21	9	Improved
AO	74	48	-26	15	Recovered
AA	63	48	-15	3	Improved
BJ	108	92	-16	16	Improved
CA	75	37	-38	16	Recovered
Mean	75.72	59.78	-15.94	10.00	

Table 14 OQ-45 Scores Pre- and Posttreatment Scores by Outcome

Client	Pretest	Posttest	Change	# of Sessions	Outcome
OD (I)	75	57	-18	13	Recovered
AJ (I)	72	56	-16	9	Recovered
BA (III)	77	40	-37	9	Recovered
AO (IV)	74	48	-26	15	Recovered
CA (IV)	75	37	-38	16	Recovered
Mean	74.60	47.60	-27.00	12.40	
BB (I)	50	26	-24	8	Improved
OH (II)	61	37	-24	2	Improved
AF (II)	116	83	-33	12	Improved
BC (III)	110	77	-33	16	Improved
OB (IV)	35	14	-21	9	Improved
AA (IV)	63	48	-15	3	Improved
BJ (IV)	108	92	-16	16	Improved
Mean	77.57	53.86	-23.71	13.2	
AG (I)	104	101	-3	3	No Change
OC (II)	64	64	0	16	No Change
OG (II)	83	76	-7	5	No Change
CO (II)	76	78	+2	7	No Change
AH (III)	70	62	-8	16	No Change
Mean	79.40	76.20	-3.20	9.4	
OJ (III)	50	80	+30	5	Deteriorated

Table 15 Client Helpful Incidents

Content	% of Responses	Definition	Example
Therapist Guidance	27.5%	Provided direction, feedback, suggestions, or solutions	Alternative perspective or information; identified patterns; explained something
Progress/Goal Orientation	15.9%	Reviewed progress, homework, and goals, or set goals	Processed the course of treatment; identified lessons learned; focused on accomplishing goals
Gained Deeper Understanding or Insight	12.1%	Trainee helped client gain deeper understanding or insight regarding issues	Deeper processing led to insight; realized why
Catharsis	11.5%	Talking about issues, letting things out, or having a safe place to vent	Gained release from talking about the past; processing issues and feelings
Trainee Attentive to the Therapeutic Process	10.4%	Trainee seemed interested, attentive, or competent	Wanted to help; remembered details; really listened; was competent and helpful
Clarification	9.8%	Clarified problems, issues, or goals	Identified core issue; clarified problem; increased clarity or focus
Received Support/ Validation	7.7%	Received support, validation, acceptance, reassurance, or encouragement	Felt accepted and not judged; reassurance felt encouraging; felt validated
None	4.3%	No helpful event	Could not find an answer; nothing was helpful
Other	0.5%	Response did not fit any categories	Something helpful, but not sure what; vague response; response did not fit categories

Table 16 Client Hindering Incidents

Content	% of Responses	Definition	Example
None	61.5%	Nothing was hindering	Don't know; nothing was hindering
Lack of Finesse/Skill	9.3%	Therapist displayed lack of clinical finesse or skill	Rushed the client through issues; was defensive; asked questions in a judging way
Client Behaviors	8.8%	Client defenses or issues with motivation hindered work	Avoidance; rambling; hates homework; reluctant to work
Client's Needs Unmet	6.6%	Not enough structure, direction, or feedback	Roles and purpose were unclear; not enough direction; want more feedback
Painful Topics	6.0%	Pursuing painful topics or emotions	Digging into past brought up painful memories; trainee brought up painful issues
Time/Attendance	3.8%	Issues related to time or attendance	Not enough time to do desired work; client was late
External Issues	2.2%	Issues external to counseling relationship or process	Clock ticked loudly; being taped for the study
Working Alliance	0.5%	Aspects of therapeutic working alliance hinder work	Fear therapist's judgment; feel uncomfortable sharing some issues
Other	1.1%	Response did not fit any categories	Something hindering, but not sure what; vague response; response did not fit categories

Table 17 Client Helpful and Hindering Thoughts and Feelings: Self

Helpful Thoughts/Feelings	% of Responses	Hindering Thoughts/Feelings	% of Responses
Good/Uplifted	16.3%	None	59.2%
Goal Oriented	15.6%	Vulnerable/Painful	13.9%
Release/Relief	10.4%	Anxious/Apprehensive	9.4%
New Insights	9.6%	Anger/Frustration	7.0%
Anxious/Apprehensive	8.5%	Other	4.5%
Vulnerable/Painful	8.1%	Gained Something Positive	3.5%
Validated/Supported	6.3%	Thoughts/ or Feelings About Trainee/Relationship	2.5%
Positive Self-Concept	5.6%		
None	5.2%		
Other	4.4%		
Positive About Trainee	3.7%		
Anger/Frustration	2.6%		

Table 18 Therapist Helpful Incidents

Content	% of Responses	Definition	Example
Catharsis	23.1%	Talking about issues, letting things out, or venting	Gained release from talking; let out or processed feelings
Trainee Guidance	22.0%	Provided direction, feedback, suggestions, or solutions	Alternative perspective or information; identified patterns; explained something
Gained Deeper Understanding or Insight	17.6%	Trainee helped client gain deeper understanding or insight regarding issues	Deeper processing led to insight; realized why
Trainee Attentive to Relationship/ Supportive	16.5%	Trainee attentive, supportive, or encouraging	Really invested; caring; accepting; validating; reassuring; encouraging
Progress/Goal Orientation	14.3%	Reviewed progress, homework, and goals	Processed course of treatment; reviewed growth; redefined goals
Client Motivated/ Invested	3.8%	Client motivated to do work or displays investment in the counseling process	Does work outside sessions; accomplished goals for the week; openly faces issues
None	2.2%	No helpful event	Could not find an answer; nothing was helpful
Other	0.5%	Response did not fit any categories	Something helpful, but not sure what; vague response; response did not fit categories

Table 19 Therapist Hindering Incidents

Content	% of Responses	Definition	Example
Lack of Finesse/Skill	25.3%	Trainee displayed lack of clinical finesse or skill	Had no idea what to say; not connecting with client; therapist talked too much
Client Behaviors	24.2%	Client defenses or issues with motivation hindered work	Avoidance of work or issues; rambling; resists interventions
Client's Needs Unmet	13.2%	Not enough structure, direction, or feedback	Did not provide answers or give test results as promised; client wanted more
Time Issues	13.2%	Issues related to time or attendance	Not enough time to cover issues; lack of time management; client was late
None	13.2%	Nothing was hindering	Don't know; nothing was hindering
External Issues	5.5%	Issues external to counseling relationship or process	Constraints of study; time of day; room temperature
Power/Control Issues	2.7%	Issues related to power or control of relationship or process	Client controlled session, not therapist; client asked personal questions
Other	1.62%	Response did not fit any categories	Something hindering, but not sure what; vague response; response did not fit categories
Painful Topics	1.1%	Pursuing painful topics or emotions	Client cried over sensitive issues; client embarrassed about talking

Table 20 Therapist Helpful and Hindering Thoughts and Feelings: Client

Helpful Thoughts/Feelings	% of Responses	Hindering Thoughts/Feelings	% of Responses
Positive About Therapist/ Therapist's Work	17.7%	None	17.2%
Release/Relief	15.8%	Nervous/Anxious	10.2%
Positive About Progress	12.4%	Frustrated/Disappointed	9.8%
Positive About Self	11.3%	Concerned About Trainee/Trainee's Work	9.3%
Anxious/Apprehensive	8.6%	Overwhelmed/Upset/Sad	8.8%
Sad/Upset	8.6%	Client Defenses	8.4%
Negative About Work/ Relationship	5.3%	Negative About Self	7.0%
Negative About Self	4.5%	Positive About Trainee/ Trainee's Work	6.0%
Frustrated/Disappointed	4.5%	Positive About Self/Own Work	5.6%
Seeking Direction/Answers	3.0%	Want More Time	4.6%
Concerns About Progress	3.0%	Relief/Relaxed	4.6%
None	2.2%	Other	3.2%
Other	0.8%	Confused/Surprised	3.2%
		Insight/Understanding	1.9%

Table 21 Therapist Helpful and Hindering Thoughts and Feelings: Self

Helpful Thoughts/Feelings	% of Responses	Hindering Thoughts/Feelings	% of Responses
Positive About Client/ Relationship	19.1%	Negative About Self/Work	15.0%
Positive About Self/Work	18.8%	Frustrated/Disappointed	15.0%
Validate/Support	13.3%	What to Do	13.5%
Positive About Progress/Goals	12.6%	Concerned About Client/ Work	9.7%
What to Do	8.1%	None	9.7%
Relieved/Relaxed	6.8%	Concern About Time Use	7.1%
Concerns About Self/Work	5.5%	Empathy	5.2%
Insights/Conceptualizations	3.6%	Insight/Conceptualization	4.9%
Frustrated/Disappointed	3.6%	Nervous/Anxious	4.9%
Concerns About Progress/Goals	2.9%	Other	4.9%
Nervous/Anxious	2.3%	Positive About Client/Work	3.4%
Session Lack of Depth	1.6%	Positive About Self/Work	2.2%
None	1.3%	Relieved/Relaxed	2.2%
Other	0.3%	Justified Intervention	2.2%

Table 22 Client Regrets in Psychotherapy Category System

Content	% of Responses	Definition	Example
No Regrets	67.0%	No regrets for self in session	Would not have done anything differently; nothing comes to mind
Be More Prepared, Motivated, or Focused	13.1%	Be more work oriented in the treatment process	More prepared, alert, or cooperative in session; actively work toward treatment goals; less avoidant rambling, or unfocused
Be More Insightful or Expressive of Here and Now Feelings	8.8%	Be more open and willing to go deeper into issues	Talk about feelings, core or important issues, or awareness; ask for feedback from and give feedback to therapist (i.e., personal reactions, frustrations)
Other	7.1%	Does not fit into any category	Have regrets but not anything specific; give therapist a hug
Boundary Issues Related to Use of Time and Attendance	3.8%	Issues related to attendance use of session time	Wish for more time or longer sessions; wish they had come or ended on time; wished they had been more consistent with attendance

Table 23 Client Regrets of Therapist Behavior in Psychotherapy

Content	% of Responses	Definition	Example
None	72.0%	No regrets	No regrets for therapist behavior during session
Provide More Guidance and Direction in Session	16.5%	Wished therapist had provided more guidance or taken a more active or directive role in session	Give advice, solutions, answers, quick fixes, or feedback; be more active, assertive, in charge, focusing, or directive
Have More Expertise, Finesse, or Maturity	7.7%	Wished therapist had more expertise, maturity, or clinical skills	Be more comfortable, relaxed, experienced, or older; stare less; be less judgmental (i.e., keep religious views to self) or labeling of client/others
Other	1.6%	Does not fit into any category	Have regrets but not specific
Boundary Issues Related to Use of Time and Attendance	1.1%	Issues related to attendance use of session time	Wish for more time or longer sessions; wish they had come or ended on time; wished therapist had not been late or missed session
Disclose More About Self	1.1%	Wished therapist had been more self-disclosing or open	Wish for more personal information from therapist or for a less neutral stance

Table 24 Therapist Self Regrets in Psychotherapy

Content	% of Responses	Definition	Example
Better Management of Session	26.9%	Be better at managing or conducting the session	Manage session structure, content, flow, focus, or pace; be more focused, goal oriented, or didactic
Be More Prepared, Skilled, or Invested	12.6%	Be better prepared, invested, or skilled in dealing with client or issue	Felt inexperienced, ill prepared, or not motivated to deal with client issues or interpersonal dynamics
Elicit Deeper Focus	12.1%	Wished they had facilitated the session going deeper into client emotions or issues	Focus on core issues or affect; go deeper with reflections or probes; processed the here and now
Be More Aware or Present in Session	10.4%	Wished they were more aware or present/in the moment during the session	Felt distracted by session content or personal, external, or environmental stimuli
None	10.4%	No regrets for how they behaved in the session	Would not have done anything differently
Modify or Use Different Intervention	6.6%	Changed delivery or use of an intervention	Modify or fine tune the timing or delivery of an intervention, not use an intervention, or use a forgotten intervention
Be More Interpersonally Responsive	6.6%	Be more responsive to client emotional needs in session	Be more supportive, empathic, understanding, gentle, or sensitive
Handle Boundaries Better	5.5%	Handle professional boundaries of time and relationship dynamics better	Address lateness, attendance, or running over time; be more professional/less casual; process client personal questions of therapist better
Let Client Lead or Focus the Content of the Session	4.9%	Be less structuring or leading of client work in session	Let client talk, elaborate, or direct focus of session; be less active, directive, or talkative
Other	3.8%	Does not fit into any category	Have regrets but not specific

Table 25 Therapist Regrets of Client Behavior in Psychotherapy (N=182; Inter-rater Reliability of all Regrets tables 87.7%)

Content	% of Responses	Definition	Example
None	37.4%	No regrets for client behavior	Would not have client change or do anything differently
Disclose More	17.0%	Wished client had been more open or disclosing	Be more open, honest, or comfortable with expressing feelings, thoughts, or needs
Demonstrate Motivation or Commitment to Treatment Process	10.4%	Wished client was more motivated or committed to the treatment process	Complete homework or follow directions; be active or self-initiating vs. passive; be more committed to treatment
Be More Direct or Focused	9.3%	Wished client was more direct and focused in sessions	Not go off on tangents or avoid issues/ questions; be clearer; be ready to work
Respect Boundary Issues	8.8%	Respect boundaries of therapy time and relationship	Be on time, attend sessions, call to cancel, end on time, don't test limits, don't ask personal questions
Be More Insightful or Reflective	8.8%	Wished client would go deeper into issues and therapy process	Focus inward on self rather than on others; go deeper with emotions, content, process, or issues; be open to and display a broader perspective; discuss transference
Other	4.4%	Does not fit into any category	Have regrets but not specific; want to change something but can't say what
More Positive View of Self and Progress	3.8%	Wished client displayed a more optimistic view of self or their treatment progress	Be more self-accepting; give self credit for progress or difficulty of issues; display higher self-esteem

Table 26 Positive Things Therapists Learn from Conducting Therapy

Content	% of Responses	Definition	Example
Increase in Confidence	46.0 %	Increasing confidence in professional proficiency and effectiveness	Witnessing client progress; receiving client confirmation of empathic understanding, conceptualization, and inference
Awareness of Self and the Therapeutic Process	28.0 %	Increasing awareness of the therapeutic process and of the therapist role within it	Exploring therapist identity and other aspects of self; recognizing varying levels of client and therapist investment; understanding process of losses and gains in therapy
Relationship Development	9.0 %	Becoming aware of and working with the therapeutic relationship in sessions	Witnessing clients' comfort in session; feeling connected and building rapport; witnessing increased client disclosure
Evaluation of Skills/Approach to Client	7.0 %	Realizing and analyzing therapeutic skills and application of approaches to clients	Noting increased conceptualization skills; developing and integrating new skills; identifying helpful and meaningful client issues
None Identified	5.0 %	Indicating that the therapy session had no positive influence on trainee's professional development	"I don't think it was positively influenced"
Other	5.0 %		Perceiving client's "no-show" as positive influence, as trainee learns not to "take it personally" e.g., stating that everything is positive without offering specific response

Table 27 Negative Things Therapists Learn from Conducting Therapy

Content	% of Responses	Definition	Examples
None Identified	49.0%	Indicating that the therapy session had no negative influence on the trainee's professional development	"Can't think of anything that influenced my development negatively"
Awareness of Self and the Therapeutic Process	23.0%	Processing personal reactions to dynamics in therapy sessions that seem unsettling to trainee	Struggling with countertransference issues and their negative impact on professional self-image, bond, and client progress; realizing therapist role in eliciting client issues and in dealing with growth edges
Evaluation of Skills/Approach to Client	22.0%	Emphasizing lack of skills or experience and criticizing applied approaches to clients	Noting unsuccessful implementation of skills; emphasizing lack of experience; feeling unprepared to handle certain situations; recognizing missed opportunities
Other	5.0%		Feeling that all sessions will somehow influence trainee's development positively by learning from it; feeling put down by client's "snide comments"; feeling like carrying an extra load because of the research study and not having learned how to put aside all that comes out in the sessions
Decrease in Confidence	1.0%	Doubting own professional proficiency and effectiveness	Feeling responsible for client's lack of progress; self-doubting when client "no-shows"

Table 28 Trainee Interpersonal Response Modes

I. Information Giving
   a. Therapy- Conceptualization- Facts and Observations
      Statement about the client or session based upon a concept conceived in the trainee's mind. These are centered on events that have actually occurred and are discernable during the therapy session. (e.g., "He said that because he is angry at his father.")
   b. Therapy- Conceptualization- Hypothesis and Clinical Assessments
      Statement about the client or session based upon a concept conceived in the trainee's mind. These are centered on opinions, thoughts, perceptions, or assumptions. (e.g., "She does not seem to understand what I am saying.")
   c. Therapy- Treatment- Facts and Observations
      Statement made by the trainee pertaining to the act of treating clients, including techniques or actions applied to a specific situation. These are centered on events that have actually occurred and are discernable during the therapy session. (e.g., "I tried using reflective listening.")
   d. Therapy- Treatment- Hypothesis and Clinical Assessments
      Statement made by the trainee pertaining to the act of treating clients, including techniques or actions applied to a specific situation. These are centered on opinions, thoughts, perceptions, or assumptions. Future plans for treatment would be included here. (e.g., "A behavioral intervention might work really well with him.")
   e. Supervision
      A statement that describes the trainee's experience of the supervision process. (e.g., "I feel like fifty minutes isn't enough time to discuss all four of my clients.")
   f. Personal and Professional
      Self disclosures pertaining to the trainee's personal and professional experiences. (e.g., "This is an easy case for me," "I really enjoyed working with this client.")
   g. Trainee Evaluation- Positive Feedback
      The trainee's expressed belief that he or she did well during therapy or supervision. (e.g., "I did a good job handling the suicide assessment.")
   h. Trainee Evaluation- Critical Feedback
      The trainee's expressed belief that he or she could have done better or done something differently during therapy or supervision. (e.g., "I think I could have handled my client's rudeness more professionally.")
II. Information Gathering
   a. Therapy- Conceptualization-Facts and Observations
      Inquiry about the client or session based upon a concept conceived in the trainee's mind. These are centered on events that have actually occurred and are discernable during the therapy session. (e.g., "Why do you think she said it like that?")

b. Therapy- Conceptualization- Hypothesis and Clinical Assessments

Inquiry about the client or session based upon a concept conceived in the trainee's mind. These are centered on opinions, thoughts, perceptions, or assumptions. (e.g., "Do you think he's depressed?")

c. Therapy- Treatment- Facts and Observations

Inquiry pertaining to the act of treating clients, including techniques or actions applied to a specific situation. These are centered on events that have actually occurred and are discernable during the therapy session. (e.g., "Should I have told him that?")

d. Therapy- Treatment- Hypothesis and Clinical Assessments

Inquiry pertaining to the act of treating clients, including techniques or actions applied to a specific situation. These are centered on opinions, thoughts, perceptions, or assumptions. (e.g., "Should I try using a relaxation technique to treat her anxiety?")

e. Supervision

An inquiry about the supervisor's experience of the supervision process. (e.g., "Do we have enough time to talk about one more client?")

f. Personal and Professional

Inquiry concerning self disclosures pertaining to the supervisor's personal and professional experiences. (e.g., "Have you ever felt like a session got out of control?")

g. Trainee Evaluation

Inquiry concerning the supervisor's thoughts on the trainee's performance in therapy or supervision. (e.g., "How do you think I handled his crisis in this session?")

III. Attempt to Demonstrate Understanding

The trainee relays to the supervisor what the trainee is hearing the supervisor say. This must go beyond the supervisor's own words, not an exact echo, more of an elaboration (such as reflective listening, restatement, shared laughter and empathetic responses). (e.g., "I see what you mean," "That makes sense now.")

IV. Techniques

The trainee prompts or initiates a specific course of action within the supervision session (such as tape review, role-play, or 2 chair technique). (e.g., "I think we should try a 2 chair technique to help me understand her point of view.")

V. Minimal Encourager

A verbalization that is an echoing of the exact words of the supervisor or some notable indication that the supervisor should continue. The echoing uses the supervisor's words but does not qualify as an "attempt to demonstrate understanding." Offers no content to the discussion. (e.g., "Mhmm," "Ooh," "Right," "Yes").

VI. Idiosyncratic Responses

Verbalizations that can stand alone but have no real meaning and offer no content to the discussion. (e.g., *sometimes:* "Know what I'm saying," "I don't know").

(continued)

Table 28 (continued) Trainee Interpersonal Response Modes

VII. Silence

Five seconds of time in which neither the trainee nor the supervisor speaks. Must be the trainee's "turn" to speak.

VIII. Other

Statements that do not attend to the supervision or therapy work being discussed (i.e., scheduling, talking about the weather) and incomplete or inaudible phrases. (e.g., "It sure is a nice day today.")

Table 29 Supervisor Interpersonal Response Modes

I. Information Giving

a. Therapy- Conceptualization- Facts and Observations

Statement about the client or session based upon a concept conceived in the supervisor's mind. These are centered on events that have actually occurred and are discernable during the therapy session. (e.g., "He was telling you that because he was scared.")

b. Therapy- Conceptualization- Hypothesis and Clinical Assessments

Statement about the client or session based upon a concept conceived in the supervisor's mind. These are centered on opinions, thoughts, perceptions, or assumptions. (e.g., "This is a textbook case of borderline personality disorder.")

c. Therapy- Treatment- Facts and Observations

Statement made by supervisor pertaining to the act of treating clients, including techniques or actions applied to a specific situation. These are centered on events that have actually occurred and are discernable during the therapy session. (e.g., "I noticed that you paused for a while after asking that question.")

d. Therapy- Treatment- Hypothesis and Clinical Assessments

Statement made by the supervisor pertaining to the act of treating clients, including techniques or actions applied to a specific situation. These are centered on opinions, thoughts, perceptions, or assumptions. Future or hypothetical plans for treatment would be included here. (e.g., "Just listening would be of great benefit to your clients.")

e. Supervision

A statement that describes the supervisor's experience of the supervision process or that directs the supervision process. (e.g., "Lets talk about that for he last 20 minutes of today's session," "We will make optimum use of the time we have together.")

f. Personal and Professional

Self disclosures pertaining to the supervisor's personal and professional experiences. (e.g., "I had a similar experience the first time I did counseling.")

g. Trainee Evaluation- Positive Feedback

The supervisor's expressed belief that the trainee did well during counseling or supervision. Statements that encourage, validate, or support the thoughts or actions of the trainee. (e.g., "That's a normal reaction," "You handled that very well," "Hang in there," "You are very therapeutic with them.")

h. Trainee Evaluation- Critical Feedback

The supervisor's expressed belief that the trainee could have done better or done something differently during therapy or supervision. (e.g., "I don't think that is the best way to handle that type of situation.")

II. Information Gathering

a. Therapy- Conceptualization Facts and Observations

Inquiry about the client or session based upon a concept conceived in the supervisor's mind. These are centered on events that have actually occurred and are discernable during the therapy session. (e.g., "What was going through your mind when she said that?")

b. Therapy- Conceptualization- Hypothesis and Clinical Assessments

Inquiry about the client or session based upon a concept conceived in the supervisor's mind. These are centered on opinions, thoughts, perceptions, or assumptions. (e.g., "How do you think she reacted to that statement?" "What diagnosis would you give him?")

c. Therapy- Treatment- Facts and Observations

Inquiry pertaining to the act of treating clients, including techniques or actions applied to a specific situation. These are centered on events that have actually occurred and are discernable during the therapy session. (e.g., "What did he say first?" "Where was she sitting?")

d. Therapy- Treatment- Hypothesis and Clinical Assessments

Inquiry pertaining to the act of treating clients, including techniques or actions applied to a specific situation. These are centered on opinions, thoughts, perceptions, or assumptions. (e.g., "What do you think would be the best way to address the issue of personal hygiene with your client?" "How do you plan to handle this?")

e. Supervision

An inquiry about the trainee's experience of supervision process. An inquiry pertaining to trainee's understanding of what is being discussed. (e.g., "What do you think we should do with our time together?" "Do understand what I mean?")

f. Personal and Professional

Inquiry concerning self disclosures pertaining to the trainee's personal and professional experiences. (e.g., "Have you ever had an experience like this before?")

g. Trainee Evaluation

Inquiry concerning trainee's thoughts on own performance in therapy or supervision. (e.g., "How do you think that approach worked with her?")

(continued)

Table 29 (continued) Supervisor Interpersonal Response Modes

III. Attempt to Demonstrate Understanding

The supervisor relays to the trainee what the supervisor is hearing the trainee say. This must go beyond the supervisor's own words, not an exact echo, more an elaboration (such as reflective listening, restatement, shared laughter, and empathetic responses). (e.g., "I feel the same way," "You have some tough clients," "I know you don't always feel that way.")

IV. Techniques

The supervisor prompts or initiates a specific course of actions within the supervision session (such as tape review, role-play, or 2 chair technique). (e.g., "Why don't you role-play your client and I'll role-play the therapist.")

V. Minimal Encourager

A verbalization that is an echoing of the exact words of the trainee or some notable indication that the trainee should continue. The echoing uses the trainee's words but does not qualify as "attempt to demonstrate understanding." Offers no content to the discussion. (e.g., "Mhmm," "Ooh," "Right," "Yes.")

VI. Idiosyncratic Responses

Verbalizations that can stand alone but have no real meaning and offer no content to the discussion. (e.g., *sometimes:* "Know what I'm saying?" "I don't know.")

VII. Silence

Five seconds of time in which neither the trainee nor the supervisor speaks. Must be the supervisor's "turn" to speak.

VIII. Other

Statements that do not attend to the supervision or therapy work being discussed (i.e., scheduling, talking about the weather) and incomplete or inaudible phrases. (e.g., "Let's meet at 4:00 next week.")

Table 30 Content of Trainee Nondisclosures in Supervision

Content	% of Responses	Definition	Example
Nothing	37.8%	No reported nondisclosure	Nothing; I really can't think of anything
Issues About work With Client	23.3%	Comments related to client behaviors, interventions, therapy process, assessment, countertransference issues	Something that happened in [the client's] childhood that was significant; how much I felt like I related to one of the clients
Negative Feelings Toward Supervisor or About Supervision	16.7%	Unpleasant or critical thoughts or feelings related to supervisor or supervision session	I was picking up that he wasn't happy that I was late; how I feel kinda like we don't really have a connection
Trainee's Personal Issues	13.3%	Issues that pertain only to the trainee	That my personality is that I just want to keep striving to do better; that I was supposed to be somewhere else today
Positive Feelings Toward Supervisor	4.4%	Pleasant thoughts or feelings about the supervisor	How helpful she was to me; how much I appreciate how invested he has been
Concerns About Supervisor's Personal Issues	2.2%	Issues that pertain only to the supervisor	He appears to have a lot on his mind; I know he's been really struggling
Other	2.2%	Trainee's thoughts or feelings that didn't fit into above categories	I was just like, "Okay, okay" (Agreement with supervisor)

Table 31 Reasons for Trainee Nondisclosures in Supervision

Reason	% of Responses	Definition	Example
No Reason Given/Other	37.9%	No definitive reason for content of nondisclosure	I don't know why we didn't talk about that; I don't really want to talk about it
Not Important/ Less Relevant	15.5%	Information seemed less important to disclose than other information	It didn't seem like a really big deal; since we were on a time constraint, that would waste the time instead of talking about the client, which I felt was more important
Negative Reaction by Supervisor	11.2%	Trainee anticipated negative response by the supervisor	It might have added to the frustration the supervisor feels; certainly didn't want to create friction for any reason
Impression Management	10.3%	Thoughts indicating need to uphold particular impression given by trainee	I don't want to give him a sense that I'm trying to dwell on negative things; it's not professional
No Time	7.8%	Lack of time during supervision session	We already ran out of time; we just didn't have the time
Not Comfortable/ Confidentiality Concerns	7.8%	Thoughts indicative of discomfort felt by the trainee, either due to lack of confidentiality in research study or other concerns	I didn't feel there was enough privacy to maintain the confidentiality; I don't think I felt comfortable talking to a guy about that
Disclosure Wouldn't Change Anything	6.9%	Trainee's perception that disclosure wouldn't help trainee get needs met	I don't know what I would expect him to say; I didn't think that my saying that would change anything
Forgot/Thought About Later	2.6%	Comments relating to forgetfulness during supervision or later discovery	I didn't really think about it until just now; I don't really think I thought about it a whole lot

Table 32 Content of Supervisor Nondisclosures

Content	% of Responses	Definition	Example
Nothing	56.5%	No reported nondisclosure	I don't think there was anything; nothing
Supervisor's Personal Issues	11.8%	Issues that pertain only to the supervisor	That I am going through the same [situation] as the client; how drained I am
Information About Trainee's Work With Client	9.4%	Comments related to trainee behaviors with client, interventions, therapy process, assessment, counter-transference issues	The challenge is for the trainee to learn and to identify what the meaning of [the client's] story is in context; whether or not [the trainee] will be able to deal with some of the issues that might come up in that client's situation
Concerns About Trainee's Personal/ Professional Issues	7.1%	Comments related to trainee's personal or professional develop-ment or work	If she doesn't take the time to do this, it's going to make her not enjoy her work; I was a little worried about that…injuring trainee at such an early stage in training
Positive Feedback	4.7%	Positive thoughts or feelings about the trainee	How likable the trainee was; giving trainee some reinforcement and positive feedback
Negative Feelings About Psychotherapy or Supervision Session	3.5%	Unpleasant or critical thoughts or feelings about trainee's psychotherapy sessions or super-vision sessions	Some concern that trainee might not be disclosing some things; I was feeling bad about last week
Concerns About Trainee's Performance in Supervision	3.5%	Specific comments expressing disap-proval of trainee's behavior in supervision	After all these weeks in supervision, trainee won't just say [how trainee feels]; how much latitude trainee really has

(continued)

Table 32 (continued) Content of Supervisor Nondisclosures

Content	% of Responses	Definition	Example
Supervisor's Expertise/Orientation	2.4%	Thoughts pertaining to supervisor's area of expertise or theoretical orientation	I don't think I ever told trainee how much experience I have...in that area; I didn't tell [the trainee] much about my orientation
Technical Issues	1.2%	Comments about technical or mechanical aspects of sessions	I had my watch over here; I am used to my clock in my office

Table 33 Reasons for Supervisor Nondisclosures

Reason	% of Responses	Definition	Example
No Reason Given	54.7%	No definitive reason for content of nondisclosure	(No response given)
Negative Reaction by Trainee	12.6%	Supervisor anticipated negative response by the trainee	I didn't want him to have sympathy or anything that might prevent him from asking for things that he needed; he would experience that very negatively
Not Important/less Relevant	10.5%	Information seemed less important to disclose than other information	Didn't seem necessary; [the trainee] wasn't seeing the client I thought it might impact
No Time	6.3%	Lack of time during supervision session	We had spent so much time on the tape issue and then on basic structure that there wasn't as much time; there's no time to do that kind of thing

(continued)

Table 33 (continued) Reasons for Supervisor Nondisclosures

Reason	% of Responses	Definition	Example
Forgot	5.3%	Comments relating to forgetfulness during supervision or later discovery	I just never thought to do it; I didn't conceptualize it until I was talking to [interviewer] about it
Negative Effect on Trainee's Work With Client	3.2%	Thoughts or feelings that disclosure would disrupt trainee's psychotherapy work	I didn't want it to affect his motivation with the client; I thought it might hinder the process
Keep Focus on Trainee	3.2%	Expressed concern about keeping focus of session on trainee	I didn't want to put the focus off of the trainee and on to me; wanted him to make sure he got what he wanted
Disclosed Indirectly	2.1%	Disclosed in ways other than direct expression of thoughts or feelings	I kind of addressed it in a different way; I didn't do it overtly
Waiting for Better Time to Raise Issues	2.1%	Comments indicative of supervisor preferring a future session or period of development to broach issue	I wanted to make sure we got through [other] information before going off into what happened; I'll wait until she sees that other client

Table 34 Trainee and Supervisor Identified Parallel Processes (N = 351; Inter-rater Reliability = 92.6%)

Content	% of Responses	Definition	Example
Invested & Collaborative (Client, Therapist, & Supervisor)	11.1%	Showed investment in the treatment or supervision process	Displayed commitment, motivation, interest, or engagement in a cooperative or helpful way
Didactic Approach (Therapist & Supervisor)	9.1%	Take an instructional approach to treatment or supervision	Provide instruction about what they (client in therapy or therapist in supervision) are not seeing or should do differently; Direct, structure, or lead session (therapist in therapy or supervisor in supervision)
Deferred to Authority (Client & Therapist)	7.7%	Defer to power differential	Being agreeable, passive, or compliant; letting or asking other to guide, dominate, or structure session (client in therapy or therapist in supervision)
Resistant or Avoidant of Work(Client & Therapist)	7.1%	Resistant to or avoidant of doing meaningful work in treatment or supervision	Guarded, avoidant, or resistant to therapy or supervision; keeping session content at intellectualized or superficial level (client in therapy or therapist in supervision)
Attentive to Trainee or Client Needs (Therapist & Supervisor)	6.8%	Actively attending to the needs of the other	Attending to emotional needs, listening intently, or being empathic, responsive, caring, or validating (therapist in therapy or supervisor in supervision)

(continued)

Table 34 (continued) Trainee and Supervisor Identified Parallel Processes (N = 351; Inter-rater Reliability = 92.6%)

Content	% of Responses	Definition	Example
Similar Issues or Emotions (Client & Therapist)	6.8%	Experiencing similar issues or affective responses	Feeling same emotions (i.e., anger, frustration, sadness) or issues (i.e., loss, death); similar transferential and countertransferential reactions (client in therapy or therapist in supervision)
Empowered (Therapist & Supervisor)	6.3%	Client (in therapy) or trainee (in supervision) was empowered during the session	Was encouraged to talk or run session, find own answers, or express conflicting feelings or opinions (by therapist in therapy or supervisor in supervision)
Provided Suggestions or Increased Perspective (Therapist & Supervisor)	5.7%	Helped provide increased perspective on how to understand or deal with issues	Give suggestions, examples, alternative perspective, or interpretations without giving direct advice (therapist in therapy or supervisor in supervision)
Similar Style of Interaction (Client & Therapist)	5.4%	Similarities between the sessions interactional styles and interpersonal dynamics	Similar speaking style, speed of speech, posture, timing, or therapeutic stance (by client in therapy or therapist in supervision)
Insight Facilitated Through Deeper Focus (Therapist & Supervisor)	5.1%	Insight gained from moving focus of session to a deeper level of analysis	Discussed transference & ountertransference issues; asked thought-provoking questions that move session to deeper level of intimacy or affect (therapist in therapy or supervisor in supervision)

(continued)

Table 34 (continued) Trainee and Supervisor Identified Parallel Processes (N = 351; Inter-rater Reliability = 92.6%)

Content	% of Responses	Definition	Example
Provided Feedback (Therapist & Supervisor)	3.7%	Provide feedback or focus on progress and strengths	Provided feedback about behavior or interpersonal dynamics; discussed progress or strengths (therapist in therapy or supervisor in supervision)
Facilitated Positive Relationship (Client, Therapist, & Supervisor)	3.4%	Ways in which the therapeutic or supervisory alliance is strengthened	Behaviors, interactions, or dynamics that are experienced positively and serve to strengthen the relationship, including feeling comfort, openness, rapport, trust, and genuineness in the session (client and therapist in therapy or therapist and supervisor in supervision)
Sought Assistance (Client & Therapist)	2.6%	Sought some kind of assistance from the other	Seek support, reassurance, feedback or perspective (client in therapy or therapist in supervision)
Other	2.3%	Did not fit any category	Obscure response that did not fit with any others
None	16.8%	No parallel processes identified	Stated that there were "none"

Table 35 Trainee Supervision Helpful Incidents Category System: Definitions and Examples

Content	% of Responses	Definition	Example
Supervisor Guidance	48.8%	Provided advice, information, feedback, or suggestions	Supervisor gave questions to ask, game plan, or what to do better; provided alternative perspective
Received Support/ Validation/ Reassurance	11.9%	Received support, validation, acceptance, reassurance, or encouragement	Reassured on the right track; validated trainee's thoughts; supported/understood trainee's work/struggles
Trainee Focused Supervision	10.7%	Supervision focused on trainee issues/ needs rather than on clients	Discussed how trainee was doing personally; provided career mentoring; discussed countertransference
Gained Deeper Understanding or Insight	9.5%	Trainee gained deeper understanding, insight, or client conceptualizations	Deeper processing led to insight; greater understanding of where to push; conceptualized client issues
Productive/Goal Focused	9.5%	Trainee found supervision productive or obtained goals and direction	Covered a wide range of clients; focused on one client in depth; accomplished a lot
Supervisory Working Alliance	8.3%	Addressed the tasks, goals, and bond of supervision	Agreed upon session structure; came up with supervision goals; connecting and processing relationship
Other	1.2%	Response did not fit any categories	Something helpful, but not sure what; vague response; response did not fit categories
None	0.0%	No helpful event	Could not find an answer; nothing was helpful

Table 36 Trainee Supervision Hindering Incidents Category System: Definitions and Examples

Content	% of Responses	Definition	Example
None	27.4%	Nothing was hindering	Don't know; nothing was hindering
Time Issues	25.0%	Issues related to use of time	Not enough time to cover material; Supervisor used up time talking; want more time
External Issues	21.4%	Issues external to supervision relationship or process	Technical difficulties; lack of material from client; room temperature
Working Alliance	10.7%	Aspects of therapeutic working alliance hinder work	Conflict with supervisor; Supervisor took call during session; poor communication; lack of connection
Trainee's Needs Unmet	8.3%	Not enough structure, direction, or feedback	Goals unclear or not established; therapist felt unprepared for clients; lack of direction or feedback
Trainee Attitude/ Motivation	6.0%	Trainee's attitude or lack of motivation/ investment hindered work	Trainee had "bad" or negative attitude; lacked enthusiasm/ motivation; late for session
Other	1.2%	Response did not fit any categories	Something hindering, but not sure what; vague response; response did not fit categories

Table 37 Trainee Supervision Helpful and Hindering Thoughts and Feelings Category Systems: Self

Helpful Thoughts/Feelings	% of Responses	Hindering Thoughts/Feelings	% of Responses
Positive About Supervision/ Supervisor	23.3%	Disappointed About Supervision/ Supervisor	32.3%
Release/Relieved	21.7%	None	28.1%
Preparation/Goals for Clients	17.5%	Anxious/Apprehensive	10.4%
Supported/Reassured/ Validated	13.3%	Session Time Use	9.4%
Positive About Self/Work	10.8%	Gained Something Positive	5.2%
Insights	5.0%	Other	5.2%
Frustrated/Upset	5.0%	External Events/Issues	4.2%
Anxious/Nervous	3.3%	Negative About Self/Work	3.1%

Table 38 Supervisor Supervision Helpful Incidents Category System: Definitions and Examples

Content	% of Responses	Definition	Example
Supervisor Guidance	42.2%	Provided direction, feedback, suggestions, or solutions	Alternative perspective or information; identified patterns; explained something
Gained Deeper Understanding or Insight	28.9%	Trainee gained deeper understanding, insight, or conceptualization of clients	Identified transference and countertransference patterns; deeper understanding of client dynamics
Received Support/ Validation	14.5%	Received support, validation, reassurance, or encouragement	Vented feelings about clients or study and gained support; feedback helped normalize therapist struggles
Supervisory Working Alliance	6.0%	Addressed the tasks, goals, and bond of supervision	Talked about supervision goals; established connection; shared supervision expectations
Trainee Focused Supervision	3.6%	Supervision focused on therapist issues/ needs rather than on clients	Addressed trainee's personal career concerns; let trainee lead and direct supervision session; discussed future goals
Progress/Goal Orientation	3.6%	Reviewed progress, growth, and goals or worked toward solidifying goals	Reviewed trainee's work, growth, or progress; worked out a plan for structuring next client session
Other	1.2%	Response did not fit any categories	Something helpful, but not sure what; vague response; response did not fit categories
None	0.0%		Could not find an answer; nothing was helpful

Table 39 Supervisor Supervision Hindering Incidents Category System: Definitions and Examples

Content	% of Responses	Definition	Example
Time Issues	22.9%	Issues related to use of time	Not enough time to review all clients; spent too much time talking about clients
Lack of Finesse/ Skill	12.0%	Supervisory intervention lacked finesse or was poorly timed	Supervisor too directive, didactic, or theoretical for trainee; talked too much
Trainee Behaviors	10.8%	Concerns about trainee behavior, difficulties, or work	Lack of knowledge; getting sucked into client world; stuck on trying to change something that can't change
External Issues	10.8%	Issues external to supervision relationship or process	Trainee tired or stressed out due to external constraints; frustration toward clients
Trainee's Needs Unmet	10.8%	Supervisor did not meet trainee needs	Came unprepared; avoided addressing trainee grief when working with grief clients
None	10.8%	Nothing was hindering	Don't know; nothing was hindering
Tape Issues	9.6%	Problems listening to tapes	No tape; couldn't find a tape
Working Alliance	8.4%	Aspects of supervision working alliance hinder work	Communication problems; conflict; trainee anxiety about supervisor feedback
Other	2.4%	Response did not fit any categories	Something hindering, but not sure what; vague response; response did not fit categories

Table 40 Supervisor Supervision Helpful and Hindering Thoughts and Feelings Category Systems: Self

Helpful Thoughts/Feelings	% of Responses	Hindering Thoughts/Feelings	% of Responses
Positive About Trainee/ Relationship	36.0%	Concerns About Supervisory Interventions	37.5%
Positive About Self/Work	21.0%	None	11.5%
What to Do	13.2%	Concerns About Trainee/ Relationship	9.4%
Validation/Empathy/ Understanding	11.4%	Frustrated/Disappointed	8.3%
Concerned About Trainee/Work	11.4%	Validation/Support/ Understanding	8.3%
Frustrated/Disappointed	2.6%	Nervous/Anxious	6.2%
Other	2.6%	Other	3.1%
Relieved/Relaxed	0.9%	Tape Issues	5.2%
None	0.9%	Positive About Supervision Work	4.2%
		Positive About Trainee/ Trainee's work	3.1%

Table 41 Supervisor Supervision Helpful and Hindering Thoughts and Feelings Category Systems: Trainee

Helpful Thoughts/Feelings	% of Responses	Hindering Thoughts/Feelings	% of Responses
Concerns About Self/Work	17.7%	Disappointed/Concerned About Supervision/ Relationship	37.6%
Support/Reassurance/ Validation	14.5%	Discouraged/Concerned with Self/Work	21.8%
Positive About Supervision/Relationship	13.7%	None	14.8%
Relieved/Relaxed	12.1%	Other	11.9%
Positive About Self/Work	9.7%	Positive About Supervision/Relationship	5.0%
Frustrated/Disappointed	7.2%	Relieved	5.0%
Preparation/Goals for Client Work	6.4%	Nervous/Anxious	4.0%
Nervous/Anxious	5.6%		
Insight	4.8%		
Concerns About Supervisor/ Relationship	3.2%		
Other	3.2%		
None	1.6%		

Table 42 Trainee Identified Self Regrets During Supervision

Category Content	% Hits	Definition	Example
Be More Prepared & Motivated	34.5%	Be more prepared for or motivated to engage in work during session	Have tapes prepared to play at desired section, review client notes prior to trigger memory, be more engaged in work of supervision rather than passive or avoidant
Manage Session Better	20.2%	Manage session content and flow differently or more efficiently	Bring up important topics at beginning rather than end of session, prioritize topics so time isn't wasted
Seek Feedback & Instruction	8.3%	Ask for feedback, strategies, or perceptions on the treatment process	Ask for feedback on trainee skills or progress, seek (more) suggestions on types of interventions to use, solicit help in understanding process of treatment (i.e., termination issues, process of change)
Be More Direct & Honest	5.9%	Be more direct, concise, open, or honest in disclosures	Be more focused or concise in sharing views or conceptualizations, be more direct in expressing needs, be more open or honest with disclosures
Be on Time	4.7%	Be on time to session	Keep better track of time or leave earlier so as not to be late to session
Other	3.5%	Doesn't fit into a category	Could have done some things differently but nothing specific identified, give supervisor positive feedback
None	22.6%		No regrets for session; would do nothing differently, can't think of anything to change

Table 43 Trainee Identified Regrets of Supervisor During Supervision

Category Content	% Hits	Definition	Example
Give Feedback & Instruction	15.5%	Provide more feedback, strategies, or perceptions on treatment process	Provide feedback on trainee skills, give suggestions on types of interventions to use, provide more help in understanding process of treatment
Attend More to Trainee & Working Alliance	11.9%	Be more attentive to trainee needs and supervision interpersonal dynamics	Focus on trainee personal and professional development issues that affect work, be more supportive, be more interpersonally open/warm/self-disclosing
Manage Session Better	10.7%	Manage session content and flow differently or more efficiently	Not spend all time on one topic or client, use time efficiently so as to cover more topics
Be Empowering	4.7%	Allow trainee to direct or generate session flow and content	Let trainee bring up clients or topics she/he wants to discuss, not interrupt and change direction of discussion, talk less
Other	4.7%	Doesn't fit into a category	Supervisor could have done some things differently but nothing specific identified, shared food with trainee
More Prepared	2.4%	Be more prepared for supervision session	Listen to tape prior as expected, bring promised literature
None	50.0%		No regrets for session; would not have supervisor do anything differently, couldn't think of anything to change

Table 44 Supervisor Regrets About Self in Supervision

Category Content	% Hits	Definition	Example
Technical Aspects of Session	21.45%	Better attention to issues such as taping and time.	Listen to more of the tape. Would have preferred not have taken that 15 minute phone call in the middle of the session. Look at my watch to budget time better.
Focus More on Trainee	19.4%	Attend to trainee's needs more.	Because [trainee] is still a rookie, I'm not ready to jettison the client reviews yet. Talk more about what the trainee needed to talk about.
Attend to Supervisory Alliance	16.3%	Attend to the goals and tasks of supervision.	Checked in with the trainee about what he would have wanted to do. Ask [trainee] about her hopes in terms of what she wants to learn. Make sure [trainee] got a chance to define what his goals were.
Focus More on Client or Psychotherapy Work	13.3%	Selectively attend to a client that would have lead to enhanced trainee learning.	Budget time better to focus on each client for 15 minutes. Spent a whole session on a client who hasn't shown up in three weeks rather than spending time with clients that need attention. Spent more time on the client that was more emotionally charged.

(continued)

Table 44 (continued) Supervisor Regrets About Self in Supervision

Category Content	% Hits	Definition	Example
Prepare for Supervision Session	11.2%	Better preparation.	Spent time before the supervision session and organized thoughts. Brought materials about client issues for the trainee.
No Regrets	11.2%	No regrets for session.	I don't think anything. I think it went pretty smoothly. I wouldn't do anything over, differently. That doesn't mean I had a perfect session, but I think [I would] allow the process to unfold like it did.
Attend to Supervisor Needs	7.1%	Been more focused on self in relation to the supervisory work.	I would have talked less, but I always say that! I would have had a cup of coffee before I came in so I could wake up. I would have taken notes during the session to help me keep track of what she was saying.

Table 45 Supervisor Regrets About Trainee in Supervision

Category Content	% Hits	Definition	Example
No Regrets	41.4%	No regrets about trainee's work in supervision.	…I just think [trainee] is doing a great job. For a guy at his level…I wouldn't change a hair on his head. Nothing. [Trainee] came prepared and had her tape ready to go. Had the questions she wanted to ask.
Tape Issues or Tape Preparation	20.7%	Preferred to have trainee be more prepared in relation to tapes.	I think if [trainee] had brought a tape, I think that would've just worked out better…we could've talked about what happened this past week. [Trainee] didn't cue the tape to really where he wanted me to hear…so I think he kind of deliberately or subconsciously didn't cue the tape to where he really wanted me to hear.
Trainee Express Feelings More	10.3%	Wished trainee had explored her or his feelings further.	[Trainee] probably could have talked a little bit more about the emotional impact that the last session had on him. It might be helpful for her to kind of go more into how she feels about not having this client show up.
Trainee Disclose More About Self	10.3%	Wished trainee had disclosed more.	Maybe talk a little bit more about [trainee's] own experience with grief and how that might impact her in the session with this new client. I want [trainee] to be able to talk about himself as much as he talks about his clients.

(continued)

Table 45 (continued) Supervisor Regrets About Trainee in Supervision

Category Content	% Hits	Definition	Example
Trainee Prepare More/Bring Questions	9.2%	Wished trainee had been prepared more.	I guess if [trainee] had more questions, to bring those in...I didn't feel like she had a lot to talk about today. I wish [trainee] would have been able to relate some questions about having a good client as opposed to seeing it as, "Oh, I understood [the client]," "I feel pretty confident about therapy," or "This is the way it is supposed to be."
Trainee Take More Control of Session/Lead Session	8.0%	Wish trainee had exhibited more empowerment in supervision.	I wish [trainee] had said, "Oh, I can handle this, it's okay, we don't have to talk about this; let's go and just talk about this." Maybe [trainee] could have led with what some of his needs were.

Table 46 Supervisor Negative Countertransference: Interfering Thoughts and Feelings

Content	% of Responses	Definition	Example
None	33.3%	Supervisor reported not having any interfering thoughts/feelings	Supervisor answers "none" to the question
External Events	23.8%	Distracted thoughts while attending to something outside the supervision process	Feeling tired, sick, hungry, cold; distracted by personal issues; distracted by the audio/videotape
Supervision Process/ Relationship	21.4%	Felt unsure, confused, or second-guessing interventions; feeling guilt for lack of investment	Supervisor felt guilty for having to miss a supervision session; hadn't listened to all the tapes; didn't know if the supervisory intervention was the best thing to do
View of Trainee's Counseling Behavior	8.3%	Supervisor disagreed with, felt frustrated by, or bothered by trainee's counseling work	Recognized trainee was projecting, resisting, judging, or acting on own countertransference
View of Trainee's Supervision Behavior	6.0%	Supervisor felt frustrated, curious about, or bothered by the trainee's behavior with the supervisor in session	Trainee came to supervision late; didn't appear motivated
Other	7.1%	Responses did not fit the established categories	Vague answers; uninterpretable answers; did not fit categories

Table 47 Supervisor Negative Countertransference: Interfering Behaviors

Content	% of Responses	Definition	Example
None	36.9%	Supervisor reported not having any interfering behaviors	Supervisor answered "none" to the question, or did not identify any interfering thoughts/feelings
More Authoritative	28.6%	Adopted a more directive and concrete style	Focused the trainee on a specific content area; felt pushier, rushed the session; talked more
Less Engaged	13.1%	Withdrew mentally or emotionally	Became unfocused; felt distanced; closed off; shut down
Less Authoritative	10.7%	Less didactic; less structure in style	Probed less; withheld evaluative feedback; let the trainee lead the session; less prescriptive
Other	10.7%	Responses did not fit the established categories	Vague answers; uninterpretable answers; did not fit categories

Table 48 Supervisor Positive Countertransference: Facilitative Thoughts and Feelings

Content	% of Responses	Definition	Example
Identified/ Empathized With Trainee	39.3%	Supervisor remembered experiences as a beginning trainee	Identified with trainee's experience of being new, young, nervous; empathized with trainee's struggles
Conceptualized Client/Trainee	16.7%	Supervisor noted facilitative feelings were generated from her/his conceptualization of the client or trainee	Supervisor had done reading that week about the client's disorder; the supervisor had experience working with manic depressive clients; the supervisor was very familiar with termination issues
View of Trainee's Counseling Behavior	15.5%	Became pleased with or encouraged by the trainee's work in therapy	The trainee was very good with reappraisals; the trainee is very calm in session; the trainee is very patient
View of Trainee's Supervision Behavior	10.7%	Became pleased with or encouraged by the trainee's behavior in supervision	The trainee gave the supervisor positive feedback on their supervision work together
Process Relationship	10.7%	Connection with supervision relationship; overall contentment with supervision experience	Feeling happy for growth of trainee, satisfied with trainee's general professional development
None	2.4%	Supervisor reported not having any facilitative thoughts/feelings	Supervisor answered "none" to the question
Other	4.8%	Responses did not fit the established categories	Vague answers; uninterpretable answers; did not fit categories

Table 49 Supervisor Positive Countertransference: Facilitative Behaviors

Content	% of Responses	Definition	Example
Rapport Building	31.0%	Became engaged, fun, comfortable, or sealed a collaborative connection	Supervisor called the interaction a "collaborative give and take process"; "natural flow"; build rapport
Supportive	27.4%	Provided supportive and gentle interventions with the intent to normalize an experience or communicate understanding	Told trainee not to feel worried; told trainee that supervision would be gentle
More Authoritative	27.4%	Adopted a more directive and concrete role; didactic and structured	Focused the trainee on a specific content issue; gave direct feedback; gave client realistic examples of goals
Less Authoritative	7.1%	Adopted a less didactic and less structured role	Allowed the trainee to lead the session; engaged in less probing; gave less critical feedback
None	4.8%	Supervisor did not report any facilitative behaviors	Reportedly, thoughts/ feelings did not affect behaviors; supervisor did not report facilitative thoughts/feelings
Other	2.4%	Responses did not fit the established categories	Vague answers; uninterpretable answers; did not fit categories

Table 50 Trainee (Lydia), Client, and Supervisor Characteristics

Participant	Sex	Age	Race	Ethnicity	Sexual Orientation	Highest Educational Degree Earned	Occupation	Socio-economic Class	Previous Therapy
Lydia	F	Early 20's	White	Eastern European	Heterosexual	B.S. Psychology	Graduate Student	Upper Class	Yes
Kendra	F	Early 60's	White	Eastern European	Heterosexual	2 Year Associate's	Retired	Middle Class	Yes
Ruby	F	Late 60's	White	Not Indicated	Heterosexual	Master's in Business	Retired Teacher	Middle Class	Yes
Bill	M	Early 70's	White	Mixture	Heterosexual	Ph.D.	Retired	Middle Class	Yes
Debi	F	Early 40's	White	Western European Mixed	Heterosexual	High School	Clerk	Working Class	Yes
Tricia	F	Late 40's	White	Western European Mixed	Heterosexual	M.A.	Psychologist	Not Answered	Yes
Julia	F	Early 40's	White	Not Answered	Heterosexual	Ph.D.	Psychologist	Middle Class	Yes

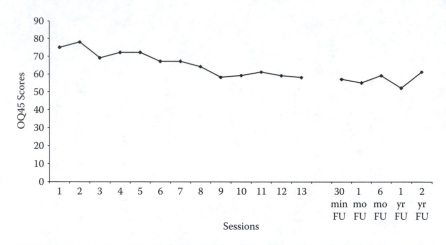

Figure A.1   Client OD – Trainee I OQ-45 Data Chart. Higher scores indicate greater client distress.

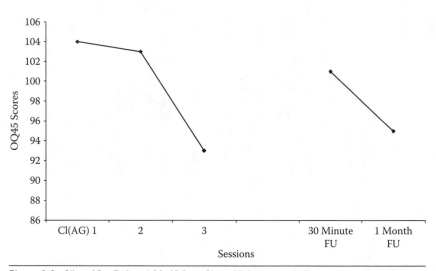

Figure A.2   Client AG – Trainee I OQ-45 Data Chart. Higher scores indicate greater client distress.

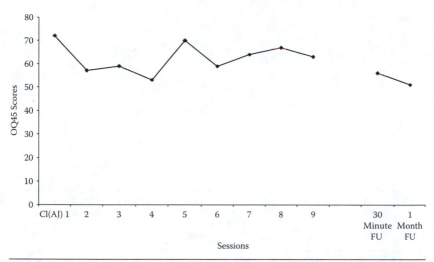

Figure A.3 Client AJ – Trainee I OQ-45 Data Chart. Higher scores indicate greater client distress.

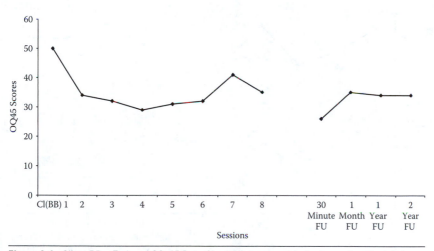

Figure A.4 Client BB – Trainee I OQ-45 Data Chart. Higher scores indicate greater client distress.

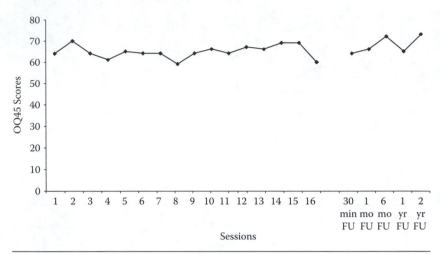

Figure A.5 Client OC – Trainee II OQ-45 Data Chart. Higher scores indicate greater client distress.

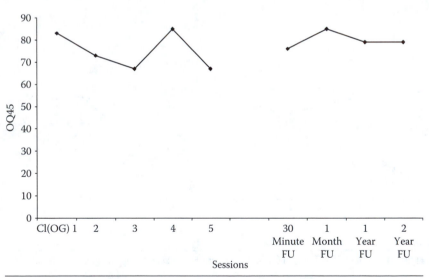

Figure A.6 Client OG – Trainee II OQ-45 Data Chart. Higher scores indicate greater client distress.

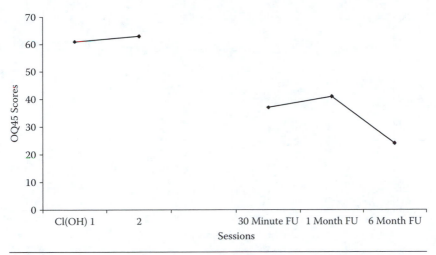

Figure A.7 Client OH – Trainee II OQ-45 Data Chart. Higher scores indicate greater client distress.

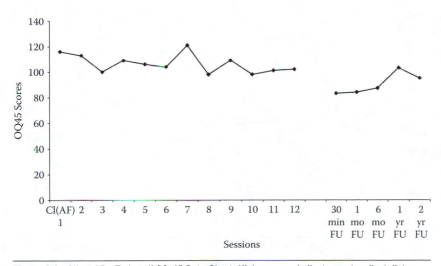

Figure A.8 Client AF – Trainee II OQ-45 Data Chart. Higher scores indicate greater client distress.

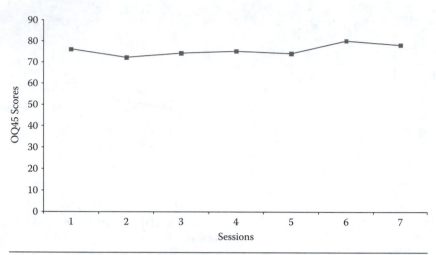

Figure A.9 Client CO – Trainee II OQ-45 Data Chart. Higher scores indicate greater client distress.

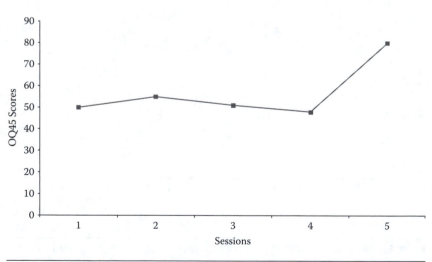

Figure A.10 Client OJ – Trainee III OQ-45 Data Chart. Higher scores indicate greater client distress.

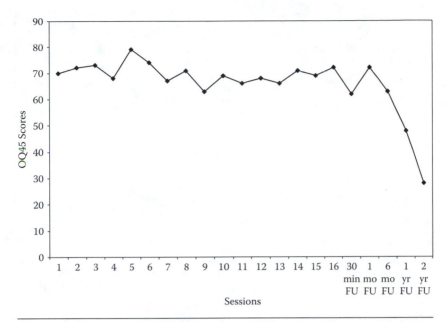

Figure A.11 Client AH – Trainee III OQ-45 Data Chart. Higher scores indicate greater client distress.

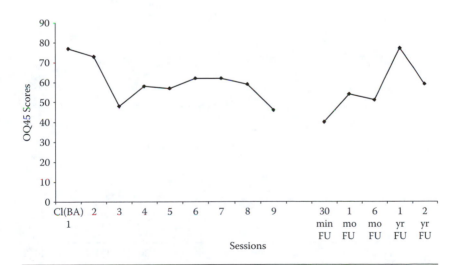

Figure A.12 Client BA – Trainee III OQ-45 Data Chart. Higher scores indicate greater client distress.

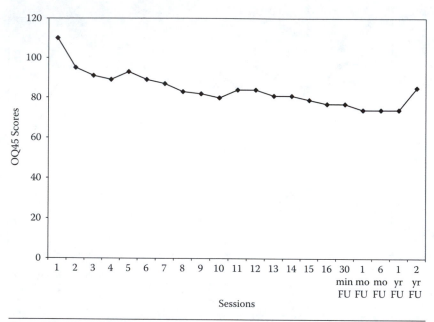

Figure A.13 Client BC – Trainee III OQ-45 Data Chart. Higher scores indicate greater client distress.

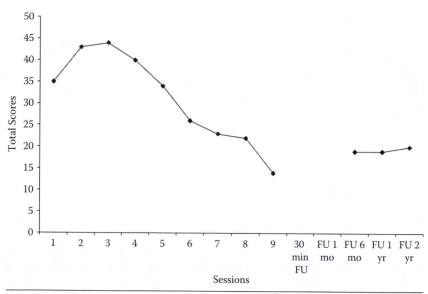

Figure A.14 Client OB – Trainee IV OQ-45 Data Chart. Higher scores indicate greater client distress.

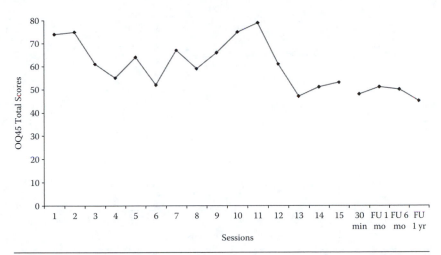

Figure A.15 Client AO – Trainee IV OQ-45 Data Chart. Higher scores indicate greater client distress.

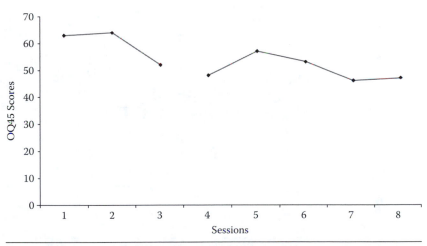

Figure A.16 Client AA – Trainee IV OQ-45 Data Chart. Higher scores indicate greater client distress.

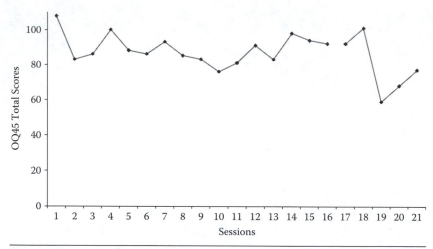

Figure A.17   Client BJ – Trainee IV OQ-45 Data Chart. Higher scores indicate greater client distress.

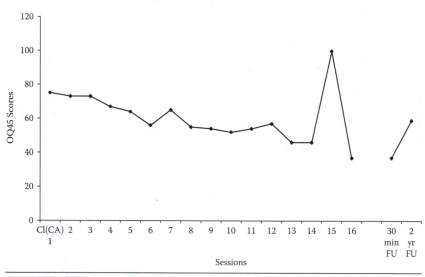

Figure A.18   Client CA – Trainee IV OQ-45 Data Chart. Higher scores indicate greater client distress.

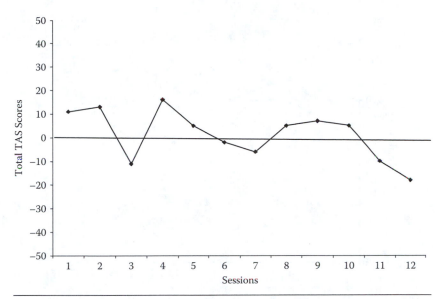

Figure A.19 Change in Anxiety for Lydia in Therapy with Kendra. TAS refers to the Trainee Anxiety Scale. Scores indicate a change in anxiety from pre-session to post-session. Positive scores indicate a decrease in anxiety from pre-session to post-session assessments.

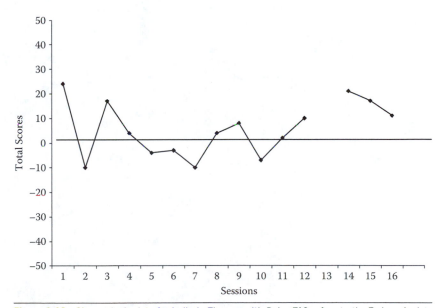

Figure A.20 Change in Anxiety for Lydia in Therapy with Ruby. TAS refers to the Trainee Anxiety Scale. Scores indicate a change in anxiety from pre-session to post-session. Positive scores indicate a decrease in anxiety from pre-session to post-session assessments.

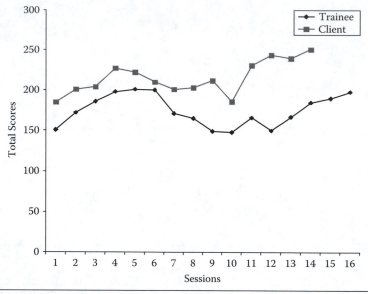

Figure A.21 Working Alliance in Therapy between Lydia and Ruby. Higher scores indicate perceptions of a stronger working alliance.

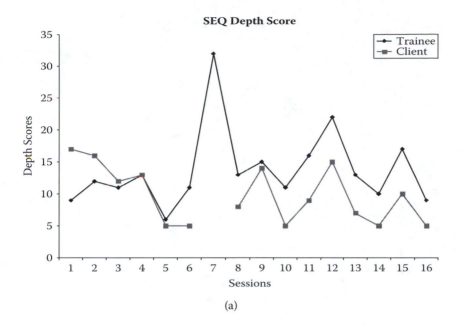

(a)

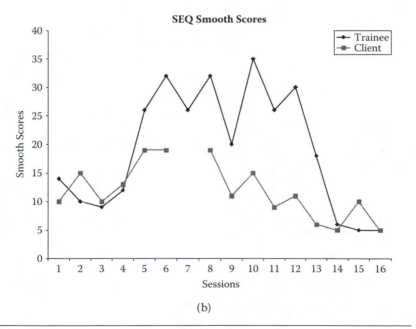

(b)

Figure A.22 Session Impact in Therapy between Lydia and Ruby. Higher scores indicate greater impact on given variable.

SEQ Positivity Scores

(c)

SEQ Arousal Scores

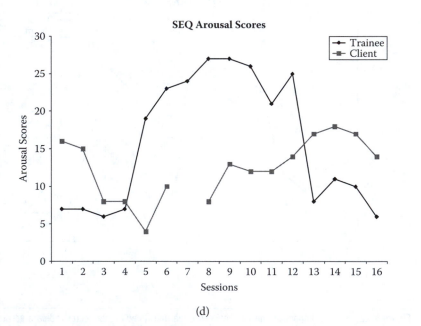

(d)

Figure A.22 (continued)

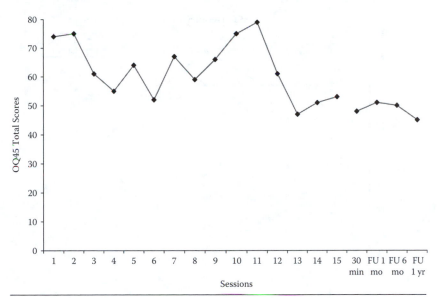

Figure A.23 Presession Level of Client Distress for Ruby. Higher scores indicate greater client distress.

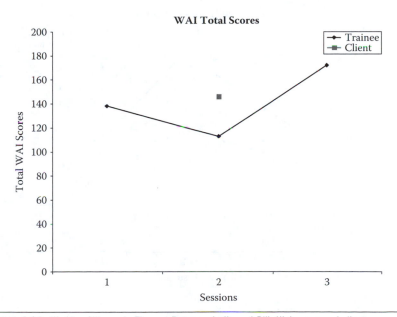

Figure A.24 Working Alliance in Therapy Between Lydia and Bill. Higher scores indicate perceptions of a stronger working alliance.

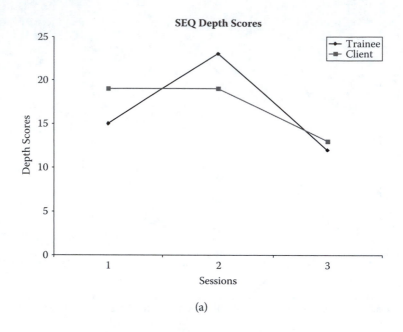

(a)

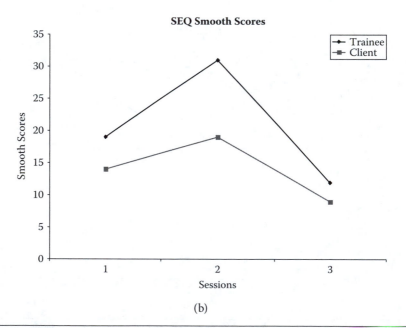

(b)

Figure A.25 Session Impact in Therapy Between Lydia and Bill. Higher scores indicate greater impact on given variable.

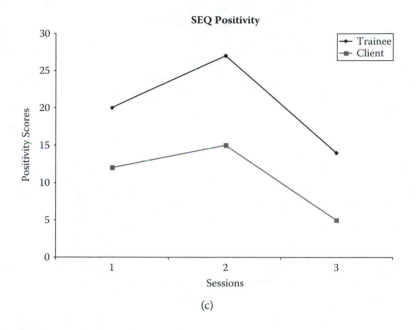

(c)

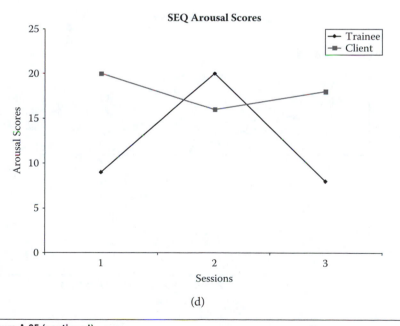

(d)

Figure A.25 (continued)

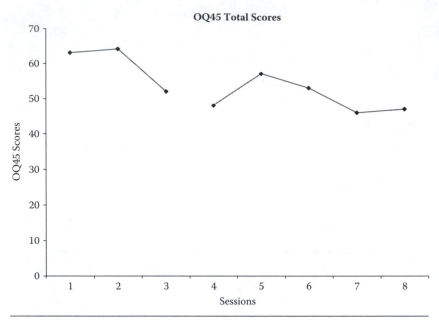

Figure A.26 Presession Level of Client Distress for Bill. Higher scores indicate greater client distress.

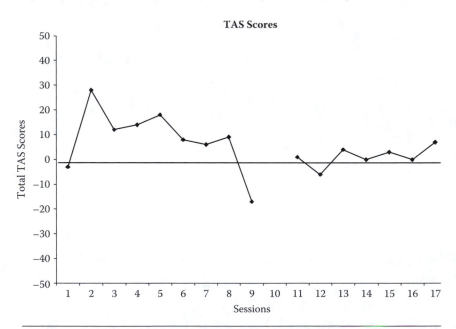

Figure A.27 Change in Anxiety for Lydia in Therapy with Debi. TAS refers to the Trainee Anxiety Scale. Scores indicate a change in anxiety from pre-session to post-session. Positive scores indicate a decrease in anxiety from pre-session to post-session assessments.

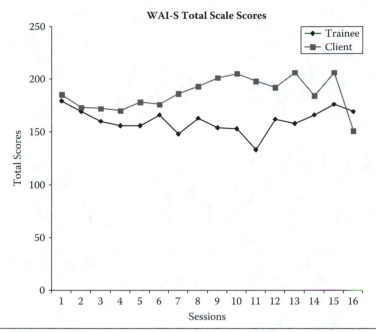

Figure A.28 Working Alliance in Therapy between Lydia and Debi. Higher scores indicate perceptions of a stronger working alliance.

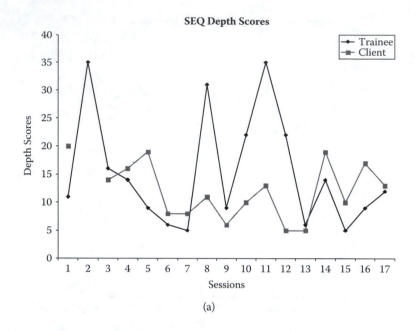

(a)

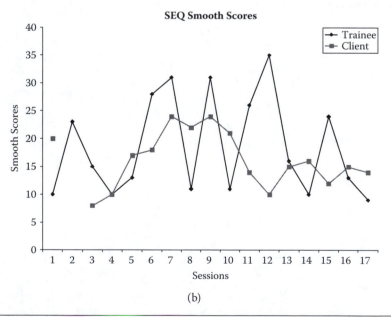

(b)

Figure A.29 Session Impact in Therapy between Lydia and Debi. Higher scores indicate greater impact on given variable.

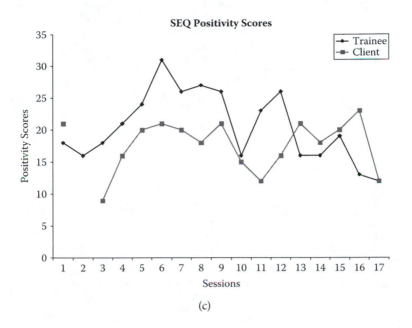

(c)

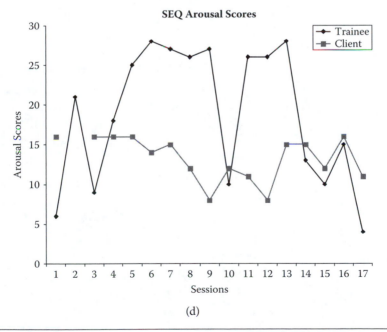

(d)

Figure A.29 (continued)

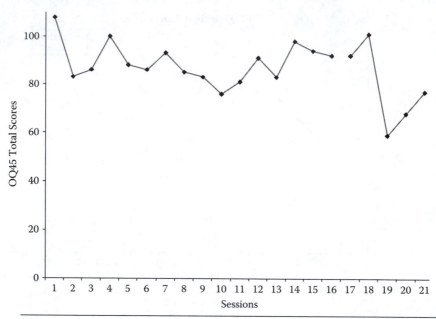

Figure A.30 Pre-Session Level of Client Distress for Debi. Higher scores indicate greater client distress.

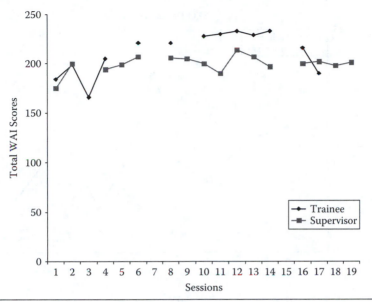

Figure A.31 Working Alliance in Supervision Between Lydia and Tricia. Higher scores indicate perceptions of a stronger working alliance.

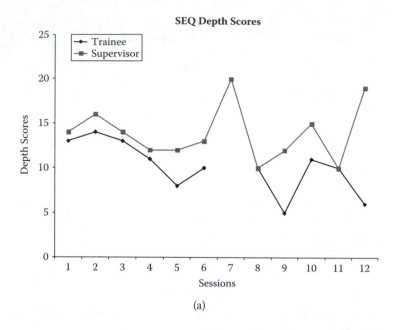

(a)

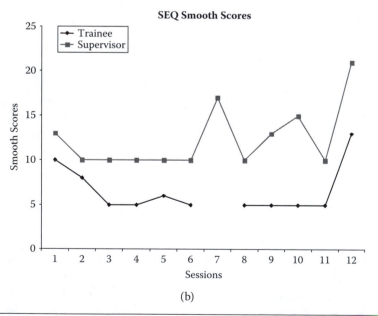

(b)

Figure A.32 Session Impact in Supervision Between Lydia and Tricia. Higher scores indicate greater impact on given variable.

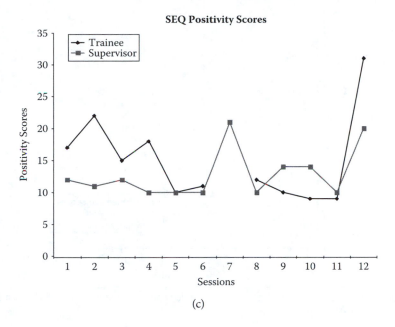

(c)

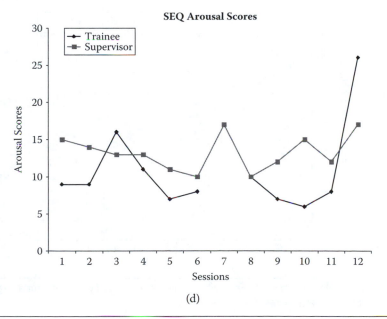

(d)

Figure A.32 (continued)

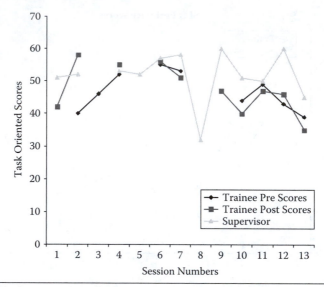

Figure A.33 Supervisor Style (Task Oriented) as Perceived by Lydia and Tricia. Higher scores indicate a greater task-oriented style.

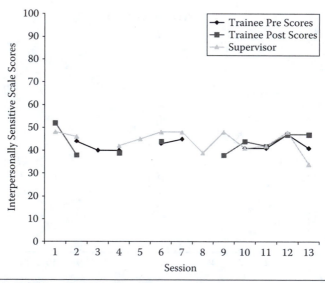

Figure A.34 Supervisor Style (Interpersonally Sensitive) as Perceived by Lydia and Tricia. Higher scores indicate a greater interpersonally sensitive style.

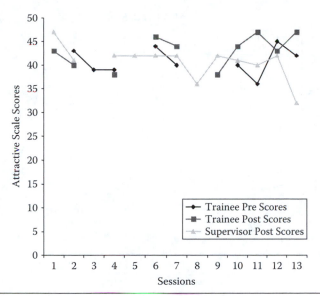

Figure A.35 Supervisor Style (Attractive) as Perceived by Lydia and Tricia. Higher scores indicate a greater attractive style.

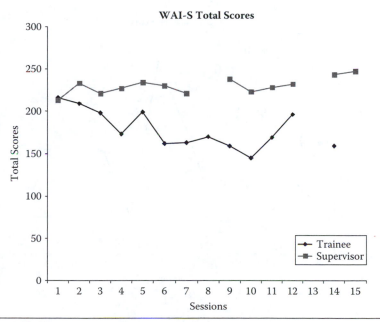

Figure A.36 Working Alliance in Supervision Between Lydia and Julia. Higher scores indicate perceptions of a stronger working alliance.

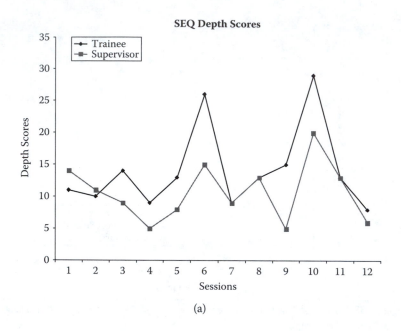

(a)

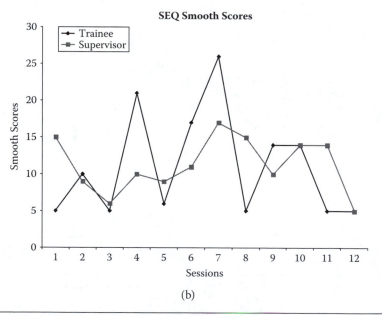

(b)

Figure A.37 Session Impact in Supervision Between Lydia and Julia. Higher scores indicate greater impact on given variable.

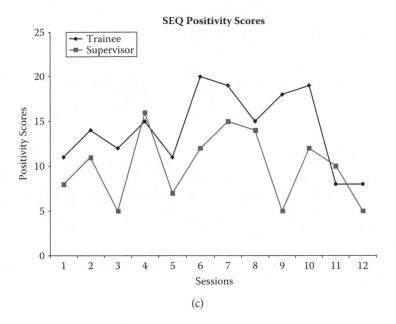

(c)

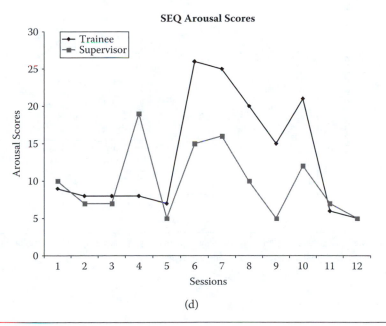

(d)

Figure A.37 (continued)

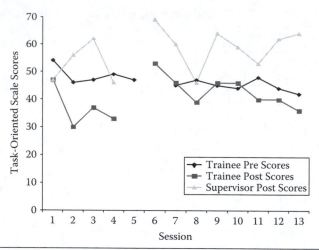

Figure A.38 Supervisor Style (Task-Oriented) as Perceived by Lydia and Julia. Higher scores indicate a greater task-oriented style.

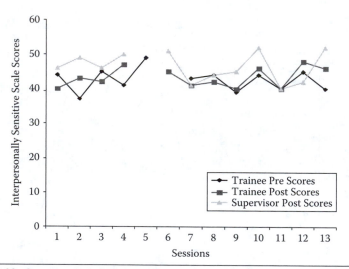

Figure A.39 Supervisor Style (Interpersonally Sensitive) as Perceived by Lydia and Julia. Higher scores indicate a greater interpersonally sensitive style.

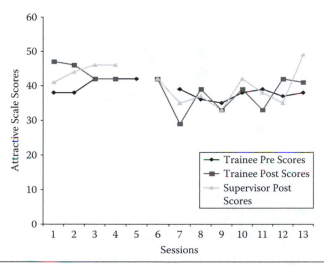

Figure A.40 Supervisor Style (Attractive) as Perceived by Lydia and Julia. Higher scores indicate a greater attractive style.

References

Ackerman, N. W. (1953). Selected problems in supervised analysis. *Psychiatry, 16,* 283–290.

Adams, D., & Carwardine, M. (1990). *Last chance to see.* New York: Ballantine Books.

Allen, G. J., Szollos, S. J., & Williams, B. E. (1986). Doctoral students' comparative evaluations of best and worst psychotherapy supervision. *Professional Psychology: Research and Practice, 17, 91–99.*

American Association of Suicidology. (2001). Warning signs. *Monitor On Psychology, 32.*

American Psychiatric Association. (2000). *Diagnostic and statistical manual of mental disorders: Text revision* (4th ed.). Washington, DC: American Psychiatric Association.

Anastasopoulos, D., & Tsiantis, J. (1999). Supervision of individual psychoanalytic psychotherapy in institutions, the setting, the dynamics and the learning process. *Psychoanalytic Psychotherapy, 13,* 167–183.

Ancis, J. R., & Ladany, N. (2001). A multicultural framework for counselor supervision. In L. J. Bradley & N. Ladany (Eds.), *Counselor supervision: Principles, process, and practice* (3rd ed., pp. 63–90). Philadelphia, PA: Brunner-Routledge.

Baker, E. (2003). *Caring for ourselves: A therapist's guide to personal and professional well-being.* Washington, DC: American Psychological Association.

Bandura, A. (1977). *Social learning theory.* Oxford, UK: Prentice Hall.

Bandura, A. (1982). The assessment and predictive generality of self-percepts of efficacy. *Journal of Behavior Therapy and Experimental Psychiatry, 13,* 195–199.

Bandura, A. (2000). Self-efficacy. In A. E. Kazdin (Ed.). *Encyclopedia of psychology* (Vol. 7; pp. 212–213). New York: Oxford University Press.

Banks, S. H. (2007). Curiosity and Narcissism as Predictors of Empathic Ability. *Dissertation Abstracts International.*

Banks, S. H., & Ladany, N. (2002, June). *Communication in the supervisory relationship: A longitudinal study of supervisor and trainee nondisclosure.* Poster accepted to be presented at the meeting of the Society for Psychotherapy Research, Santa Barbara, CA.

Benedek, T. (1954). Countertransference in the training analyst. *Bulletin of the Menninger Clinic, 18,* 12–16.

Berman, E. (2000). Psychoanalytic supervision: The intersubjective development. *International Journal of Psychoanalysis, 81, 273–289.*

Bernard, J. M. (1979). Supervisory training: A discrimination model. *Counselor Education and Supervision, 19,* 60–68.

Bernard, J. M., & Goodyear, R. K. (2004). *Fundamentals of clinical supervision* (3rd ed.). Needham Heights, MA: Allyn & Bacon.

Borders, L. D. (1991). A systematic approach to peer group supervision. *Journal of Counseling & Development, 69,* 248–252.

Bordin, E. S. (1979). The generalizability of the psychoanalytic concept of the working alliance. *Psychotherapy: Theory, Research & Practice, 16,* 252–260.

Bordin, E. S. (1983). A working alliance based model of supervision. *Counseling Psychologist, 11,* 35–41.

Bordin, E. S. (1994). Theory and research on the therapeutic working alliance: New directions. In A. O. Horvath & L. S. Greenberg (Eds.), *The working alliance: Theory, research and practice* (pp. 12–37). Oxford, UK: John Wiley & Sons.

Brown, L. S. (1992). *Personality and psychopathology: Feminist reappraisals.* New York: Guilford.

Brown, L. S. (2001). Feelings in context: Countertransference and the real world in feminist therapy. *Journal of Clinical Psychology, 57,* 1005–1012.

Chemtob, C. M., Hamada, R. S., Bauer, G. B., Torigoe, R. Y., & Kinney, B. (1988). Patient suicides: Frequency and impact on psychologists. *Professional Psychology: Research and Practice, 19,* 421–425.

Chen, E. C., & Bernstein, B. L. (2000). Relations of complementarity ad supervisory issues to supervisory working alliance: A comparative analysis of two cases. *Journal of Counseling Psychology, 47,* 485–497.

Chung, Y. B., Baskin, M. L., & Chase, A. B. (1998). Positive and negative supervisory experiences reported by counseling trainees. *Psychological Reports, 82,* 762.

Cohen, M. (1952). Counter-transference and anxiety. *Journal of Psychiatry, 15,* 231–243.

Constantine, M. G., & Ladany, N. (2001). New visions for defining and assessing multicultural competence. In J. G. Ponterotto, J. M. Casas, L. A. Suzuki, & C. M. Alexander (Eds.), *Handbook of multicultural counseling* (pp. 491–492). Thousand Oaks, CA: Sage.

Cook, D. A. (1994). Racial identity in supervision. *Counselor Education and Supervision, 34,* 132–141.

Cosgrove, L., & Riddle, B. (2004). Gender bias and sex distribution of mental disorders in the *DSM-IV-TR.* In P.J. Caplan & L. Cosgrove (Eds.), *Bias in psychiatric diagnosis* (pp. 127–140). Lanham, MD: Jason Aronson.

Crall, J., & Ladany, N. (in preparation). Interpersonal response modes in supervision.

Cutler, R. L. (1958). Countertransference effects in psychotherapy. *Journal of Consulting Psychology, 22,* 349–356.

Davison, G.C. (2005). Issues and nonissues in the gay-affirmative treatment of patients who are gay, lesbian, or bisexual. *Clinical Psychology: Science and Practice, 12,* 25–28.

Doehrman, M. J. (1976). Parallel processes in supervision and psychotherapy. *Bulletin of the Menninger Clinic, 40,* 3–104.

Dollard, J., & Miller, N. E. (1950). *Personality and psychotherapy: An analysis in terms of learning, thinking, and culture.* New York: McGraw-Hill.

Downing, N. E., & Roush, K. L. (1985). From passive acceptance to active commitment: A model of feminist identity development for women. *Counseling Psychologist Special Issue: Cross-Cultural Counseling, 13,* 695–709.

Duckworth, D. H. (1985). Is the "organizational stress" construct a red herring? A reply to Glowinkowski and Cooper. *Bulletin of the British Psychological Society, 38,* 401–404.

Ehrlich, F. M. (2001). Levels of self-awareness: Countertransference in psychoanalysis, couple, and family therapy. *Contemporary Psychoanalysis, 37,* 283–296.

Ekstein, R., & Wallerstein, R. S. (1958). *The teaching and learning of psychotherapy.* New York: Basic.

Ekstein, R., & Wallerstein, R. S. (1972). *The teaching and learning of psychotherapy* (rev. ed.). Oxford, UK: International Universities Press.

Elliot, R., Barker, C. B., Caskey, N., & Pistrang, N. (1982). Differential helpfulness of counselor verbal response modes. *Journal of Counseling Psychology, 29,* 354–361.

Elliot, R., & Shapiro, D. A. (1992). Client and therapist as analysts of significant events. In T. G. Shaké & D. L. Rennie (Eds.), *Psychotherapy process research: Paradigmatic and narrative approaches* (pp.163–186). Thousand Oaks, CA: Sage.

Ellis, A. (2001). Rational and irrational aspects of countertransference. *Journal of Clinical Psychology, 57,* 999–1004.

Ellis, M. V. (1991). Critical incidents in clinical supervision and in supervisor supervision: Assessing supervisory issues. *Journal of Counseling Psychology, 38,* 342–349.

Ellis, M. V., & Douce, L. A. (1994). Group supervision of novice clinical supervisors: Eight recurring issues. *Journal of Counseling & Development, 72,* 520–525.

Ellis, M. V., & Ladany, N. (1997). Inferences concerning supervisees and clients in clinical supervision: An integrative review. In C. E. Watkins (Ed.), *Handbook of psychotherapy supervision* (pp. 447–507). Hoboken, NJ: John Wiley & Sons.

Falender, C. A., & Shafranske, E. P. (2004). *Clinical supervision: A competency-based approach.* Washington, DC: American Psychological Association.

Fauth, J., & Williams, E. N. (2005). The in-session self-awareness of therapist-trainees: Hindering or helpful? *Journal of Counseling Psychology, 52,* 443–447.

Figley, C. R. (Ed.). (2002). *Brief treatments for the traumatized: A project of the Green Cross Foundation.* Westport, CT: Greenwood.

Finer, L. B., & Henshaw, S. K. (2003). Abortion incidences and services in the United States in 2000. *Perspectives on Sexual and Reproductive Health, 35,* 6–15.

Fitzpatrick, M. R., Stalikas, A., & Iwakabe, S. (2001). Examining counselor interventions and client progress in the context of the therapeutic alliance. *Psychotherapy: Theory, Research, Practice, Training, 38,* 160–170.

Fretz, B. R. (2001). Postural movements in a counseling dyad. In C. E. Hill (Ed.), *Helping skills: The empirical foundation* (pp. 183–194). Washington, DC: American Psychological Association.

Freud, S. (1910). The origin and development of psychoanalysis. *American Journal of Psychology, 21,* 181–218.

Freud, S. (1959). *The future prospects of psychoanalytic therapy* (standard ed., vol. 11). London, UK: Hogarth Press. (Original work published in 1910).

Friedlander M., & Ward, L. (1984). Development and validation of the Supervisory Styles Inventory. *Journal of Counseling Psychology, 31,* 541–557.

Friedlander, S. R., Dye, N. W., Costello, R. M., & Kobos, J. C. (1984). A developmental model for teaching and learning psychotherapy supervision. *Psychotherapy, 21,* 189–196.

Friedman, S. M., & Gelso, C. J. (2000). The development of the inventory of countertransference behavior. *Journal of Clinical Psychology, 56,* 1221–1235.

Frost, R. (1993). *The road not taken and other poems.* Mineola, New York: Dover.

Fukumoto, O. (2001). Experiencing a way of working through the countertransference. *Psychoanalytic Psychotherapy, 15,* 153–167.

Furnham, A. (1994). A content, correlational and factor analytic study of four tolerance of ambiguity questionnaires. *Personality and Individual Differences, 16,* 403–410.

Gabbard, G. O. (2001). A contemporary psychoanalytic model for countertransference. *Journal of Clinical Psychology, 57,* 983–991.

Gabbard, G. O. (2004). *Long-term psychodynamic psychotherapy: A basic text.* Washington, DC: American Psychiatric Publishing.

Gandolfo, R. L., & Brown, R. (1987). Psychology intern ratings of actual and ideal supervision of psychotherapy. *Journal of Training and Practice in Professional Psychology, 1,* 15–28.

Garb, H. (2005). Clinical judgment and decision making. *Annual Review of Clinical Psychology, 1,* 67–89.

Gelso, C. J., Fassinger, R. E., Gomez, M. J., & Latts, M. G. (1995). Countertransference reactions to lesbian clients: The role of homophobia, counselor gender, and countertransference management. *Journal of Counseling Psychology, 42,* 356–364.

Gray, L. A. (2005). Critical incidents in psychotherapy and supervision: A search for parallel processes. *Dissertation Abstracts International: The Sciences and Engineering, 66,* 3B, 1718.

Gray, L. A., Ladany, N., Walker, J. A., & Ancis, J. R. (2001). Psychotherapy trainees' experience of counterproductive events in supervision. *Journal of Counseling Psychology, 48,* 371–383.

Greenberg, L. S. (1986). Change process research. *Journal of Consulting and Clinical Psychology, 54,* 4–9.

Greenson, R. R. (1967). The "Something more" of Psychotherapy. *Journal of Contemporary Psychotherapy, 32,* 35–40.

Greenwald, M., & Young, J. (1998). Scheme-focused therapy: An integrative approach to psychotherapy. *Journal of Cognitive Psychotherapy Special Issue: Supervision, 12,* 109–126.

Hayes, J. A., & Gelso, C. J. (1993). Male counselors' discomfort with gay and HIV-infected clients. *Journal of Counseling Psychology, 40,* 86–93.

Hayes, J. A., & Gelso, C. J. (2001). Clinical implications of research on counter-transference: Science informing practice. *Journal of Clinical Psychology, 57,* 1041–1051.

Hayes, J. A., McCracken, J.E., McClanahan, M. K., Hill, C. E., Harp, J. S., & Caro-zzoni, P. (1998). Therapist perspectives on countertransference: Qualitative data in search of a theory. *Journal of Counseling Psychology, 45,* 468–482.

Helms, J. E. (1992). *A race is a nice thing to have: A guide to being a white person or under-standing the white persons in your life.* Topeka, KS: Content Communications.

Helms, J. E. (1994). Racial identity and career assessment. *Journal of Career Assessment, 2,* 199–209.

Helms, J. E. (1995). An update of Helms's White and people of color racial identity racial identity models. In J. G. Ponterotto, J. M. Casas, L. A. Suzuki, & C. M. Alexander (Eds.), *Handbook of multicultural counseling* (pp. 181–198). Thousand Oaks, CA: Sage.

Helms, J. E., & Cook, D. A. (1999). *Using race and culture in counseling and psy-chotherapy: Theory and process.* Needham Heights, MA: Allyn & Bacon.

Herbert, J. T., Ward, T. J., & Hemlick, L. M. (1995). Confirmatory factor analysis of the supervisory style inventory and the revised supervision question-naire. *Rehabilitation Counseling Journal, 38,* 334–349.

Hill, C. E. (1982). Counseling process research: Philosophical and methodological dilemmas. *Counseling Psychologist, 10,* 7–19.

Hill, C. E. (1986). An overview of the Hill counselor and client verbal response modes category systems. In L. S. Greenberg & W. M. Pinsof (Eds.), *The psy-chotherapeutic process: A research handbook* (pp. 131–159). New York: Guil-ford Press.

Hill, C. E. (1990). Exploratory in-session process research in individual psy-chotherapy: a review. *Journal of Consulting and Clinical Psychology, 58,* 288–294.

Hill, C. E. (Ed). (2001). *Helping skills: The empirical foundation.* Washington, DC: American Psychological Association.

Hill, C. E. (2003). Working with dreams: A road to self-discovery. *The Counseling Psychologist, 31,* 362–372.

Hill C. E. (2004). *Helping skills: Facilitating explorations, insight, and action* (2nd ed.). Washington, DC: American Psychological Association.

Hill, C. E., & Kellems, I. S. (2002). Development and use of the Helping Skills Measure to assess client perceptions of the effects of training and of helping skills in sessions. *Journal of Counseling Psychology, 49,* 264–272.

Hill, C. E., Nutt-Williams, E., Heaton, K. J., Thompson, B. J., & Rhodes, R. H. (1996). Therapist retrospective recall of impasses in long-term psycho-therapy: A qualitative analysis. *Journal of Counseling Psychology, 43,* 207–217.

Hill, C. E., & O'Brien, K. (1999). *Helping skills: Facilitating explorations, insight, and action.* Washington, DC: American Psychological Association.

Hill, C. E., Thompson, B. J., Cogar, M. C., & Denman, D. W. (1993). Beneath the surface of long-term therapy: Therapist and client report of their own and each other's covert processes. *Journal of Counseling Psychology, 40,* 278–287.

Hill, C. E., Thompson, B. J., & Ladany, N. (2003). Therapist use of silence in therapy.*Journal of Clinical Psychology, 59,* 513–524.

Hill, C. E., Thompson, M. J., & Williams, E. N. (1997). A guide to conducting consensual qualitative research. *The Counseling Psychologist, 25,* 517–572.

Hogan, R. A. (1964). Issues and approaches in supervision. *Psychotherapy: Theory, Research & Practice, 1,* 139–141.

Holloway, E. L. (1995). *Clinical supervision: A systems approach.* Thousand Oaks, CA: Sage.

Horvath, A. O. (2006). The Alliance in context: Accomplishments, challenges, and future directions. *Psychotherapy: Theory, Research, Practice, Training, 43,* 258–263.

Horvath, A. O., & Greenberg, L. S. (Eds.). (1994). *The working alliance: Theory, research, and practice.* Oxford, UK: John Wiley & Sons.

Horvath, A. O., & Symonds, B. D. (1991). Relation between working alliance and outcome in psychotherapy: A meta-analysis. *Journal of Counseling Psychology, 38,* 139–149.

Hutt, C. H., Scott, J., & King, M. (1983). A phenomenological study of supervisees' positive and negative experiences in supervision. *Psychotherapy: Theory, Research and Practice, 20,* 118–123.

Issacharoff, A. (1984). Countertransference in supervision: Therapeutic consequences for the supervisee. In L. Caligor, P. Bromberg, & J. Meltzer (Eds.), *Clinical perspectives in the supervision of psychoanalysis and psychotherapy* (pp. 89–105). New York: Plenum.

Ivey, A. E. (1971). *Microcounseling: Innovations in interviewing training.* Oxford, UK: Charles C. Thomas.

Javed, N. (2004). Clinical cases and the intersection of sexism and racism. In P. J. Caplan & L. Cosgrove (Eds.), *Bias in psychiatric diagnosis* (pp. 77–79). Lanham, MD: Jason-Aronson.

Jennings, L., & Skovholt, T. M. (1999). The cognitive, emotional and relational characteristics of master therapists. *Journal of Counseling Psychology, 46,* 3–11.

Jobes, D. A., & Berman, A. L. (1993). Suicide and malpractice liability: Assessing and revising policies, procedures, and practice in outpatient settings. *Professional Psychology: Research and Practice, 24,* 91–99.

Jones, F. A. (2001). Statistical risk factors for suicide. *Monitor On Psychology, 32.*

Kagan, J. (1997). Conceptualizing psychopathology: The importance of development profiles. *Development and Psychopathology, 9,* 321–334.

Kagan, N. (1984). Interpersonal process recall: Basic methods and recent research. In D. Larson (Ed.), *Teaching psychological skills: Models for giving psychology away* (pp. 229–244). Monterey, CA: Brooks/Cole.

Kaslow, F. W. (2001). Whether countertransference in couples and family therapy: A systemic perspective. *Journal of Clinical Psychology, 57,* 1029–1040.

Kennard, B. D., Stewart, S. M., & Gluck, M. R. (1987). The supervision relationship: Variables contributing to positive versus negative experiences. *Professional Psychology: Research and Practice, 18,* 172–175.

Kernberg, O. (1965). Notes on countertransference. *Journal of the American Psychoanalytic Association, 13,* 38–56.

Kiesler, D. J. (2001). Therapist countertransference: In search of common themes and empirical referents. *Journal of Clinical Psychology, 57,* 1053–1063.

Knox, S., Hess, S. A., Williams, N. E., & Hill, C. E. (2003). "Here's a little something for you": How therapists respond to client gifts. *Journal of Counseling Psychology, 50,* 199–210.

Kupers, T.A., Ross, R., Frances, A., & Widiger, T.A. (2004). Issue 2: Is there gender bias in the *DSM-IV?* In Halgin, R.P. (Ed.) *Taking sides: Clashing views on controversial issues in abnormal psychology* (3rd ed., pp. 14–40). New York: McGraw-Hill.

Ladany, N. (1993). The supervisory working alliance: Its relation to trainee self-efficacy and satisfaction with supervision. *Dissertation Abstracts International, 54,* 1B.

Ladany, N., Brittan-Powell, C. S., & Pannu, R. K. (1997). The influence of supervisory racial identity interaction and racial matching on the supervisory working alliance and supervisee multicultural competence. *Counselor Education and Supervision, 36,* 284–304.

Ladany, N., Constantine, M., Miller, K., Erickson, C. D., & Muse-Burke, J. L. (2000). Supervisor countertransference: A qualitative investigation into its identification and description. *Journal of Counseling Psychology, 47,* 102–115.

Ladany, N., Ellis, M. V., & Friedlander, M. L. (1999). The supervisory working alliance, trainee self-efficacy, and satisfaction. *Journal of Counseling & Development, 77,* 447–455.

Ladany, N., Friedlander, M. L., & Nelson, M. L. (2005). *Critical events in psychotherapy supervision: An interpersonal approach.* Washington, DC: American Psychological Association.

Ladany, N., Hill, C. E., Corbett, M. M., & Nutt, E. A. (1996). Nature, extent, and importance of what psychotherapy trainees do not disclose to their supervisors. *Journal of Counseling Psychology, 43,* 10–24.

Ladany, N., & Inman, A. G. (in press). Counselor Training and Supervision. In S. Brown and R. Lent (Eds.). *Handbook of Counseling Psychology* (4th ed.). New York: Wiley.

Ladany, N., Lehrman-Waterman, D., Molinaro, M., & Wolgast, B. (1999). Psychotherapy supervisor ethical practices: Adherence to guidelines, the supervisory working alliance, and supervisee satisfaction. *Counseling Psychologist Special Issue: Advanced quantitative methods in counseling psychology: Part I, 27,* 443–475.

Ladany, N., & Melincoff, D. S. (1999). The nature of counselor supervisor nondisclosure. *Counselor Education and Supervision, 38,* 161–176.

Ladany, N., & Muse-Burke, J. L. (2001). Understanding and conducting supervision research. In L. Bradley and N. Ladany (Eds.), *Counselor Supervision: Principles, Process, & Practice* (3rd ed., pp. 304–329). Philadelphia, PA: Brunner-Routledge.

Ladany, N., Thompson, B. J., Hill, C. E., & O'Brien, K. (2004). Therapist perspectives about using silence in therapy: A qualitative study. *Counselling and Psychotherapy Research, 4,* 80–89.

Ladany, N., & Walker, J.A. (2003). Supervisor self-disclosure: Balancing the uncontrollable narcissist with the indomitable altruist. *In Session: Journal of Clinical Psychology, 59*, 611–621.

Ladany, N., Walker, J. A., & Melincoff, D. S. (2001). Supervisory style: Its relation to the supervisory working alliance and supervisor self-disclosure. *Counselor Education and Supervision, 40*, 263–275.

Lambert, M. J., Hansen, N. B., Umphress, V. J., Lunnen, V., Okiishi, J. C., Burlingame, G. M., & Reisinger, C. W. (1996). *Administration and scoring manual for the OQ-45*. East Setauket, NY: American Professional Credentialing Services.

Lambert, M. J., & Hill, C. E. (1994). Assessing psychotherapy outcomes and processes.In A. E. Bergin & S. L. Garfield (Eds.), *Handbook of psychotherapy and behavior change* (4th ed., pp. 72–113). Oxford, UK: John Wiley & Sons.

Lambert, M. J., & Ogles, B.M. (1997). The effectiveness of psychotherapy supervision. In C. E. Watkins (Ed.), *Handbook of psychotherapy supervision* (pp. 421–446). Hoboken, NJ: John Wiley & Sons.

Lambert, M. J., Okiishi, J. C., Finch, A. E., & Johnson, L. D. (1998). Outcome assessment from conceptualization to implementation. *Professional Psychology: Research and Practice, 29*, 63–70.

Lecours, S., Bouchard, M., & Normandin, L. (1995). Countertransference as the therapist's mental activity: Experience and gender differences among psychoanalytically oriented psychologists. *Psychoanalytic Psychology, 12*, 259–279.

Little, M. (1951). Countertransference and the patient's response to it. *International Journal of Psychoanalysis, 32*, 32–40.

Llewelyn, S. P. (1988). Psychological therapy as viewed by clients and therapists. *British Journal of Clinical Psychology, 27*, 223–237.

Lower, R. B. (1972). Countertransference resistances in the supervisory situation. *American Journal of Psychiatry, 129*, 156–160.

Luborsky, L., Rosenthal, R., Diguer, L., Andrusyna, T. P., Berman, J. S., Levitt, J. T., Seligman, D. A., & Krause, E. D. (2002). The dodo bird verdict is alive and well—mostly. *Clinical Psychology: Science and Practice, 9*, 2–12.

Mahrer, A. R. (1988). Discovery-oriented psychotherapy research. *American Psychologist, 43*, 694–702.

Mahrer, A. R. (2001). An experiential alternative to countertransference. *Journal of Clinical Psychology, 57*, 1021–1028.

Mahrer, A. R., & Nadler, W. P. (1986). Good moments in psychotherapy: A preliminary review, a list, and some promising research avenues. *Journal of Consulting and Clinical Psychology, 54*, 10–15.

Mattas-Curry, L. (2000). Eight factors found critical in assessing suicide risk. *Monitor On Psychology, 31*.

McCarn, S. R., & Fassinger, R. E. (1996). Revisioning sexual minority identity formation: A new model of lesbian identity and its implications. *Counseling Psychologist, 24*, 508–534.

McNeill, B. W., & Worthen, V. (1989). The parallel process in psychotherapy supervision. *Professional Psychology: Research and Practice, 20*, 329–333.

Meehl, P. E. (1956). Wanted—a good cook-book. *American Psychologist, 11*, 263–272.

Menninger, K. (1958). *Theory of psychoanalytic technique*. New York: Basic Books.

Metcalfe, W. R., & Caplan, P. J. (2004). Seeking "normal" sexuality on a complete matrix. In P. J. Caplan & L. Cosgrove (Eds.), *Bias in psychiatric diagnosis* (pp. 121–126). Lanham, MD: Jason-Aronson.

Morrow, S. L., & Smith, M. L. (2000). Qualitative research for counseling psychology. In S. D. Brown & R. W. Lent (Eds.), *Handbook of counseling psychology* (3rd ed., pp. 199–230). Hoboken, NJ: John Wiley & Sons.

Moskowitz, S. A., & Rupert, P. A. (1983). Conflict resolution within the supervisory relationship. *Professional Psychology: Research and Practice, 14,* 632–641.

Mueller, R. M., Lambert, M. J., & Burlingame, G. M. (1998). Construct validity of the Outcome Questionnaire: A confirmatory factor analysis. *Journal of Personality Assessment, 70,* 248–262.

Munson, C. E. (2002). Child and adolescent needs in a time of national disaster: Perspectives for mental health professionals and parents. *Brief Treatment and Crisis Intervention, 2,* 135–151.

Murray, B. L., & Wright, K. (2006). Integration of a suicide risk assessment and intervention approach: The perspective of youth. *Journal of Psychiatric and Mental Health Nursing, 13,* 157–164.

Nelson, G. L. (1978). Psychotherapy supervision from the trainee's point of view: A survey of preferences. *Professional Psychology, 9,* 539–550.

Nelson, M. L., & Friedlander, M. L. (2001). A close look at conflictual supervisory relationships: The trainee's perspective. *Journal of Counseling Psychology, 48,* 384–395.

Norcross, J. C., & Goldfried, M. R. (2002). On becoming an integrative psychotherapist.*PsycCRITIQUES, 47,* 332–333.

Norcross, J. C., & Goldfried, M. R. (2005). The future of psychotherapy integration: A roundtable. *Journal of Psychotherapy Integration, 15,* 392–47.

Olk, M., & Friedlander, M. L. (1992). Role conflict and ambiguity in the supervisory experiences of counselor trainees. *Journal of Counseling Psychology, 39,* 389–397.

Orlinsky, D. E., Grawe, K., & Parks, B. K. (1994). Process and outcome in psychotherapy: Noch einmal. In A. E. Bergin & S. L. Garfield (Eds.), *Handbook of psychotherapy and behavior change* (4th ed., pp. 270–376). Oxford, UK: John Wiley & Sons.

Ossana, S. M., Helms, J. E., & Leonard, M. M. (1992). Do "womanist" identity attitudes influence college women's self-esteem and perceptions of environmental bias? *Journal of Counseling & Development, 70,* 402–408.

Othmer, E., & Othmer, S. C. (2002). *The clinical interview using* DSM-IV-TR, *Vol 1: Fundamentals.* Washington, DC: American Psychiatric Publishing.

Overholser, J. C. (2004). The Four Pillars of Psychotherapy Supervision. *Clinical Supervisor, 23,* 1–13.

Pate-Carolan, L. M. (2004). An examination of interpersonal responses during psychotherapy sessions in the context of session evaluations and working alliance. *Dissertation Abstracts International: The Sciences and Engineering, 64,* 12B.

Pate-Carolan, L. M., Walker, J. A., & Tyson, A. (June, 2002). *An examination of anxiety levels, relationships, and working alliances in novice trainees.* Paper presented at the annual international conference of the Society for Psychotherapy Research, Santa Barbara, CA.

Peabody, S. A., & Gelso, C. J. (1982). Countertransference and empathy: The complex relationship between two divergent concepts in counseling. *Journal of Counseling Psychology, 29,* 240–245.

Peltzer, K. (2003). Culture and psychiatric diagnosis: A *DSM-IV* perspective. *Journal of Psychology in Africa; South of the Sahara, the Caribbean, and Afro-Latin America, 13,* 98–99.

Ponterotto, J. G., Casas, J. M., Suzuki, L. A., & Alexander, C. M. (Eds.). (2001) *Handbook of multicultural counseling* (2nd ed.). Oaks, CA: Sage.

Prochaska, J. O., & Norcross, J. C. (2001). Stages of change. *Psychotherapy: Theory, Research, Practice, Training, 38,* 443–448.

Psychotherapy Finances Survey. (2000). *Psychotherapy Finances, 26,* 318. Juno Beach, FL: Ridgewood Financial Institute.

Reich, A. (1951). On counter-transference. *International Journal of Psycho-Analysis, 32,* 25–31.

Rhodes, R. H., Hill, C. E., Thompson, B. J., & Elliot, R. (1994). Client retrospective recall of resolved and unresolved misunderstanding events. *Journal of Counseling Psychology, 41,* 473–483.

Richard, D. H. (2001). Clinical diagnosis of multicultural populations in the United States. In L. A. Suzuki, J. G. Ponterotto, & P. J. Meller (Eds.), *Handbook of multicultural assessment: Clinical, psychological, and educational applications* (2nd ed., pp.101–131). San Francisco: Jossey-Bass.

Robbins, S. B., & Jolkovski, M. P. (1987). Managing countertransference feelings: An interactional model using awareness feeling and theoretical framework. *Journal of Counseling Psychology, 34,* 267–282.

Rosenzweig, S. (1936). Some implicit common factors in diverse methods of psychotherapy. *American Journal of Orthopsychiatry, 6,* 412–415.

Safran, J. D., & Muran, J. C. (2000). *Negotiating the therapeutic alliance: A relational treatment guide.* New York: Guilford Press.

Shanfield, S. B., Matthews, K. L., & Hetherly, V. (1993). What do excellent psychotherapy supervisors do? *American Journal of Psychiatry, 150,* 1081–1084.

Sodowsky, G. R., Kwan, K. K., Pannu, R. (1995). Ethnic identity of Asians in the united states. In J. G. Ponterotto, J. M. Casas, L. A. Suzuki, & C. M. Alexander (Eds.), *Handbook of multicultural counseling* (pp. 123–154). Thousand Oaks, CA: Sage.

Spradlin, K., Ladany, N., & Schutt, M. (2003, June). Trainee Learning—An Exploratory Investigation Into How Counselor Trainees Experience Their Learning Through Practice And Supervision. Paper presented at the meeting of the Society for Psychotherapy Research, Weimar, Germany.

Sterba, R. (1934). The fate of the ego in analytic therapy. *International Journal of Psycho-Analysis, 15,* 117–126.

Stiles, W. B. (1979). Verbal response modes and psychotherapeutic technique. *Psychiatry: Journal for the Study of Interpersonal Processes, 42,* 49–62.

Stiles, W. B. (1986). Development of a taxonomy of verbal response modes. In L. S. Greenberg & W. M. Pinsof (Eds.), *The psychotherapeutic process: A research handbook* (pp.161–199). New York: Guilford Press.

Stiles, W., Honos-Webb, L., & Surko, M. (1998). Responsiveness in psychotherapy. *Clinical Psychology: Research and Practice, 5,* 439–458.

Stoltenberg, C. D., McNeill, B., & Delworth, U. (1998). *IDM supervision: An integrated developmental model for supervising counselors and therapists.* San Francisco, CA: Jossey-Bass.

Strean, H. S. (2000). Resolving therapeutic impasses by using the supervisor's countertransference. *Clinical Social Work Journal, 28,* 263–279.

Sue, D. W. (2003). *Overcoming our racism: The journey into liberation.* San Francisco, CA: Jossey-Bass.

Sue, D. W., Carter, R. T., Casas, J. M., Fouad, N. A., Ivey, A. E., Jensen, M., LaFromboise, T., Manese, J. E., Ponterotto, J. G., & Vazquez-Nutall, E. (1998). *Multicultural counseling competencies: Individual and organizational development.* Thousand Oaks, CA: Sage.

Suman, A., & Brignone, A. (2001). Transference, countertransference, society and culture: Before and during the first encounter. *British Journal of Psychotherapy, 17,* 465–473.

Sumerel, M. B., & Borders, L. D. (1996). Addressing personal issues in supervision: Impact of counselors' experience level on various aspects of the supervisory relationship. *Counselor Education and Supervision, 35,* 268–286.

Tallent, N. (1958). On individualizing the psychologist's clinical evaluation. *Journal of Clinical Psychology, 14,* 243–244.

Teitelbaum, S. H. (1990). Supertransference: The role of the supervisor's blind spots. *Psychoanalytic Psychology, 7,* 243–258.

Tosone, C. (1997). Countertransference and clinical social work supervision: Contributions and considerations. *The Clinical Supervisor, 16,* 17–32.

Tune, D. (2001). Is touch a valid therapeutic intervention? Early returns from a qualitative study of therapists' views. *Counselling & Psychotherapy Research, 1,* 167–171.

Usher, C. H., & Borders, L. D. (1993). Practicing counselors' preferences for supervisory style and supervisory emphasis. *Counselor Education and Supervision, 33,* 66–79.

Walker, J. A. (2003). *Countertransference in therapy and supervision: Proximal parallel process.* Dissertation Abstracts International.

Wampold, B. E. (2001). *The great psychotherapy debate: Models, methods, and findings.* Mahwah, NJ: Lawrence Erlbaum Associates.

Ward, C. C., & House, R. M. (1998). Counseling supervision: A reflective model. *Counselor Education and Supervision, 38,* 23–33.

Warwar S., & Greenberg, L. S. (2000). Advances in theories of change and counseling. In S. D. Brown & R. W. Lent (Eds.), *Handbook of counseling psychology* (3rd ed., pp. 571–600). Hoboken, NJ: John Wiley & Sons.

Webb, A., & Wheeler, S. (1998). How honest do counsellors dare to be in the supervisory relationship? An exploratory study. *British Journal of Guidance & Counselling, 26,* 509–524.

Weerasekera, P., Linder, B., Greenberg, L., & Watson, J. (2001). The working alliance in client-centered and process-experiential therapy of depression. *Psychotherapy Research, 11,* 221–233.

West, W. (2004). *Spiritual issues in therapy: Relating experience to practice.* London: Palgrave MacMillan.

Williams, E. N., & Fauth, J. (2005). A psychotherapy process study of therapist in session self-awareness. *Psychotherapy Research, 15,* 374–381.

Winnicott, D. W. (1949). Hate in the countertransference. *International Journal of Psycho-Analysis, 30,* 69–74.

Worthen, V., & McNeill, B. W. (1996). A phenomenological investigation of "good" supervision events. *Journal of Counseling Psychology, 43,* 25–34.

Worthington, R. L., Tan, J. A., & Poulin, K. (2002). Ethically questionable behaviors among supervisees: An exploratory investigation. *Ethics & Behavior, 12,* 323–351.

Yalom, I. D. (2000). *Momma and the meaning of life: Tales of psychotherapy.* New York: Basic Books.

Yerushalmi, H. (2000). Psychodynamic supervision as narrative. *The Clinical Supervisor, 19,* 77–97.

Yourman, D. B. (2003). Trainee disclosure in psychotherapy supervision: The impact of shame. *Journal of Clinical Psychology Special Issue: In session: Self disclosure, 59,* 601–609.

Yourman, D. B., & Farber, B. A. (1996). Nondisclosure and distortion in psychotherapy supervison. *Psychotherapy: Theory, Research, Practice, Training, 33,* 567–575.

Yulis, S., & Kiesler, D. J. (1968). Countertransference response as a function of therapist anxiety and content of patient talk. *Journal of Consulting and Clinical Psychology, 32,* 414–419.

Zetzel, E. R. (1956). Current concepts of transference. *International Journal of Psycho-Analysis, 37,* 369–375.

About the Authors

Nicholas Ladany, Ph.D., is Professor of Counseling Psychology at Lehigh University in Bethlehem, Pennsylvania. He has served as Counseling Psychology Program Coordinator & Director of Doctoral Training, and Chair of the Department of Education and Human Services. Before his affiliation with Lehigh University, he was an Assistant Professor at Temple University and a Visiting Faculty member at the University of Maryland. He received his Ph.D. at the University at Albany, State University of New York, in 1992. He has published numerous articles and presented nationally and internationally in the area of counseling and psychotherapy supervision and training. His primary research interest and activity include the interrelationships between supervision process and outcome and counseling and psychotherapy process and outcome, including such issues as the working alliance, self-disclosures and nondisclosures, multicultural training, and ethics. He has served on the editorial board of the *Journal of Counseling Psychology* and *Counselor Education and Supervision* and currently is the Associate Editor of *Psychotherapy: Theory, Research, Practice, and Training*. He is the author of two books: *Critical Events in Psychotherapy Supervision: An Interpersonal Approach* and *Counselor Supervision: Principles, Process, and Practice*. He is a Licensed Psychologist in Pennsylvania.

Jessica A. Walker, Ph.D., is a Staff Psychologist at the University of North Carolina Charlotte's Counseling Center, where she provides leadership in the areas of outreach programming and graduate training. Prior to her affiliation with UNC-C, she served as a psychologist and instructor at UNC-Wilmington. She received her Ph.D. in Counseling Psychology at Lehigh University after completing her pre-doctoral internship at Appalachian State University's Counseling Center. She has published and presented nationally and internationally in her areas of research including psychotherapy supervision, countertransference and multicultural variables in counseling.

Lia M. Pate-Carolan, Ph.D., is a Psychologist with the ACT Medical Group, PA in North Carolina. She conducts psychotherapy with those currently residing in nursing homes and assisted living settings north of Raleigh. She completed a postdoctoral position at the New Jersey Department of Veterans Affairs focusing on Cognitive Behavioral Therapy as an intervention to reduce medical overutilization. Her research interests include the process within therapy, and the parallel process between therapy and supervision. She is a Licensed Psychologist in New York and North Carolina.

Laurie Gray Evans, Ph.D., is a Staff Psychologist at Lehigh University's University Counseling and Psychological Services, in Bethlehem, Pennsylvania. She received her Ph.D. at Lehigh University and has published articles and presented nationally and internationally primarily in the area of psychotherapy supervision and training. Her primary research interests and activities include the interrelationships between supervision and psychotherapy processes and outcomes, with particular interest in such issues as critical incidents, parallel processes, transferential and character dynamics, and gay affirmative attitudes.

Subject Index

level 4: strategies and techniques,
24–25, 109–111
Professional informational interviewing
(exercise), 6
Prognosis, 70
Progress notes, 70–72
Progress to date, client's, 74–75
Proposed treatment strategy, 75
Psychodynamic approach, 24, 73–74
Psychotherapy and Supervision
Research Project
protocols and methodology, 2–3,
188–191
therapy and supervision variables,
192–193

Q

Questions, uncomfortable (exercise), 176

R

Race Is a Nice Thing to Have, A (Helms),
55
Regrets, 91–94
client, 216–217
supervision and, 114, 241–246
therapist, 218–219
Relationship, therapeutic, *see* Alliance,
working
Resolution phase, 111
Response modes
exercise, 29
in supervision, 108
in therapy, 18–22
Role-playing exercises, 28

S

Self-awareness, 4; *See also*
Countertransference
multicultural identities and, 45–50
during sessions, 26–27
tolerance of ambiguity, 51–53
Self-care, 184–186
Self-disclosure, 21–22

Session Evaluation Questionnaire (SEQ),
263–264, 266–267, 270–271,
274–275, 278–279
Silence, 21, 29
Skills, supervision
level 1: nonverbal behaviors, 107
level 2: response modes, 108
level 3: covert processes, 108–109
level 4: strategies and techniques,
109–111
Skills, therapy
level 1: nonverbal behaviors, 17–18
level 2: response modes, 18–22
level 3: covert processes, 22–24
level 4: strategies and techniques,
24–25
Strengths, client, 70
Study, *see* Psychotherapy and
Supervision Research Project
Style, supervisor, 119, 276–277, 280–281
Suicidal risk
assessing in first session, 16
conceptualization and, 70
Supervision
countertransference and, 119–124
ethics and, 104–107
managing, 124–125
outcomes, 112–117
parallel process and, 111–112
process skills, 107–111
sample conceptualization outline,
131
sample evaluation forms, 127–130,
132
structure and function, 102–103
supervisor style and, 119
variables in, 7
as working alliance, 103–104,
133–134
Supervision case study, 136–138
client: Bill, 154–156, 180
client: Debi, 160–165, 167–169
client: Kendra, 144–147, 151–154,
177–180
client: Ruby, 147–149, 172
first therapy session, 142–144
overview, 135–136
supervisor: Julia, 157–158, 169–171,
172–174, 173–174, 181

Author Index